The Digital Logic of Death

The Digital Logic of Death

Confronting Mortality in Contemporary Media

Steven Pustay

BLOOMSBURY ACADEMIC

NEW YORK • LONDON • OXFORD • NEW DELHI • SYDNEY

BLOOMSBURY ACADEMIC
Bloomsbury Publishing Inc
50 Bedford Square, London, WC1B 3DP, UK
1385 Broadway, New York, NY 10018, USA
29 Earlsfort Terrace, Dublin 2, Ireland

BLOOMSBURY, BLOOMSBURY ACADEMIC and the Diana logo
are trademarks of Bloomsbury Publishing Plc

First published in the United States of America 2021
This paperback edition published in 2022

Copyright © Steven Pustay, 2021

For legal purposes the Acknowledgments on p. ix constitute an
extension of this copyright page.

Cover design by Steven Pustay
Cover image © Steven Pustay

This work is published open access subject to a Creative Commons Attribution-NonCommercial-NoDerivatives 3.0 licence (CC BY-NC-ND 3.0, https://creativecommons.org/licenses/by-nc-nd/3.0/). You may re-use, distribute, and reproduce this work in any medium for non-commercial purposes, provided you give attribution to the copyright holder and the publisher and provide a link to the Creative Commons licence.

Bloomsbury Publishing Inc does not have any control over, or responsibility for, any third-party websites referred to or in this book. All internet addresses given in this book were correct at the time of going to press. The author and publisher regret any inconvenience caused if addresses have changed or sites have ceased to exist, but can accept no responsibility for any such changes.

ISBN:	HB:	978-1-5013-6408-2
	PB:	978-1-5013-7238-4
	ePDF:	978-1-5013-6406-8
	eBook:	978-1-5013-6407-5

Typeset by Integra Software Services Pvt. Ltd.

To find out more about our authors and books visit www.bloomsbury.com
and sign up for our newsletters.

For Madeleine and Scottie

CONTENTS

Acknowledgments ix

Introduction: The Digital Logic of Death 1
    Knowing Death 1
    Showing Death 4

1 The Trauma of Digital Death 9
    In Effigie, In Absentia 9
    The *Jouissance* of Death (Witnessing) 12
    The Pornography of Death (Representing) 19
    The Sublimity of Death (Simulating) 32
    Time Destroys Everything 47

2 The Digital Path to Death 53
    Death in Digital Games 53
    Re-animation 56
    Compossibility 60
    Recurrence, Subjectivity, Contemplation 63
    The Path to Death 72
    After the Game is Before the Game 78

3 The Potential of Digital Death 89
    Possibilistic to the Limit 89
    Anxiety and Angst (Possibility and Authenticity) 92
    Being-toward-Death (Potentiality, Resoluteness, Immanence) 104
    Split Subjectivity (Potentiality, Reflection, Ecstasis) 114
    The Road to Awe 122

4 The Event of Digital Death 133
   The One or the Multiple 133
   Cyborgs, Androids, and Immortal Machines 137
   Being as Multiplicity (Axiomatic vs. Problematic) 146
   Death as Event (Consistency and Inconsistency) 153
   Everything That Has a Beginning Has an End 162

Conclusion: The Fractal Logic of Life 167
   The Micro and the Macro 167

Notes 174
Bibliography 196
Index 203

ACKNOWLEDGMENTS

This project would not have been possible without the support of a large group of people, many of whom were probably unaware of how much their interest and concern encouraged me during the difficult and long process of writing. First and foremost, I want to thank my committee at Georgia State University. My advisor, Angelo Restivo, not only guided this project, but also inspired a young grad student to look upon the world with a critical eye and a passion for nuance. Likewise, Alessandra Raengo has long been a constant supporter and friend, helping me to grow as a scholar and as a person. I may not have ever been a student in Jennifer Barker's classroom, but even our most casual conversations have had a profound impact on my scholarship and my approach to media. Greg Smith's straightforward and honest writing style has long been something I've attempted to imitate, and it was Ian Bogost's work that first turned me on to reading popular media through the lens of critical theory.

Equally important were the friendship and support of my cohort at Georgia State – Drew Ayers, Karen Petruska, and Kris Cannon – whom I've long relied upon for advice and empathy, and whom I will always greatly admire. Likewise, the encouragement of my colleagues Justin, Collin, Darcey, and Sam helped to spurn this project forward even when it was barely more than an idea. Thanks also to my many great friends, including Adam, Ryan, Barry, Traci, Ben, Joe, Bill, Pete, Steve, Casey, Jessica, Katie, Leslie, and Mandy, all of whom continually expressed interest in my work, and never once rolled their eyes or pretended to fall asleep as they listened to me describe this project for the thousandth time. Among them, a special shout-out to Kurt for his willingness to directly engage with my work, and to my sister Kelly and my brother-in-law Nick, who were always willing to listen and help.

Many thanks are also owed to my editor at Bloomsbury, Katie Gallof, whose support for this project brought a book about death back to life in more ways than one, and to her assistant, Erin Duffy, for her patience and editorial guidance. Elsewhere, my gratitude to Richard Pult for his assistance and support of this project on its journey toward publication, and to the team at Integra, especially Shanmathi Priya, for their diligent edits which helped the final book take form.

Lastly, my biggest thanks to my mom, who once told me to 'just get it done' and then continued to tell me the same thing over and over for the next three years (I love you mom!), and to my dad, who always agreed to listen to yet another revision, always thoughtfully engaged with my ideas no matter how strange or esoteric, and who has often been the only person I could count on to understand and alleviate my frustrations and my fears. Thank you.

Introduction
The Digital Logic of Death

Knowing Death

One of the most profound yet critically overlooked consequences of the birth of the motion picture was that it, together with the rise of modern medical science, fundamentally uprooted our relationship with death. Indeed, one's understanding of mortality had long been grounded in a common though crucial act of looking, of bearing witness to the passing of loved ones and friends, of standing in the presence of death. Yet at the turn of the twentieth century, as the act of dying withdrew from the communal space of the home into the private space of the hospital, that ability to look suddenly and violently disappeared. No longer was it deemed necessary or even respectable to witness the passing of others, yet anxieties regarding death never waned and the desire to look upon its face never diminished. So the public turned to the moving image to satisfy their curiosity, and what followed was a century in which death was utterly abject yet intensely visible, the event itself increasingly hidden from everyday life even as its fictional representations became all the more frequent and all the more fetishized.

Despite the significant repercussions, this transition went largely unnoticed and unremarked. Instead, a perilous gap opened up between scholarly studies of death and those of popular media, preventing us from fully accounting for the role that moving images play in our understanding of mortality. On one side were the existentialists, thanatologists, and continental philosophers who gave rise to critically important questions regarding the influence of death upon our subjectivity, yet who so often failed to recognize how our collective cultural logic is shaped by our consumption of popular media. On the other were the film and media scholars who explored the impact of moving images on our experience of everyday life, without recognizing that those same images had entirely reconfigured our understanding of life's inevitable conclusion. As we push further into a new digital age, it is essential that we begin to bridge this gap, especially given that our impression of death is once again shifting in response to new technologies of the image. This is the critical and urgent aim of this book, to not only unpack the nature of the relationship between death and the moving image, but also reveal how electronic media and digital technologies are transforming our ability to represent, contemplate, and confront the finiteness of the human experience, so much so that our contemporary media landscape has produced an entirely new understanding of mortality: a *digital logic of death*.

To confront the consequences of our mortality has been and forever will be a central philosophical concern of the human condition. Yet to study death — to attempt to truly *know* death — is an overly grand endeavor, overwhelming in its intense scope and magnitude, unsettling in its inconsistencies and implications. As a subject, death crosses all social and cultural boundaries, traversing the realms of philosophy, art, politics, science, religion; as an event, it remains painfully out of reach, visible to all yet objectively indefinable. To contemplate our mortality is to grapple with the ultimate contradiction, to glimpse the only event which is absolutely known (in its certainty) and absolutely unknowable (in its experience). It's for this very reason that death fascinates us, that we surround ourselves with its veiled presence. In our digital age, it seems impossible to watch a film, turn on a television, or play a game without being confronted by the image of death, at times indirectly or abstractly, but more often than not through an unabashedly direct representation.

While we know that the overwhelming majority of these images are pure fiction, we often fail to acknowledge that they reflect only a most basic understanding of the actual processes of death. In fact, our obsession with representations of death betrays a significant problem which lies at the heart of our contemporary relationship with mortality: despite the fact that we purposefully distance ourselves from the painful and uncomfortable realities of dying, we so often assume that we know death because we are inundated with its fictional image. To address this problem, this book takes as its subject not death itself, but rather our collective *logic of death* — i.e., the culturally constructed characteristics and implications of the event of death — and a privileged space in which this logic is continually formed and reformed: the moving image.

To speak of our logic of death is to refer not only to our understanding of what death is or the many forms that it can take, but also to the myriad and endless ways in which it affects our lives and culture. So much of our experience is informed by the notion that our time is fragile and finite, that the boundaries of our lives are frustratingly unknowable and yet painfully obvious. When we look ahead to our educations and careers and retirements, for example, we arrange our lives toward an end. When we write in our diaries, take photographs, or create social media posts, we're structuring our legacies and leaving behind traces that we hope will outlast us. When we wear our seat belts, change our diets according to new science, or lock our front doors, we are acknowledging and protecting ourselves against the many ways in which death can come sooner than we would like. When we emphasize the importance of children, families, and societal structures, we're recognizing that our own time on this planet is fixed and that others will endure after we are gone. In all of these ways and more, our lives are immeasurably shaped by our recognition of death.

Yet the immensity and complexity of the influence of death on our lives is far too great (and far too uncomfortable) for us to collectively comprehend. As such, our logic of death can perhaps best be thought of as our limited social recognition of mortality and its effects, of the ways in which we allow certain properties of death to proliferate around us while we acknowledge other facets only in the cracks of culture. In fact, our logic of death is but one component of our broader *cultural logic* — our implicit social agreement to share certain assumptions and interpretations of the world around us — which has, since the early 1990s, become slowly saturated by the effects of digital processing, as personal computers have become an essential part of daily life, as the internet has fractured our lives into online and offline components, as computer-generated images have changed our capacity to represent the world as it is and as we imagine it to be.[1] Throughout this project, then, I'll use the term *digital logic* to refer to the current state of our collective thinking, in which we've come to adopt certain digital processes like compression and binary thinking in order to make more of the world accessible and comprehensible, at the expense of seeing redundancies where we once saw nuance. In this sense, "the digital" can be read as a shorthand not only for computers and microprocessors, but also for a new current of social relations and cultural assumptions that have been over-determined by digital technologies.

Although media plays a considerable role in shaping our cultural logic (and vice versa), it is also influenced by many other factors including politics, economics, religion, and so on. Yet our discomfort and reluctance to engage with the realities of dying have ensured that our logic of death is profoundly and disproportionately influenced by the ephemera of popular culture, by the accumulation of images and narratives which titillate and placate rather than inform. This is why films, television shows, and digital games are so important to this study, because our logic of death is always in the process of shifting and reorganizing in response to new representations in popular media, including radically new depictions brought about by the communications and image-making technologies of the digital age. Not every piece of contemporary media that we'll explore in this book has been created using digital tools, yet they are all nonetheless informed by our digital logic, they illustrate how our relationship with death has shifted from the other to the self, from the private to the public, from the unexpectedly traumatic to the traumatically anticipated, from the abject to the essential.

Showing Death

While the cinematic technologies of the twentieth century shifted our proximity to death, simultaneous advancements in medical science all but ensured that "questions of what *constituted* human death and how we could determine its occurrence," as David DeGrazia puts it, "had emerged as issues both philosophically rich and urgent."[2] For example, debates as to whether death is primarily a neurological or cardiopulmonary phenomenon have inspired vast controversies in science, law, medicine, and even art. In turn, our inability to objectively define death has long made the attempt to study the *image* of death — even before the eruption of the digital — highly problematic. If we can't seem to decide how or when the physical body transitions from being alive to being dead, how do we capture that moment within the image?

Many of the debates surrounding the definition of death arise from the fact that death exists as not a concrete thing that can be captured and studied, but rather a transformation which involves both subtle and profound changes to the body. So to avoid becoming bogged down in the huge expanse of scientific, political, social, and philosophical definitions of the moment of one's passing, let's turn the problem of the event of death on its head, asking not "what is the definition of death" but rather "how do we attempt to define and understand death?" This project is far less interested in what death is than in how we come to recognize it's inevitability, how our knowledge of mortality is influenced by specific drives or shifts in culture, and how we've negotiated, repressed, and confronted that knowledge through media and the moving image. Put another way, this project is an attempt not to lay bare the ontology of death so much as its epistemology, the way in which our understanding of death was organized in the past and the way in which it continues to be structured in the here and now. This strategy allows us to mirror recent developments in our logic of death by doing something that even thanatological studies so often fail to achieve: to discuss mortality not only in reference to the deaths of others — i.e., how we care for the dying, structures of grief, funerary practices, religious doctrines, etc. — but also in regard to ourselves as finite individuals, to examine how we rely on media and moving images to explore our own mortality and the frailty of our own bodies.

This project, then, is a study of how we "image" death and how those images reflect and influence our anxiety regarding our own mortality. Yet for all intents and purposes it's clear that capturing the fullness of death within an image, even with the tools of the digital age, is virtually impossible. In her examination of documentary representations of death, for example, Vivian Sobchack acknowledges this impossibility by addressing only what she calls the "thickness" of death found in certain images (rather than, say, their supposed "truth-value").[3] Like Sobchack, I too hope to avoid the search for some universal truth of death, yet I take the opposite path by avoiding documentary representations and instead focusing on the "thickness" of the *fictional* renderings through which we establish our collective logic. This choice certainly leaves behind some fruitful and compelling examples of how we choose to recognize and face the fact of death in the digital age, such as news footage from disasters and terrorists attacks or the myriad executions videos that have accumulated online. Yet I'm searching for the manner by which we (vainly, naively) attempt to *control death* by turning it into a socially acceptable image, a goal we relentlessly pursue despite our implicit recognition that death defines us just as much as we define death.

Over the next four chapters, we'll work our way toward a fuller understanding of the digital logic of death, concerning ourselves not only with the digital's impact on our ability to represent death within the image, but also with its effect on our subjectivity and our very understanding of the nature of Being. In fact, in the same moment that we find ourselves capable of producing ever-more "realistic" and "immersive" images of world around us, in the same moment that we find ourselves capable of accessing more of that world than ever before, we also find ourselves splitting apart, our subjectivity fracturing into actual and virtual components that each have their own relationship to finitude and the fact of mortality. Coming to terms with the digital logic of death is therefore more than simply recognizing our relationship to death, it's an attempt to understand how death shapes our culture, how it inaugurates our individuality, how it defines our humanity.

To that end, our first chapter will look to the increasingly visceral images of death that have appeared in the digital age, images which are as concerned with the breakdown and collapse of the *interior* of the body — bones, muscles, organs, fluids — as they are with the closed eyes, torn flesh, and inanimate limbs that were once the preferred signifiers of death. To unpack the trauma such images aim to inspire, I'll trace our relationship with the event of death from the nineteenth century to the present, along the way demonstrating how the perceptually thick and incredibly common experience of witnessing the death of others was replaced, at the turn of the twentieth century, by moving images which failed to capture the biological realities of dying. This account of the changing nature of witnessing will draw on several theoretical traditions — from psychoanalysis to poststructuralism to new media theory — in order to reveal a contemporary dissatisfaction with *representations of death* and a push toward *simulations of death*. These autonomously generated images echo the traumatic, unanticipated, and over-stimulating details that accompany the living body's transition into nonbeing, once felt only through the strange, difficult, and intense pleasure of witnessing.

A particular form of simulation will be the focus of our second chapter, that of the digital game and its radically new employment of death as both a narrative and a mechanical trope. In games, death is both inconsequential and essential, a mistake which is easily rewound and overwritten as well as an indispensable indicator of the goals and obstacles of gameplay. Looking closely, we'll find that the re-animation prevalent in games — where "dying" provides an opportunity to reshape the present using knowledge of both the past and the future — fundamentally challenges the traditions of death found in moving images of the twentieth century. Drawing on Nietzsche's concept of the eternal return and Freud's theory of the death drive, we'll see how this process of re-animation acts as a digital "path to death," through which game players attempt not to survive indefinitely but rather to establish and reach a narratively satisfying end to life.

Our third chapter will expand upon the first two by arguing that the moving image's fetishization of traumatic death increased our awareness of death's possibility (i.e., the fact that our lives can end at any moment) at the expense of our awareness of death's potential (i.e., the myriad ways in which our knowledge of mortality affects and influences our lives and culture). In the digital age, we seek out relays through which we can re-encounter that potential, whether it be through narratives of characters who are anxiously aware of their own impending deaths or through the establishment of our own virtual subjectivities in digital games and online spaces — subjectivities that are, unlike our own fleshy bodies, impervious to death. We'll trace these relays with the help of existential thinkers like Kierkegaard, Heidegger, and Sartre, whose work linked anxiety to authentic subjectivity while arguing for an ecstatic relationship to time and finitude, and the metaphysics of Bergson, Deleuze, and Massumi, which established clear distinctions between possibility and potential while promoting a recognition of the world as immanently interconnected.

Finally, our fourth chapter will explore not a new image of death, but rather a new concept of immortality: the artificially intelligent machine, for whom consciousness is entirely divorced from frail and fragile bodies. The networked intelligence of the digital age is both an extension of the cyborgs and androids of popular culture and a radically new notion of life, a shift in the long-established parameters of Being. To better understand this shift, I'll turn to Deleuze and Alain Badiou, who agreed that all Being is pure multiplicity while disagreeing on the ontological status of *the event*, a debate that echoes the breakdown between the networked multiplicity of the machine and the event of death that haunts our very Being. Contemporary narratives of the organic and the inorganic tell us that what separates us from the machine is nothing less than our mortality, and in doing so they reveal a notion that drives both this project and the digital logic of death, that to be human is to know that you will die.

In laying out the ways in which we yearn to return to a more personal and direct relationship with death, my hope is that the observations presented in these chapters can renew an existential line of inquiry that was once a pivotal undercurrent of critical theory, phenomenology, psychoanalysis, and metaphysics, one with the potential to greatly inform key conversations surrounding identity and subjectivity in film and media studies, cultural studies, posthumanism, and (in the form of thanatology) cultural anthropology. From psychoanalysis and phenomenology I borrow a recognition of language and the perceiving body as the basis of human experience, consciousness, and subjectivity. Through thanatology I emphasize the twentieth century's widespread repression of death, and proceed to investigate changes in this repressive impulse which have appeared in response to digital technologies. From the metaphysics of thinkers like Kierkegaard, Heidegger, Deleuze, and Badiou, I form an understanding of the ontology of Being and the meaning of being human. Finally, I respond to central issues raised by posthumanism and recent branches of cultural studies regarding the contemporary association between the fleshy biological body and the mechanical/digital body of the machine.

Although these traditions provide the central philosophical underpinnings through which we'll explore our response to death and the digital, this book follows many branches of theory when needed. No single study of death can provide us a complete picture, but by drawing out the digital logic of death, I believe this project will provide a vantage point that is sorely needed in both our contemporary thanatological landscape and our current conversations on the cultural impact of popular media. Indeed, treatises on death and mortality are too often brushed aside as little more than morbid meditations, a remnant of the repression of death that was a defining characteristic of the last century. Likewise, a presumption has emerged that the digital is robbing us of our humanity, that the more we embrace new technologies the more we lose sight of our own individuality and subjectivity. This project looks to demonstrate precisely the opposite, that our digitally mediated culture does not rob us of our humanity but rather brings us closer to the very thing that defines us as being human: our recognition of the inevitability of death.

1

The Trauma of Digital Death

The images are all-too-familiar: stabbings, strangulations, bludgeonings, poisonings, and other forms of murder; mutilations, amputations, asphyxiations, beheadings, and other varieties of torture; cuttings, jumpings, hangings, overdoses, and other methods of suicide; car crashes, falls, drownings, chokings, and other tragic accidents; heart attacks, cancer, AIDS, Ebola, and other diseases both mundane and exotic; and the gun violence and shootings … the many, many shootings. In an increasingly violent world, we believe that we know the face of death, for we believe that we've seen it — the eyes slowly closing, the last gasps for breath, the bodies pierced and torn apart, the insides made suddenly, sickeningly visible. No matter that the images are fiction, the bodies props, the wounds makeup, the blood a thick red dye, the torn flesh a digital effect. No matter, for death is all around us (a false proximity, sure, but always nearby nonetheless). Yes, in the digital age, we believe that we know death, despite the fact that so few of us have actually *witnessed it*.

In Effigie, In Absentia

The first strike is, quite literally, a stunning blow: it knocks the would-be rapist on his back while the onlookers — whose rowdy cries and crude gestures precipitated the violence — suddenly grow quiet, only serving to reinforce the nauseating repetition of the wailing soundtrack. The camera, too, seems momentarily stunned; it struggles to find a subject, hovering between the assailant, the fire extinguisher, and his victim, whose slack jaw already bears the trace of concussive trauma. As the extinguisher swings down for second blow, and then a third, and a fourth, and a fifth, we too become stunned, nauseated, disorientated; helplessly bearing witness as the face, its square jaw and sharp nose so distinct only moments ago, becomes deformed — the flesh above the mouth torn away, the teeth cracked and knocked out, the jawbone crushed and compacted to the side. And yet, from somewhere within the victim, there is movement, there remains a hint of *life*. His tongue protrudes as he gags and grasps for breath, the muscles in his face twitch visibly as flesh is ruptured, his hand, out of focus and distorted, juts up in front of the lens as if to push us, to beg us to look away. But the film won't let us, the shot refuses to cut, and instead the camera echoes our disorientation by spinning upside down and then back again, pulling up as the extinguisher rises and smashing down as it makes contact. There is *weight* behind every impact, both the weapon and the camera feel excessively heavy, and each strike grows exceedingly visceral. By now the face is gone, the forehead cracked open, flaps of tissue and bits of bone and blood and brain violently spatter about. As a last rush of air escapes the victim's throat, all signs of struggle finally, mercifully disappear, and what is left is no longer the face of man but rather the face of death.

At least we think it is, maybe. Well, to be honest, upon watching this early scene from Gaspar Noé's 2002 film *Irréversible* — in which one of the protagonists enacts misguided revenge for another equally violent and reprehensible transgression — we're not quite sure what we saw, though we hope to never see it again just as much as we want to watch it again immediately. It's only fiction, we assure ourselves, yet it *looks* so real and *feels* so real that we can't stop replaying it in our minds. We've seen death depicted before — many, many times in many, many ways — but there's something different about this image, something haunting, something shocking, something we can't quite put into words. In fact, the only thing we can say for certain about this scene is that it's *traumatic*: on the one hand we have the visible, physiological trauma that plays out within the frame — that unrelenting depiction of flesh pushed so far beyond its limits as to not simply fail but rather utterly fall apart at the seams, to disintegrate before our very eyes — while on the other we have the invisible, psychological trauma suffered on the part of the audience, not simply a feeling of disturbance but rather an overwhelming shock to the senses. When we look a bit closer (as uncomfortable as that might be), we find this sensation to be the result of a carefully orchestrated series of excitations and stimulations, a calculated image of death — *a simulation of death* — so intensely visceral and so disturbingly verisimilar that its veracity becomes almost impossible to gauge, leaving us convinced that we've seen the very thing that we know we've not. Utterly overcome in this moment of witnessing, it's only later that we can ask ourselves if this is what death really looks like — a question which implies an ignorance every bit as painful as the image that inspired it — and because the answer never comes, we cannot seem to stop asking.

So, let's try asking different questions. In fact, let's change the whole conversation, for whenever the subject of violence in moving images comes up, the narrative seems always already determined: contemporary society, having been exposed to increasingly violent imagery over the last century, has become increasingly numb to not only those images but also violence as a whole. Indeed, though few would deny the fact that images of death have grown ever more gruesome (for lack of a better word) in the digital age, fewer still see such images as anything more than indications of a culture desensitized to violence and gore. Putting aside such notions, I seek a more nuanced account of our desire to *see and feel death* in popular media, first by observing that in the digital age we no longer aim to simply *represent* the end of life but also *simulate* death, and second by arguing that such simulations are, thanks in part to their increased viscerality and hapticity, symptoms of a desperate struggle to reassert the intensely painful pleasure — the *jouissance* — that was once found in the act of *witnessing death*, lost over the course of the twentieth century when that common experience was rapidly replaced by the production of images capable of displaying only the pain of *trauma*.

When Lacan first approached the issue of trauma in his 1964 seminar on "Tuché and Automaton," he was quick to remind us of Freud's observation that "nothing can be apprehended *in effigie, in absentia*" — that encounters with the sign and the symbol are not equal to encounters with the real.[1] Yet a confusion between representation and reality lies at the very heart of our relationship to death in contemporary culture: we find ourselves profoundly curious about and perversely titillated by death because its reality has been repressed and replaced by endless effigies, erected in the absence of an experience that has long been declared offensive and abject. Put more simply, we're drawn to images of death because we no longer have direct, unmediated encounters with the actual processes of dying. It's no wonder then, that so many of us fail to "apprehend" mortality — to understand, even at a rudimentary level, its complex physiological processes, to grasp its vast and far-reaching effects on our lives and our culture, or even to catch-it-in-the-act — because, for us, death has never been more than an image, just as it's always been absent from our lives. This is not to say that the *loss* that accompanies death (especially the passing of loved ones and friends) does not have a direct and profound impact on our lives, but rather that the actual *event* of dying — the moment that one's Being transitions into nothingness — is veiled, hidden, and repressed. And so to understand how this veiling of death has impacted our understanding of mortality, we must look back to a time when death was not absent but rather intensely *present*, a time before the image of death rendered the reality of death obscene.

What follows in this chapter, then, can perhaps best be described as *a longue durée of death* in three parts, each unpacking a different attitude toward mortality during a given century from the nineteenth to the twenty-first, each drawing upon different branches of theory and philosophy (from psychoanalysis to poststructuralism to new media theory), yet each also connected by a central theme: the trauma of witnessing death and the impact of that experience (or the absence of that experience) on our relationship to the very act of dying, whether as concept or as event. To that end, the first section will illustrate *what we've lost*: the thick experience of death once found in the act of witnessing, which provided opportunities (however traumatic they may have been) to glimpse the full processes of dying. The second section will explore *how we've lost it*: the emergence of new technologies during the late nineteenth and early twentieth centuries — chief among them the rise of hospital and the advent of the moving image — that allowed us to repress the thought of mortality and conceal the act of dying while simultaneously, and rather perversely, fetishizing the notion of traumatic death. The third section will cover *how we struggle to get it back*: the aesthetic and narrative strategies in contemporary moving images — namely, the push toward simulation, but also the increase of viscerality — through which we attempt to reassert both the painful trauma and the pleasurable *jouissance* of witnessing death. Along the way, we'll continue to wrestle with the issue of trauma and its connection to the image of death in contemporary culture, leading to a brief coda that will return us to the very spot from which we began: the physical and psychological trauma contained within a particularly visceral simulation of death.

The *Jouissance* of Death (Witnessing)

Let's begin as I suggested we should, by asking new questions about representations of violence and changing the conversation about death in moving images. In doing so, we must remember to consider trauma in both its forms: the physical violence that so often defines contemporary images of death and the psychological shocks that continue to resonate even after the screen has gone dark. Why, for example, are so many contemporary depictions of death fixated upon anatomical and biological details that were all but absent from moving images prior to the digital turn — not the tearing of flesh or the spilling of blood but the making visible of bones, muscles, organs, fluids, and other viscera under the skin? If we find these increasingly visceral depictions of death to be so uncomfortable to watch, why are we also so clearly attracted to them, both as audiences and as artists? Likewise, if the act of viewing verisimilar depictions of death is so painful, why are we subsequently compelled to repeat the experience (even if only in our minds)?

Perhaps it might be easiest to start with that last question, whose answer is both "shocking" and yet hardly surprising, for Freud's elaboration of traumatic neurosis — the foundation of numerous philosophical approaches to trauma throughout the twentieth century — hinged upon a similar question: Why does the unconscious mind repeat or replay traumatic experiences? In his influential essay *Beyond the Pleasure Principle*, Freud proposed that conscious experience is punctuated by the undesirable accumulation and subsequent cathexis of various energies or tensions. As such, one of the primary purposes of the structures of consciousness is to act as shield against "excessive amounts of stimulation" that might disproportionately add to such tensions, in particular through the pre-conscious reception and dismissal of vast amounts of stimuli that are deemed inconsequential or unnecessary for the conscious interpretation of experience.[2] According to this schema, one's typical experiences and memories are constituted only by those stimuli that pass through this pre-conscious screening process and enter into conscious thought or consideration. Trauma, on the other hand, is the result of stimuli whose "amplitude" is so intense as to overwhelm our defenses — forcefully bypassing the pre-conscious, flooding the conscious, and spilling over excess excitations into the unconscious in the form of psychic wounds. This is why Freud argued that "*protection* against stimuli is an almost more important function for the living organism than *reception* of stimuli," for the individual is always under threat of becoming overwhelmed, always "threatened by the enormous energies at work in the external world."[3] This notion was borrowed several years later by Walter Benjamin, who wrote that "the threat from these energies is one of *shocks*. The more readily consciousness registers these shocks, the less likely are they to have a traumatic effect."[4] When we're shocked by the images of *Irréversible*, it is not simply because we find their content disturbing, but also because the film overwhelms us with stimuli of such intensity that it cannot be easily or readily processed, leaving behind traumatic wounds in the form of questions that we cannot seem to answer and curiosities that we cannot seem to satiate.[5]

Considering that traumatic events greatly increase our tensions, we might assume that, in an attempt to somehow manage these tensions, traumatic wounds would be repressed or pushed aside within the unconscious. Yet Freud was surprised to find that this was frequently not the case. Instead, his initial encounters with trauma — first the analysand's transference of affect unto the analyst, which he read as an unconscious attempt to reproduce the circumstances a troubling relationship within the boundaries of analysis, and second the uncontrollable recollection of distressing events, such as the intense flashbacks experienced by veterans of combat or the debilitating nightmares suffered by victims of abuse — all shared in common an act of *repetition*, in which the circumstances of the traumatic event are not repressed but rather pushed to the fore and reproduced or re-experienced.[6] And so Freud arrived at that crucial question: If recollections of trauma build upon painful tensions, why does the unconscious mind repeat or replay traumatic experiences?

The answer was to be found in the now-famous example of the child's "fort-da" game, in which a well-behaved child of one and a half years old (who "above all never cried when his mother left him for a few hours") was observed repeatedly throwing a wooden spool tied to a string over the edge of his cot, such that it was out of view and therefore effectively absent, and then taking great delight in pulling it back — fort-da, fort-da, gone and back, gone and back.[7] The game, according to Freud, was an unconscious re-staging of a traumatic scene for the boy — that of the mother's uncontrollable absence, which instilled in the boy an anxiety regarding loss — and "he compensated for this, as it were, by himself staging the disappearance and return of the objects within his reach."[8] What is important here is not that the boy gained mastery over the toy's "existence" (an act which did not in any way negate his lack of agency in regard to his mother's presence and absence), but rather that he was able to stitch the notion of loss into his understanding of everyday experience, as rudimentary as it might yet have been, by creating a *symbol* that represented or, more astutely, stood in for the root cause of his pain and anxiety. As upsetting it may have been, the boy was no longer *overwhelmed* by his mother's absence because he had created a symbol which made the very concept of absence (and thus the experience of loss) far more easily negotiable and understandable.[9] Likewise, in cases of transference, flashbacks, and nightmares, Freud surmised that the unconscious continually reasserts traumatic experiences in order to provide opportunities to symbolize and negotiate the trauma, to give context and meaning to that which initially overwhelmed the primary (meaning-making and tension-reducing) processes of the conscious mind.

"The problem," as Žižek would later tell us, "is *how* to symbolize the trauma, how to integrate it into our universe of meaning and cancel its disorienting impact."[10] Or, perhaps, the problem is actually *when* to symbolize the trauma, as we find in Žižek's descriptions of disaster films that, in trying to *anticipate* mass trauma, failed to prepare us in any way for the horrors of 9/11.[11] But let's not get ahead of ourselves. If we assume that the answer to Freud's inquiry is the same as the answer to our own — why are we compelled to replay the shockingly visceral images of death found in contemporary moving images? — we might conclude that we "re-stage" the images in order to consciously negotiate or reflect upon that which had originally overwhelmed us and prevented conscious interpretation. Certainly there is truth here — we run through the distressing images of *Irréversible* again and again in our minds in order to "make sense" of something so violent that it initially stunned and nauseated us — and yet something about this analysis feels incomplete, there's something that we're clearly missing.

It's only when we look a bit closer at the cause of our trauma, at the very thing which we are attempting to symbolize and digest through contemplation and recollection, that it suddenly hits us: the traumatic image that we witnessed was itself already a symbol, a representation, and a substitute for another, greater trauma which many of us have never even experienced, namely, *the act of witnessing the actual death of another human being*, once an exceptionally common experience, yet now regarded as utterly abject. Moreover, if the image that felt so traumatizing — *the image that was designed to traumatize us* — was itself merely a stand-in for an encounter that we imagine to be intensely unpleasant even as we seem to unconsciously long to experience it, then we find that before we can fully address the role or function of trauma in contemporary images of death, we need first to explore how death was experienced *before* the moving image inundated us with its symbols, how we understood and related to death when its reality (and not just its image) was readily available to all.

In the opening of his seminal text *Discipline and Punish*, for example, Michel Foucault brutally yet eloquently describes a visceral scene of death, in which a man is tortured in front of a crowd with burning pinchers, covered in boiling oil and sulfur, has his limbs stretched by horses and hacked off by knives and saws, and is finally burned alive.[12] Although the details are every bit as gruesome and as painful as those of *Irréversible*, if not more so, Foucault's scene is no work of fiction; it's an account of the execution of Robert-François Damiens, the Frenchman charged with regicide after a botched attempt to assassinate King Louis XV in 1757. For Foucault, Damiens's execution — the last time the French government sanctioned the use of several brutal methods of torture, most specifically drawing and quartering — marked the start of a significant transition in which "the entire economy of punishment was redistributed" and subsequently hidden from the public within the invisible, panoptic systems of control favored by the modern prison complex and the neoliberal surveillance state.[13] Yet what strikes me about the event, and what warrants mention of it here, is not only the ensuing repression of the spectacle of death but also the very *public* from which it was hidden: the crowds and spectators who came to *see and feel death* and who thus desired to bring themselves *into contact with death* in a manner almost entirely unavailable in contemporary Western culture.

As was the case with the majority of executions from the medieval period through the late nineteenth century, the execution of Damiens was a public event, one in which the working class and the aristocracy alike witnessed firsthand the destruction of the human body and the difficult processes of dying. Among the crowd that day was the infamous womanizer Giacomo Casanova, who described the event as "an offence to our common humanity" — drawing and quartering having already been out of fashion, so to speak, for at least a century — yet also noted that his companions "did not budge an inch" as they watched.[14] Despite the severe brutality suffered upon Damiens's body or the disgust that such violence likely aroused, the fascination implied by Casanova was nonetheless a common characteristic of all who attended, regardless of gender, class, or occupation. "Nothing was noticed more in the vast concourse that saw it done," Dickens wrote of the event in *A Tale of Two Cities*, "than the crowd of ladies of quality and fashion, who were full of eager attention to the last ... until nightfall, when he had lost two legs and an arm, and still breathed!"[15] "Was it because their hearts were hardened?" Casanova asked.[16] Or were they, even unconsciously,

PORTRAIS DES · SOUFRANCE·DE·R·F·DAMIEN· ATTANTATEUR·DE·LAS
PERSONNES· SACRE'DU ROY·LOUIS·XV·LE· 5·JEANVIER.··· 1757

FIGURE 1.1 *The torture and execution of Damiens, March 2, 1757.*

drawn to the execution not to see the punishment of an infamous criminal, but instead simply drawn to *witness death*?

Today it strikes us as cruel, uncivilized, and unhealthy to desire to witness the death of another human being, but "for a very long period" — many centuries, as Philippe Ariès tells us — "death was a public spectacle from which no one would have thought of hiding and which was even sought after at times."[17] In this regard, the public execution is perhaps too easy an example; we recognize its graphic details because execution scenes have become a common trope in many historical dramas, where they adhere closely to the notions of traumatic death privileged by the moving image (we feign astonishment at the fictional spectators who cheer on the executioners, yet delight ourselves in the violence). When we extend our gaze further back in history, we find that we are similarly well-versed in the "bloodlust" that spurred ancient gladiatorial combat — where the traumatic destruction of the human body was (and remains, in fictional representations) the central attraction — and with the practice of human sacrifice, prevalent not only in our narratives of ancient tribal cultures but also in many of our most celebrated religious texts.[18] Despite being a bit on-the-nose, these examples nonetheless hint at a desire that has always accompanied the conscious recognition of mortality — to stand in the presence of death — that was also on display more recently, though less transparently, in nineteenth-century examples like public surgeries and autopsies or in the desire to observe combat, such as the picnic-basket-toting spectators who went to watch the opening battle of the American Civil War in July of 1861.[19]

Significantly more prominent in our past, though far less represented today, was the experience of natural death, the anticipated passing which occurred in the home, in bed, and in the presence of *witnesses*. Far and away the most common manner of dying for centuries, the "deathbed" held an especially prominent role in the literature, theater, and art of the mid-to-late nineteenth century — immediately prior to the advent of the moving image and its fetishization of traumatic death — when it became "a key set piece" for many Victorian and Edwardian artists.[20] According to Geoffrey Gorer, the reason for this was simple: "it was one of the relatively few experiences that an author could be fairly sure would have been shared by the vast majority of his readers," a universal familiarity afforded by its status as an overtly *public* ceremony.[21] Indeed, before the hospital became the primary and private domain of death, the dying person's bedchamber was always "a public place to be entered freely" and an intimate space where they were always "at the center of a group of people" — not just family, but also friends, neighbors, acquaintances, and even curious strangers.[22] Children, too, were exposed to death, and it was considered so integral a part of the experience of adolescence that until the turn of the twentieth century "no portrayal of a deathbed scene failed to include children."[23] Though the experience of death has never been *comfortable*, to witness the passing of others was once at the very least *common*, a standard rite of passage for the young and an anticipated sacrament for the old.

The former ubiquitousness of the deathbed ritual betrays the fact that it was once considered a necessary and even essential event, but for what purpose and to what end? On the surface, we can attribute this omnipresence to the fact that several important social functions were made possible by the deathbed.[24] First and foremost, it facilitated the farewells desired by both the dying and their kin, allowing for the necessary gratitudes, praises, apologies, and forgivenesses that accompany a social life, as well as the opportunity for reflection and prayer.[25] At the same time, it was often the preferred moment to announce the "redistribution of social roles and property rights," which, according to Elisabeth Bronfen, helped to "close the gap in social relations produced by death" and ensure the continuation of significant social and familial structures.[26] Finally, on a less practical and more existential level, to be surrounded in one's last moment was also thought to be the final assurance of a meaningful and successful life, for before the image of trauma turned the sudden possibility of death into a terrifying specter, the primary fear regarding one's mortality was the fear of dying alone. So to die "at home in the bosom of one's family" was often considered to be the very definition of "the good death," which was more than a privilege, it was an aspiration, the goal of well-lived life, the final opportunity to resolve lingering tensions and ensure the continued subsistence of family and community.[27] Yet today, in an age when the act of witnessing death is anything but quotidian, we can begin to look beyond these obvious benefits and recognize that the deathbed ritual was far more than a simple custom. It was, rather, for hundreds if not thousands of years, an indispensable ritual that eased the pain of knowing death just as much as it eased the passing of the aged, the sick, and the injured, for it provided an opportunity to *viscerally and haptically experience* an event that is, consciously or not, the central concern of every human life.[28]

The experience of witnessing death would have been, we can imagine, rather intense under such intimate circumstances. Various sensations would have emerged: a visible blotchiness of the skin as it mottled, the sound of heavy and irregular breathing — the infamous death rattle — as the lungs began to fill with fluid, a coolness of the skin as circulation began to slow, a mustiness in the air as the body sweat and lost bladder and bowel control, strange tremors which shook the bed as muscles convulsed and spasmed. *It was in this close proximity that death was not only seen and heard but touched, smelled, and tasted.* Yet any lasting impression — the shock of witnessing, as it were — would have originated not from one phenomenon alone but rather from their constant and continuous co-mingling, for to witness the passing of another was always far more than a simple series of sensations, it was a vivid act of perception that expanded and perhaps even enabled one's knowledge of death. Whether in the home or in the square, whether it be natural or traumatic, the importance of witnessing death was that very thickness of experience: death, that ultimate unknown, that fleeting moment which separates our lived reality from the abstractness of non-existence, could at the very least be *perceived* even if it could not be caught, captured, or studied.

We might say, in fact, that the importance of witnessing was the strange and difficult comfort that accompanied such perception, clearly felt in one of Ariés's most potent examples of the deathbed scene. Present for her husband Albert's death from pulmonary consumption in June of 1836 (alongside his priest, parents, siblings, and friends), Alexandrine de La Ferronay observed the slow agony brought about by both his disease and his treatment — including violent fevers, agonizing coughs, and "extensive bloodlettings." Rather than pain or heartache, however, she found herself taken aback in the moment of his passing: "His eyes, already fixed, were turned to me ... and I, his wife!, felt something I would have never imagined: I felt that death was happiness."[29] Certainly Alexandrine was relieved to see her husband's suffering abated, but the happiness that she felt was something far more powerful — it was an altogether new understanding of death, a recognition that to die is not necessarily the culmination of our fears, but also often the answer to our prayers. The event itself was shocking (as the experience of witnessing always was) but this trauma was different, not only of intense pain or confusion but also of intense pleasure — it was an experience of *jouissance*.

Although the concept was first developed in his seminar on "The Ethics of Psychoanalysis," let's sneak up on Lacan's understanding of *jouissance* by briefly turning to Roland Barthes, whose work on *The Pleasure of the Text* outlined a clear distinction between *plaisir* and *jouissance* or, as translator Richard Miller puts it, pleasure/contentment vs. bliss/rapture.[30] As Miller's dichotomy suggests, *plaisir* is quotidian, the enjoyment of the comfortable experience, whereas *jouissance* is excessive, a disturbing and overwhelming ecstasy, and although Barthes's analysis was grounded in literature and other forms of the text, it's clear in his writing that *plaisir* is born in the security of contemplation, whereas *jouissance* comes from the vulnerability of embodied perception, such that "you cannot speak 'on' [*jouissance*], you can only speak 'in' it."[31] We find *jouissance*, then, in "that moment when my body pursues its own ideas — for my body does not have the same ideas I do."[32]

This is not so different from the understanding we find in Lacan, who saw *jouissance* as an experience that exceeds the comfortable boundaries of pleasure and thus pushes *beyond the pleasure principle*, to the point where it becomes painful and distressing. That Lacan's reading of *jouissance* is strongly linked to the sexual drives — Alan Sheridan reminds us that its French root "*jouir* is slang for 'to come'" — should not deter us from finding *jouissance* in the experience of witnessing death, for the pleasurable trauma of sex is a bodily ecstasy, and in the presence of death one's ecstasy comes not from the contemplation of finitude so much as it comes from the full bodily perception of the physical and biological processes of death, the minute details of the breakdown of the body which are concretely accessible to the senses and yet so difficult to capture using mere words or representations.[33] Indeed, we'll come to find that *jouissance* is almost entirely unavailable in representations, and so as we turn our attention to twentieth century images of death, let's add one more crucial question to our list: how does our awareness and comprehension of mortality change when the traumatic pleasure of witnessing is replaced by the painful image of trauma?

The Pornography of Death (Representing)

Over the course of last century, death has become both aggressively clinical and violently unruly, a private and abject event subject to stringent rules and restrictions even as we imagine it to be uncontrollably chaotic and destructive. Of course death has always been a contradictory, paradoxical figure — ever hovering just out of reach and just beyond understanding — but today, in the age of medical science, in the age of contamination and sterilization, *in the age of the hospital*, the domain of death has become a private space, a quarantined space, visited only by the dying person and their practitioners, those scant few deemed worthy of death's presence because they have devoted their lives not simply to comprehending and confronting it, but more importantly to *containing* it, so that the masses need not be burdened with the details — "an interdiction of death in order to preserve happiness."[34] For the rest of us, then, death is a distant thing, a shameful failure of the body, a (supposed) struggle that (apparently) happens behind closed doors, between walls of white curtain, and under oppressive fluorescent lighting ... though it's hard to be certain of the details because we are so often denied access in the final moments. And so we rely upon the fictions that surround us on television screens and in movie theaters, transforming death into something altogether different, a sudden and malevolent event that exists only in the dominion of sickness, accidents, malice, and cruelty.

This was, as we have seen, not always the case. Prior to the twentieth century, death was present, it was public, and it was explicitly visible; not some thief in the night who came to steal you away without warning but instead a constant companion whose existence was *experienced* (rather than inferred or suspected) through the common, social ritual of witnessing of the death of others. In this light, there was no shame to death — rather than a "failure" of the body, death was the body letting go of bonds that were never meant to be permanent — and so it played out in the home, a public event anticipated and attended by a community. This was the death that Ariès refers to as "the tame death," the death that gave "advanced warning of its arrival" and consequently "could not be sudden" because it was always present, always expected, always familiar.[35] "When we call this familiar death the tame death," Ariès explains, "we do not mean that it was once wild and that it was later domesticated. On the contrary, we mean that it has become wild today when it used to be tame."[36] Only since the start of twentieth century have we come to assume that death is wild, because only then did death become *hidden, repressed, and denied* — hidden by technologies that aim to defeat or replace it, repressed by a culture that fetishizes its bitterness while forgetting its sweetness, denied by the individual who "at heart ... doesn't feel that *he* will die" but instead "only feels sorry for the man next to him."[37] Today, we fail to recognize the possibility of the tame death because *we fail to recognize death at all*, we have removed its actual presence from daily life to such an extent that we have forgotten what death is and remember only what we imagine it to be.

This repression has not gone entirely unobserved. The first to note its onset was the aforementioned anthropologist Geoffrey Gorer, whose slight but influential 1955 essay "The Pornography of Death" argued that death had become the central taboo of the twentieth century, much as sexuality had been in the nineteenth. "There seems to have been an unremarked shift in prudery;" he observed, "whereas copulation has become more and more 'mentionable,' particularly in the Anglo-Saxon societies, death has become more and more 'unmentionable' as a natural process" — a radical overturning of social attitudes toward propriety and a conspicuous reversal of thinking in regard to the body.[38] Particularly striking is his reference to the "natural process" of death, which brings to mind two implications: first that death is, like sex, a fundamental aspect of the natural world whose consequences must eventually be thought through regardless of their "seemliness" (as Gorer would put it), and second that only natural death has become repressed in contemporary culture, whereas traumatic death has become increasingly symbolized to the point of fetishization.

In a culture where the reality of death has all but disappeared, it is of the utmost importance to recognize that biological trauma is and has long been *the* defining characteristic of the image of death. In fact, traumatic death is so fundamental to the tradition of the moving image that it would be nearly impossible to count the number of popular films, television shows, and digital games which revel in the spectacle of the body's destruction (whether in the form of action heroes who avoid danger while indiscriminately doling out death, horror starlets who watch as friends are poached and gored one by one, or dramatic leads who struggle with the illness or injury of friends and lovers), resulting in an immeasurable database of fictional bodies battered and torn apart by gunfire, car accidents, explosions, and other equivalent forms of violence which have only increased in viscerality in the digital age. Yet this move toward the fetishization of trauma was so radically different from prior, long-standing attitudes toward death that Ariès describes it as no less than "a brutal revolution in traditional ideas and feelings."[39] Looking back to the Middle Ages, Ariès reminds us that traumatic death was deemed, for hundreds of years, as the abject event par excellence — an attitude born from a religious viewpoint that thought of sudden death as a direct punishment from God — and the narratives of those who were unfortunate enough to die by random trauma were subject to repression and denial. "In this world that was so familiar with death, a sudden death was a vile and ugly death; it was frightening; it seemed a strange and monstrous thing that nobody dared talk about," and even the victims of violent crime were subjected to such repression, "inescapably dishonored by the vileness of [their] death."[40] The heroes of literature, songs, and folk tales, on the other hand, were always fully cognizant of their immanent death, whether through an awareness of natural signs from the body such as pain, bleeding, and fever, or from more supernatural inclinations like visions, dreams, and premonitions — though this distinction is, Ariès warns, "probably an anachronism; in those days the boundary between the natural and the supernatural was indefinite."[41] Regardless, the death worthy of remembrance was one which the dying person approached calmly and with dignity, a death marked by acceptance rather than struggle, by *recognition rather than denial*.

Consider, then, the complete reversal of this attitude in contemporary culture, where to fight against death is considered not only brave but honorable and praiseworthy, where the natural death warrants little more than a small notice in local obituaries while the sudden or traumatic death is widely reported, discussed, and memorialized. Bearing in mind that traumatic injuries, whether accidental or intentional, account for less than 10 percent of the deaths in the contemporary United States, this constant bombardment of stories and images of trauma (murders, freak occurrences, automobile accidents, natural disasters, etc.) serve not to make death more present in our lives but rather to veil the realities of death, to deny that it is ever natural to begin with and instead turn it into something that can be prevented with better treatment and more vigilance (what Ariés refers to as "the return of warning").[42] For more than a century, then, natural death has been all but absent from the cultural imaginary, whereas traumatic death has become a central fear and a key form of titillation.

Titillation is, in fact, a vital aspect of Gorer's reading of the repression of death, which he brings into play when he argues that representations of traumatic death quickly transitioned from being merely obscene (as in a failure to observe social codes which results in "shock, social embarrassment, and laughter") to being pornographic (the "description of tabooed activities" which gratifies personal fantasies and produces a "pleasurable guilt or a guilty pleasure").[43] While we typically associate pornography with graphic depictions of sexuality, "there seem to be," Gorer argued, "a number of parallels between the fantasies which titillate our curiosity about the mystery of sex, and those which titillate our curiosity about the mystery of death."[44] In particular, both tend to ignore "the emotions which are typically concomitant with the acts ... while the *sensations* [of the event] are enhanced as much as a customary poverty of language permits."[45] For Gorer, this meant that the psychological aspects of sex and death — such as love, grief, angst, and anxiety — are denied in their pornographic depictions, whereas the physical sensations are fetishized and fixated upon, they become the central characteristics of the representation. To Gorer's observation we can add our own: in fetishizing the sensations of physical trauma, what was lost was at the turn of the twentieth century was the perceptual thickness that came with witnessing the natural processes of death, and by extension the pleasurable trauma that was once an essential component of the contemplation of mortality (the implications of which we'll return to shortly).

Gorer's investigations into the repression of death were followed in the 1960s by Herman Feifel's collection on *The Meaning of Death* (featuring essays by Carl Jung and Herbert Marcuse, among others), which laid the groundwork for the field of thanatological study by arguing that death plays an essential role in human psychology and that its repression shuts down several avenues for understanding basic human behavior, and by Jessica Mitford's exposé on *The American Way of Death*, which shed light upon the sudden commercialization and industrialization of death that had been made possible by the refusal to discuss or acknowledge the "secret" practices of the funerary profession.[46] Then, of course, there was Elizabeth Kubler-Ross's *On Death and Dying*, which (aside from its introduction of the now-famous "five stages of grief") argued for the return of an increased awareness of the implications of death for both society and the individual.[47] Yet the most thorough analyses of the repression of death would appear in the 1970s, particularly in the psychoanalytic and anthropological work of Ernest Becker and Philippe Ariès.

In *The Denial of Death*, Becker drew on Freud, Kierkegaard (who he saw as a precursor to psychoanalysis and a religious counterpoint to Freud), and Otto Rank to diagnose mass culture as little more than a series of "immortality projects" — specific acts or actions through which the individual could strive for a symbolic immortality long after the decay of the body — designed to assuage the need to contemplate the inevitability and finitude of mortality. In other words, the ultimate goal of many human endeavors — whether they be grand in scale, like becoming a war hero or having a building named after you, or humble, like taking a photograph or keeping a diary — has long been to leave behind self-causing (*causa sui*) objects or impressions which can continue to organize or define the meaning of our lives even after our deaths, effectively denying one of death's most terrifying capacities: erasure.[48] History is of course filled with such death monuments, but the common individual's capacity for preserving fragments of their life increased significantly in the transition from the nineteenth to the twentieth century, and only continues to expand in the twenty-first. Equally intriguing for this project is Becker's argument, early in the text, that a repressive society constructs two images of those who contemplate death: the "healthy-minded" person who maintains that the "fear of death is not a natural thing for man," and the "morbidly-minded" person for whom death is not only natural and ever-present, but also "the basic fear that influences all others."[49] In fact, since the turn of the twentieth century, the acute awareness of death has often been categorized (erroneously or not) as a neurosis, a notion that Becker returned to throughout his text to paint well-established neuroses like depression and schizophrenia as possessing more and more extreme perspectives on death and futility.

Yet while Becker was relatively successful in highlighting the repressive aspects of the twentieth century's immortality projects, he nonetheless failed to contextualize them in relation to earlier preoccupations with mortality.[50] To fill in the historical gaps, one could turn to Ariès (as I so often have) and his rather grand pronouncement that "the historian of death must not be afraid to embrace the centuries until they run into a millennium," which he backed up with research that traced Western culture's attitudes toward death over the course of several hundreds years.[51] Along the way, Ariès was able to demonstrate that our relationship with death "may appear almost static over long periods of time ... and yet, at certain moments, changes occur, usually slow and unnoticed changes, but sometimes, as today, more rapid and perceptible ones."[52] In his classic thanatological tome *The Hour of Our Death*, for example, Ariès sketches out an epistemology of death in which a series of subtle shifts and variations on specifics themes — the role of the church in shaping our conception of death, the image of the corpse and other elements of the *macabre*, the last rights and judgments of the dying — are punctuated by moments of rupture, the most severe being the aforementioned "brutal revolution" of the early twentieth century, when, as I argue, we swung from the abject view of trauma to its fetishization. In fact, if there is anything we can take away from the scholarship produced by Gorer, Becker, Ariès and others, it's that the sudden concealment of the realities of death just over a century ago was in every way an unprecedented event, a reversal of attitude so violent and so sudden as to not simply change our understanding of death but to entirely reshape our relationship to it.

How did this shift come to pass? How did we transition so rapidly from the notion that witnessing death was an essential aspect of the human experience to the belief that death should be utterly concealed from respectable society? The most obvious and most often cited answer, as I made more or less explicit above, is that the embrace of modern medical science at the turn of the twentieth century ensured that the hospital became not only death's *primary* domain, but also its *private* domain as well. Indeed, the move from a visible death to an invisible specter of death was largely instigated by a shift in medical thinking, which declared witnesses to the dying to be not a comfort and a necessity but rather a danger and a risk — carriers of germs, microbes, and bacteria that would only increase both the pace and the pain of death, which could in turn be abated only by the expertise of the hospital staff. This much was obvious to Becker and Ariès, the former dying of cancer when he wrote *The Denial of Death*, the latter calling the state of death in the twentieth century a "technical phenomenon" which occurs not as a result of internal, natural causes but rather from the "cessation of care ... determined in a more or less avowed way by a decision of the doctor and the hospital team."[53] Foucault, too, was aware of the immense influence of the hospital. In *The Birth of the Clinic*, he wrote of the adoption of new medical practices in the nineteenth century as an epistemological rupture in which the regimes of the visible became divorced from the regimes of knowledge, such that sickness and illness could no longer be "seen" by the untrained eye but were instead visible only to those with a mastery of medical science.[54] As the sole possessors of this "medical gaze," the authority of doctors and clinicians was certainly increased, yet at great cost, for it also implied that the average person was incapable of comprehending the natural processes of the body through perception alone. Witnessing death, once a requisite experience which inaugurated one's subjective yet essential knowledge of mortality, was quickly territorialized by doctors who veiled its reality and claimed dominion over its very existence (in the process transforming hospitals into what Foucault called "temples of death," far removed from "the familiar surroundings of [the] home and family").[55]

Yet this is clearly not the whole story, for we've seen that the trauma of witnessing played an essential role in our contemplation of mortality — so essential that it couldn't be denied or repressed without, at the very least, some sort of substitute sensation. Enter the moving image, whose representations of death *facilitated* the disappearance of our actual encounters by providing that alternate experience, which is not to say that they negated our fascination with the processes of dying, but rather that they gave us just enough of a glimpse to satisfy our curiosity. The problem, of course, is that that glimpse was pure fantasy — images of eyes closing and bodies going limp with little correlation to the actual processes, appearance, or experience of death — and thus a substantially poor substitution. Worse yet, over time we seem to have lost sight of (or perhaps even *chosen to ignore*) the very fact that these images are a substitution.

Before we can examine those images in detail, however, it's important to note that the roots of the relationship between death and the moving image began many years before Edison and the Lumiéres first began to experiment with strips of celluloid, for death was one of the primary fascinations of the photographic technologies which preceded the motion picture. "Ever since cameras were invented in 1839," Susan Sontag tells us, "photography has kept company with death," perhaps because it had "the advantage of uniting two contradictory features. [Its] credentials of objectivity were inbuilt. Yet [it] always had, necessarily, a point of view."[56] The photograph, though *less perceptually thick*, could at least do something that the often-overwhelming experience of witnessing could not: it could draw one's focus to a particular sensation — the paleness of the skin, the stiffness of the postmortem expression, the eerie lifelessness of the eyes of the corpse — and then allow one to fixate upon or contemplate that sensation in perpetuity. It should be no surprise, then, that something which had been so notoriously difficult to pin down would become a steady fixture of popular photographs during the nineteenth century, nor that the medium only truly took root in the public consciousness after the onset of the American Civil War, when pictures of corpse-strewn battlefields were highlighted in newspapers and journals across the country and around the world.[57]

Yet a photograph need not contain a dead body in order to signify death. For example, when Barthes set out to uncover why we are drawn to certain photographs — why one image strikes us as profound, sad, terrifying, or exhilarating when a whole world of other images do little more than give us pause — he came upon the notions of the *studium* and the *punctum*, the former being the collective content of an image which inspires only a "docile interest," the latter that rare detail within an image which strikes us in an "unexpected flash" and thus shocks us, disturbs us, pricks us.[58] In his analysis of the *punctum*, Barthes came to realize that it need not be a physical detail but could be (and often is) something less tangible and less material. "This new *punctum*, which is no longer of form but of intensity, is Time, the lacerating emphasis of the *noeme* ('*that-has-been*')."[59] Within every photograph there is a co-mingled sense of time, a past moment that meets with the present and a suggestion — no, an argument — that time moves ever forward, that *what-has-been* is life and *what-will-be* is death. "Whether or not the subject is already dead" — whether or not there even *is* a living subject, Barthes came to recognize — "every photograph is this catastrophe."[60] Why a catastrophe? Because the implication of death within the photograph is not reserved only for its subject, but instead "each photograph already contains this imperious sign of *my* future death."[61]

Regardless of whether or not we view death as a catastrophe, Barthes showed us that the power of the image (still or moving) is not found in the thing or event that it depicts, but rather in those intense details which prick and shock us. Seeing as it is both *subjective* and *shocking*, the punctum of representations is somewhat akin to the trauma of witnessing — but does this mean that representations can also arouse the *jouissance* that once made standing in the presence of death so important and so essential? To find out, let's look a bit closer at a rather obvious characteristic of twentieth-century depictions of death, one which not only distinguished them from their photographic counterparts of the nineteenth but also had a profound affect on the nature of our understanding of death in contemporary culture — namely, that they were, on the whole, overwhelmingly *fictional*.

The initial reasons for this are apparent, as the technological limitations of early motion pictures — the expense and rarity of celluloid film stock, the amount of light needed to achieve a properly exposed image, the short lengths of film which could be loaded into the camera — prohibited improvisational shooting and made it extremely difficult to capture live events without first staging the scenario (sure, the Lumiéres wanted to reflect back to us the *"actualités"* of the world, but their images were every bit as carefully composed and micro-managed as those made by Edison and Dickson in their Black Maria studio). Yet by mid-century, when new technological advancements, such as smaller, lighter cameras and faster, cheaper film stocks, made the capturing of live events less challenging, the reality of death had already receded into the realm of the unspoken and unseen — what was once so natural a subject for the still photograph remained far more elusive for the moving image.

Perhaps, then, it's all the more surprising that the fictional representations of death in moving images seemed to possess the same "credentials of objectivity" that defined the still photograph — credentials which they maintained on the back of misidentifications and misunderstandings. To clarify, let's turn once again to the "easy example" of public executions, and in particular to the rather infamous death of Mary Stuart, one-time queen of Scotland, whose beheading both shocked and delighted many early film viewers in 1895 thanks to the Edison Manufacturing Company's short recreation of the event. With direction credited to Alfred Clark and cinematography by William Heise — who also shot *The Kiss*, another scandalous early short film — *The Execution of Mary, Queen of Scots* is known as much for its violence as it is for being one of the earliest examples of filmic editing and special effects. The film itself is rather simple: several spectators (wearing anachronistic costuming) stand against a white background at the rear of the frame, watching as the character of Mary kneels, in an austere black dress, before an executioner in an equally stark robe and mask. Mary places her head upon a block as the executioner raises an axe above his, which, with nary a moment of hesitation, is brought down upon her neck. Her head, cleanly and bloodlessly severed from her body, rolls onto the floor, where it is snatched up by the executioner, the film abruptly ending just as he begins to raise it into the air for display. More complex than the film itself was the public's reaction to it, which, depending on the source, is reported to have been a mixture of nervous laughter, disbelief, and revulsion — a variety of responses owing largely to the question of whether or not those early spectators, unschooled in the visual duplicity of filmmaking, believed that an actual woman gave her life for the film.

FIGURE 1.2 *The "fatal" blow in* The Execution of Mary, Queen of Scots.

Yet duplicity it was, for not only was the character of Mary played by a male actor in drag, but frame by frame analysis clearly reveals the moment when the actors froze in place, the camera turned off to allow for "Mary" to replaced by a dummy, then restarted just in time for the "fatal" blow to be struck — perhaps our earliest example of a substitution splice.[62] For those peeping into a Kinetoscope in 1895, however, the ability to pause the film for study would have been just as foreign a notion as "editing" itself, and thus they "may not have noticed, for example, the slight mismatch of the raised scepter one moment with no raised scepter the next," which, according to Scott Combs, is "the one 'glitch' that tells on the film."[63] As a result, he argues, "spectators may have believed that [Mary's] decapitation looked as real as any other subject," which is to say that it looked as real as the photographs of death which had proceeded it, whose truth-value (at least as far as the public was concerned) had been clearly established.[64] As the ancestor of that technology, the moving image *inherited* the credibility of the photograph, even if it had most certainly not earned it.

Despite the fact that it *looked* real, however, the perceptual thickness of Edison's film would have surely paled in comparison to the actual event upon which it was based. Having been convicted of plotting to usurp the throne of England from her cousin Queen Elizabeth, Mary Stuart was brought by her executioners before a large body of witnesses (mostly local nobles and dignitaries, but also a small group of her servants whose attendance she personally requested) on February 8, 1587. There, she was rather embarrassingly disrobed in front of the crowd, kneeling before the block not in the plain black dress of Edison's film, but rather a satin bodice. Despite joking that she had "never had such grooms before to make her unready," Mary's nervousness and fear must have been felt by the crowd, especially in her hurried prayers as she awaited the executioner's stroke.[65] Yet what came brought no end to the ordeal, for the headsman's first swing missed her neck and struck the back of her head — "one account," according to John Guy, "says Mary made a 'very small noise,' but another says she cried out in agony."[66] A second swing nearly finished the job, if not for the small strips of flesh and sinew that needed to be crudely cut apart with the axe's blade. Next, when the executioner lifted Mary's severed head for presentation, "an audible gasp went up from the hall because Mary's lips were still moving" — a postmortem spasm that many in the crowd interpreted as a continued prayer. Worse yet, the hair which the executioner grasped turned out to be a wig, Mary's secret revealing itself to the world only when it detached from her scalp, her grey and balding head falling unto the floor and awkwardly rolling away. And, as if this scene where not horrific or harrowing enough for the crowd, Mary's small dog, which had apparently hidden itself under her petticoat, ran toward her body and, after several failed attempts to corner or contain it, "lay down in the widening pool of blood between her severed head and shoulders."[67]

However we might imagine our own reaction to such an event, this much is certain: "No one who witnessed Mary's last day could ever have forgotten it."[68] Not the sound of the axe striking bone nor that of Mary's painfully muttered cry, not the slowness of time as the executioner recognized his error and pulled back for a second blow, not the sight of her face tumbling across the floor nor the smell of her thickly spilled blood, not the sting of the winter air in the hall nor the chill that rippled through the crowd as a nobleman shouted "so perish all the Queen's enemies!"[69] On the flip side, we have the simplicity of Edison's representation — the promptness with which Mary relents to her killer, the cleanliness of his stroke, the lack of emotion or reaction from the rather small crowd — which, under any form of reflection, lends the film an air of inauthenticity. Sure, it's shocking when we first see it, but it's also strangely anticlimactic, especially considering the fact that we are given very little time to truly anticipate the event. In fact, when we watch the film over again (as if, say, on a loop, the way it would've actually been exhibited in nickelodeons of the era) it's hard not to notice other telltale signs of the film's deception. Combs undersells the "glitchiness" of the splice, for example, as not only does the position of a guard's spear jump a bit, but so too does the executioner's backswing –moving from precisely vertical to an angled downward strike — and nearly every member of the crowd, most of whom are shuffled some degree to their left or right. Even Mary's body shifts strangely, her face pressed flatter against the block and her dress much fuller as if her hips were suddenly propped further up and back (either that or she gains about 50 pounds in a fraction of a second). Equally telling is the reaction of the executioner after completing his task, who appears to look up directly at the camera, perhaps in excitement at the success of his swing, or perhaps to check with someone off frame to ensure that everything went according to plan. Realizing that the cameras are still rolling, he quickly remembers his second task and scoops up the fake head — the final "proof" of death demanded by the film.

Whether grinning or grimacing, however, it's safe to assume that the most common response to *The Execution of Mary* was shock, just as it would have been the most common reaction to the actual death of Mary Stuart. Yet it's also clear that these two shocks had almost nothing in common, the former one of simple surprise at what amounts to little more than a visual hoax (which ultimately leaves very little in the way of lasting impression), the latter a shock of intensity, an overwhelming perceptual thickness that assaulted the senses and burrowed its way into the unconscious. As the twentieth century came and went, however, it brought with it only the shock of the hoax — gunmen tossing dummies off a train (or pretending to fire directly at the audience) in Porter's *The Great Train Robbery*, noisy yet bloodless drive-bys in Hawk's original *Scarface* (whose potency came more from pointing to real-life events than it did from any sort of verisimilitude), inexplicable explosions of blood and bodies ridiculously flung through the air in Peckinpah's *The Wild Bunch*. To these oft-cited examples we could undoubtedly add countless other images that feel somehow equally provoking and unfulfilling, but we've little need to walk step-by-step through this familiar, escalating trajectory of violence.[70] Instead, what we should and will do is look to the consequences of this trajectory, to the false consciousness that results from these endless and infertile hallucinations.

"False consciousness" is exactly what Guy Debord saw in the mediated culture of the mid-twentieth century, a "society of the spectacle" in which "everything that was directly lived has receded into a representation."[71] Crucially, this "spectacle" is one that expressly denies direct perception in favor of the contemplation of discrete sensations:

> Since the spectacle's job is to use various specialized mediations in order to *show* us a world that can no longer be grasped, it naturally elevates the sense of sight to the special pre-eminence once occupied by touch: the most abstract and easily deceived sense is the most readily adaptable to the generalised abstraction of present-day society.[72]

Our recognition of the world, then, comes not from our *being-present* with it, but rather from quick glances to the other side of the room, from staring not through a window but at a screen. For Debord, what was at stake was not simply the notion that reality is masked by these sensationalized deceptions, but more importantly that it had come to be defined by them — "reality emerges within the spectacle, and the spectacle is real."[73]

This failure to distinguish the image from the actual is equally accounted for in the poststructuralism of Jean Baudrillard, whose development of the four "successive phases of the image" was a direct commentary on the lost connection to reality at the heart of the postmodern condition. In fact, when I stated a moment ago that there was little need to lay out the history of death in moving images, I did so not only because its trajectory has always been explicitly visible, but also because even a cursory reading of Baudrillard's essay on "The Precession of the Simulacra" provides an exceptional periodization of the image of death (even if death itself was not explicit in the study). In its first phase, for example, Baudrillard argued that the image appears as a "reflection of a profound reality," and in regard to death, this was the era of the still photograph, when pictures of corpses and battlefields were meant to safeguard the memory of those who were lost — not a replacement for the experience of witnessing so much as an extension of it.[74] Baudrillard names this phase "the sacramental order," when the image was "a *good* appearance" because its intentions were pure (or, perhaps, its intentions were to maintain the purity of the thing or event depicted). In the second phase, however, the image "masks and denatures a profound reality," it was "an evil appearance."[75] Counted amongst this "order of maleficence" would be early motion pictures like *The Execution of Mary*, whose depictions of death *perverted its reality* not simply because they were a hoax, but because that hoax forced its audience to question and doubt their own ability to recognize death. This led to the third stage, when the image "masks the *absence* of a profound reality," when its very purpose was to disguise that which it deemed inconsequential or abject.[76] This was the era of Gorer's pornography, those mid-century depictions of violence that were designed to titillate only in service of satisfying our curiosity, such that the veiled realities of death would not be missed. In this, the "order of sorcery," the image merely "plays at appearance," whether it held any allegiance to reality was of little consequence, for its very existence concealed that of its long-forgotten referent.

By the fourth stage, however, there was no more uncertainty: the image held "no relation to any reality whatever: it [was] its own pure simulacrum."[77] Implicit in this statement is Baudrillard's unique definition of the simulacrum — not merely a representation but a signifier without a signified, an imitation that has assumed the throne of reality (in a coup that is by no means bloodless) and thus declared itself *truth* — and also an indication of what Baudrillard termed "the precession of simulacra," that moment when representations begin to *precede* their referents, when the image defines the real rather than the other way around. Baudrillard's well-known example is borrowed from Jorges Louis Borges, a fable in which a map becomes so large and so exquisitely detailed that it blankets the empire it was made to represent, and in time "it is the real, and not the map, whose vestiges persist here and there in the deserts ... *the desert of the real itself*."[78] Like Borges's map, the images of death that grew from the roots of films like *The Execution of Mary* are no longer even recognized as representations, but are instead believed to *be death itself* (while the vestiges of actual death persist only for those who are lost or who have chosen to go exploring).[79]

Indeed, by the postmodern era, few could say that they had actually witnessed or experienced the death of another, despite the fact we had become encumbered by images upon images upon images of death and dying, pure simulacra with no relation to real bodies ceasing to function, a collectively invented conception of the final event of life. We've already seen that what we lost during the twentieth century was the trauma and *jouissance* of witnessing that once inaugurated our knowledge of mortality, but now we can also see *how we lost it*: the influence of the hospital and the inescapabilty of the moving image, which together hid from us a truth that we once thought so essential. Yet our profound lack of understanding only fuels a desire for a new experience of mortality, even if such desire is unconscious and we're not quite sure how to satisfy it. Perhaps there was a clue in Baudrillard's name for the fourth phase of the image: *the "order of simulations."*

The Sublimity of Death (Simulating)

In the two decades since the digital turn, the image of death has changed — on the one hand doubling down on the physical trauma that has long been its defining characteristic, while on the other attempting to recapture the (perversely pleasurable) psychological trauma that once accompanied the actual event of death. In fact, if we can say anything about our contemporary relationship to death, it's that we are constantly and continuously searching for a way to bring the image of death into alignment with the actuality of death, to reinstate the knowledge and the *jouissance* once associated with the act of witnessing. In *Welcome to the Desert of the Real*, for example, Žižek followed Baudrillard in mapping out a persistently shifting relationship between our desire to comprehend the richness of lived reality and our desire to reproduce or represent that reality, what he called (borrowing from Alain Badiou) our "passion for the Real" and our "passion for semblance," respectively. What began in the modern period as a push to replicate the phenomenological experiences of reality through the new technologies of the image — photographs, cinema, television — morphed over time into a postmodern obsession with representing the abject or traumatic aspects of life and death through relatively harmless (if also inherently dishonest) spectacles. Seeing as those spectacles were little more than signposts pointing to our lack of immediate, first-hand experiences with the very things that we are most ashamed or afraid of, over time our obsession with representations has unintentionally and conversely fostered "a violent return to the passion for the Real," a desire to peel off "the deceptive layers of reality" in order to directly encounter the world "in its extreme violence."[80]

As we have already seen, events that were once a common aspect of lived experience, such as the witnessing of the death of others, have receded so far into the image — into the world of semblance — that their reality has become both abject and yet simultaneously (and passionately) desired. Žižek referred to this mediated state of being constantly represented yet experientially absent as a new form of "virtual reality," an encounter that is "deprived of its subject, of the hard resistant kernel of the Real."[81] "It is not that reality entered our image," he continued, but instead that "the image entered and shattered our reality."[82] Take, for example, the central object of his text, the terrorist attacks of September 11, 2001, an event that appeared on the surface as the radical inverse of public desire, yet which Žižek found to be the ultimate fulfillment of the American fantasy, a televised spectacle which provided the "uncanny satisfaction" of a disaster movie:

> For the great majority of the public, the WTC explosions were events on the TV screen, and when we watched the oft-repeated shot of frightened people running towards the camera ahead of the giant cloud of dust from the collapsing tower, was the framing of the shot not reminiscent of

spectacular shots in catastrophic movies, a special effect which outdid all others, since — as Jeremy Bentham knew — reality is the best appearance of itself.[83]

Žižek reminds us that, despite the frequent positioning of 9/11 as a shocking, unexpected event — "how the unimaginable Impossible happened" — we can clearly see that it was frequently and graphically predicted or anticipated within moving images, not only through the constant warnings of possible terrorist attacks from the news media but also through the myriad Hollywood blockbusters that situated mass-scale chaos and destruction as part and parcel of the pleasures of spectacle.[84] "The unthinkable which happened *was the object of fantasy*, so that, in a way, America got what it fantasized about, and that was the biggest surprise."[85]

Our fantasy, of course, is not to be terrorized or attacked. It is, rather, *to bear witness* — to stand in the presence of that which gives us anxiety *so as to better know or understand it* — and our renewed passion for the Real has cultivated several new avenues through which we attempt to re-encounter the trauma of witnessing. Not the least of these is the reappearance of the actual experience of witnessing, for at the same moment that the digital is transforming the images that once facilitated the hospital's veiling of death, so too is medical science's approach to the event itself changing by way of an increased interest in (and the increased availability of) palliative care and hospice. The goals of hospice are clearly designed to benefit the sick and the dying — to lessen the symptoms of their illnesses, to cease treatments which decrease quality of life while providing only marginal increases to life expectancy, and to improve end of life experiences by promoting the presence and participation of loved ones. Under the surface, however, we also find *a return of the deathbed event*, an encouragement to not only perceive the extensive processes of death, but also contemplate and form our own unique attitudes toward it (even if doing so is positioned only as a way to help ease the suffering of the dying). The twentieth century's repression has by no means worn off, but at the very least conversations regarding natural death are being renewed, and for the first time in over a century the curtain surrounding death is being lifted.

Then again, the technological advancements of the digital age might be forcing the issue. For instance, the constantly improving quality and accessibility of digital cameras has made them an omnipresent aspect of contemporary culture, while at the same moment the barriers for dispersing and distributing video have all but disappeared. Consequently, we've witnessed a sudden proliferation of images of *actual death*, particularly in the form of execution videos and eyewitness footage of accidents and acts of violence — once kept from the public by the gatekeepers of media, now available to anyone interested enough to seek them out online. With hospice, witnesses to death are rarely if ever encouraged to promote their experience as personally beneficial (let alone pleasurable), yet in a strange way that is often how we frame this footage of real-world violence. News programs, for example, may pause graphic footage moments before the event occurs, but they also consistently report that the uncensored images are easily found online, rendering their very existence as a challenge, a test of will in the face of horror. What is on display, and in fact the display itself, is still widely regarded as taboo, but for those few with the "strength" to stomach the images, they are assumed to reveal some "truth" about reality (bitter though that truth may be). For the many who choose not to look, however, their presence serves only to amplify the curiosity — the passion for the Real — that drives contemporary representations (the first person at a party to admit that they watched an execution video becomes the instant center of attention).[86]

Despite our renewed passion for the Real, however, hospice is not yet the preferred practice of death in the medical community, and images of actual death continue to circulate primarily on the periphery of culture. As such, our desire to re-encounter the trauma of witnessing remains, as Žižek showed us, firmly grounded in *fantasy*, and our modern attempts at witnessing have resulted not in a richer or more complete understanding of mortality, but rather a demand for greater *intensity* in the fictional images that continue to define death — images which have, in turn, attempted to match *the shock of the real* with an increase in both *viscerality* and *verisimilitude*.

As we've seen, our knowledge of death was long born from our traumatic encounters with the dying, and in trying to replicate that trauma the moving image has, from *The Execution of Mary* forward, long had an obsession with shock. In many ways, viscerality *is* shock — that moment when you become overwhelmed to the point of being physically affected by an experience — and as Jennifer M. Barker explains, by visceral "we often mean our 'gut reaction,' a general feeling that begins deep inside but makes its way to the surface."[87] Put another way, the visceral reaction is that initial or primary feeling which seems to come from the stomach (rather than the mind) because it *precedes thought or contemplation*. This holds true even when we use the word to describe an experience itself (rather than our response to that experience), for the *visceral moment* is one that is so sudden or unexpected that it denies us the opportunity to process our perceptions.

Viscerality has, therefore, a temporal component, and the visceral image of death is that which startles because it occurs *rapidly*. In her study of documentary images of actual death, Vivian Sobchack observed that "the most effective cinematic representation of death in our present culture is inscribed on the lived body in action that is *abrupt*," which "denies formal reason and connotes the 'irrationality,' 'arbitrariness,' and 'unfairness' of death."[88] The same certainly holds true in fiction, and since the digital turn, representations of death have attempted to replicate the traumatic experience of witnessing by greatly increasing the suddenness or abruptness of their violence. Consider the moment toward the end of Catherine Breillat's coming-of-age fable *Fat Girl*, when two sisters, pulled over in their car at a rest stop, sleepily discuss the loss of the older girl's virginity. Suddenly, in a matter of mere seconds, a man smashes through the windshield and hacks at the older sister's head with an axe, the audience — given no opportunity to process this abrupt turn of events — feeling the blow as if they were the victim. Or perhaps Nicolas Winding Refn's *Drive*, which shifts into slow motion to tell us that its hero has realized that he's about to be attacked, yet before he can act (or before the audience has any chance to prepare themselves for what they might see or feel) a shotgun blast explodes not just a window, but literally the entire head of his companion. Or John Hillcoat's *The Proposition*, where a shocking injury to the lead character is matched seconds later by an even more gruesome and unexpected gunshot wound to the head of one of his attackers, both instances lacking the customary shot of someone aiming a weapon which we typically expect to forecast such moments of violence.

A favorite example of mine comes not from the art-house, but rather from the first film of Peter Jackson's *The Lord of the Rings* trilogy, the epitome of digital-age blockbuster filmmaking. In its climactic fight, the ranger Aragorn faces off against an enormous brute of an orc, and as the battle builds in intensity, we reach a moment where generic expectation dictates that our hero will be physically overwhelmed before miraculously and triumphantly rising to victory. Instead, it is *us* who are overwhelmed, caught off guard when Aragorn takes one unexpectedly masterful swing that lops off the orc's head, and with barely a moment of hesitation (or, more importantly, barely a moment for us to recognize that the fight is over) he runs off to help a friend. Imagine that this film were made a mere decade or two earlier, when Aragorn would have undoubtedly pinned his opponent, exchanged words about something important like the fate of humankind, and then struck the fatal blow exactly when we expected and desired it. Instead, in its suddenness we find a death that is far more visceral and even brutal, because it defies anticipation and denies contemplation.

Certainly the "shock of the hoax" is intense in all of these examples because of the swiftness of their violence, but at the same time the viscerality of the *physical trauma* on display has increased as well, with fleshy bodies ripped apart and exposed like never before. In fact, Barker reminds us that the visceral is not only a "gut reaction," but also *the guts themselves*, the *viscera* that hides beneath the skin and which we "hardly notice ... under normal circumstances."[89] In the digital age, however, those insides are being frequently and graphically revealed, as new representations of death often emphasize and fixate upon the interiors of the body that went more or less un-depicted in the moving image for over a century. Aside from the gunshot wounds and sliced-off limbs that disclose blood, bone, and muscle, most striking is the aesthetic technique of replaying or, more accurately,

FIGURE 1.3 *A bullet (and the camera) passes through the viscera of a human body in* Three Kings.

re-examining traumatic deaths from *inside* the body, first developed on cinema screens in David O. Russell's *Three Kings*, popularized on television with Jerry Bruckheimer's *CSI: Crime Scene Investigation*, and adapted into gaming with the latest incarnations of Ed Boon's iconic *Mortal Kombat* series. No matter the medium, we find in each case a camera that peers or even traverses *into and through* the interior of the body, following the ricocheting path of bullets or the rippling effect of blunt force trauma as every tear of the flesh, every break of the bones, and every puncture of the organs is scrutinized by its lens. And, as we follow the camera's trajectory, we also notice a desire for greater *verisimilitude*, for whether or not these images accurately reflect the true reality of trauma, they nonetheless aim to expose the biological processes that occur during death, the breakdown and failure of the intricately complicated systems of the organic body.

Whether through an abrupt eruption of violence or the exposure of the unseen interior of the body, *increased viscerality* is a significant component of contemporary representations of death, yet one that is at best an extension of prior strategies for inspiring the psychological trauma of witnessing, and at worst satisfied with (or perhaps only capable of) portraying the pain of physical trauma. In this regard, digital representations possess only small advantages over their forebears of the twentieth century, which could occasionally shock the senses but rarely provide anything approaching the thickness of witnessing or the intense pleasure of *jouissance*. To truly capture the trauma of death, the digital image must first become something *radically different and new*, and to find out what that is, let's return not only to the question of the essence of trauma, but also to another previously posed inquiry: What happens when the trauma of witnessing death is replaced by the image of trauma? If Lacan has anything to say about the matter, the effects are rather profound.

On the one hand, Lacan's observations in "Tuché and Automaton" are very much an extension of Freud's view of trauma as an overwhelming tension resolved only through the process of symbolization (his employment of the Aristotelian concept of the automaton, for example, is a clear reference to the spontaneous and automatic return or repetition of trauma). On the other, Lacan's structuralist approach to the processes of consciousness brings to light nuances that are essential for understanding how the eruption of representations impacted our relationship to death in contemporary culture, especially when viewed through the lens of his well-known declaration that "the unconscious is structured like a language" and his elaboration of the three registers of the Imaginary, the Symbolic, and the Real.[90] Together, these strands of thought present the landscape of human experience as fundamentally grounded in language and representation, and position trauma as those experiences which lie *beyond language* and *beyond representation*, so much so that Lacan gave a new name to trauma: the tuché, *the encounter with the Real*, that which cannot be contained within the realm of the sign and the symbol.

Like Freud, Lacan saw the procedures of the conscious mind as a screening process, but under his schema the screen is language itself, and the complexities of everyday existence are categorized, conceptualized, and contained within the boundaries of discrete signifiers. As such, he argued that our complex yet illusory interpretations of everyday life (i.e., the Imaginary) are separated from the overwhelming experience of actual existence (i.e., the Real) by the order of language and representation (i.e., the Symbolic, which also includes the practice of traditions, rituals, and law, and which Lacan pointedly referred to as the "insistence of the signs"). When we step outside, for example, rarely are we overwhelmed by the intricate geometric shapes, innumerable swaths of color, or flowing, undulating movements that appear before us, nor are we shocked by wafting scents, tickling breezes, or distant songs. Instead, we immediately and effortlessly digest the scene by situating each sensation within the confines of a word: a porch, a table, a grill, grass underfoot, leaves overhead, birds chirping, and wind blowing. If the scene were suddenly interrupted by a strange crack and a brilliant light, a sharp and inexplicable stinging sensation, dizziness, and the smell of some foreign thing burning and smoking, then we might begin to enter the realm of trauma, for in our refusal to recognize unpleasant possibilities, we so often fail to create terms which easily categorize and contain such intense experiences (ask Freud's soldiers or abuse victims to explain the circumstances of their trauma in detail, and you would invariably hear them say something along the lines of "I can't quite put it into words").

Lacan was not the only one to note the connection between the limits of language and the forms of trauma that so often frame death. Gorer, for example, told us not only that "the sensations [of images of death] are enhanced as much as a customary poverty of language permits," but also that "most languages are relatively poor in words or constructions to express intense pleasure or intense pain."[91] With the very first line of *The Birth of the Clinic*, Foucault made explicit that his book was "about space, about language, and about death," for the hospital's self-declared jurisdiction over the latter was a shift on two fronts: a shift in setting, whereby its domain moved from the public to the private, and a shift in *representation*, in that the contemplation of the processes of death could occur only within the boundaries of the language of medicine (leaving the masses, as I argue, with naught but the fictions of the moving image).[92] In structuralism, Merleau-Ponty found an uneasy ally to his phenomenology, and when he argued that the body "signifies" in much the same manner as words and utterances — "language as/of corporeality," as Kristen Brown Golden puts it — we can see how physical trauma begets psychological trauma, for the loss of a limb or the paralysis of the face disavows the bodily significations that connote subjectivity.[93] Most aligned with Lacan, however, are Barthes and Sobchack, the former arguing, in his analysis of photographs of traumatic events such as "fires, ship-wrecks, catastrophes, [and] violent deaths," that "trauma is just what suspends language and blocks signification," such that "the shock photo is by structure non-signifying," it has "no value" and produces "no knowledge."[94] Sobchack, in turn, maintained that "the representation of the event of death is an indexical sign of that which is always in excess of representation and beyond the limits of coding and culture: Death confounds all codes."[95]

Of course, that doesn't prevent us from trying. Returning to Lacan, we find an expansion of Freud's notion that the repetition and subsequent symbolization of trauma is an attempt to resolve lingering tensions, for if trauma is that which is beyond language, then to represent trauma is to wrench it away from the realm of the Real and forcefully insert into the Symbolic (after which it can be easily and readily stitched into the comfortable fabric of the Imaginary). Yet to symbolize is also to negate the trauma of the encounter with the Real by turning it into an effigy, so what now do we make of Lacan's reminder that "nothing can be apprehended *in effigie, in absentia*"? Earlier, I paraphrased this statement as a warning that encounters with the sign and the symbol are not equal to encounters with the real, and now we can see not only that the Symbolic can never fully contain (and therefore is always less than) the Real, but also, and more importantly, that we can never truly know a thing or event if we meet it only at the level of representation, if we refuse to first submit to its trauma.[96] In a culture where the encounter with the Real of death remains largely absent, representations will never be able to provide the knowledge that we seek, and so we turn to a new form of the image that, like trauma itself, pushes *beyond* representation: we look to *simulations*.

For Baudrillard, the "order of simulations" was the last phase of the image, that moment when the representation becomes utterly divorced from the reality it once meant to signify, emerging on the other side a simulacrum. The *simulation*, meanwhile, is nothing less than the revolution itself, the process through which one reality is destroyed and another is born. We've already discussed one implication of this process — that the resulting simulacra come to precede reality rather than the other way around — but we've yet to grasp an equally important consequence, that the simulation is thus *affective* in ways that the representation can never be, as we see in this quote from *Simulacra and Simulation*:

> Simulating is not pretending: "Whoever fakes an illness can simply stay in bed and make everyone believe he is ill. Whoever simulates an illness produces in himself some of the symptoms" (Littre). Therefore, pretending, or dissimulating, leaves the principle of reality intact: the difference is always clear, it is simply masked, whereas simulation threatens the difference between the "true" and the "false," the "real" and the "imaginary."[97]

It's interesting that Baudrillard positions simulations as a threat, for as we begin to simulate, we must also stop pretending, and when we stop pretending, we begin to *experience*. Rather than being frightened by that possibility, however, in the digital age we have embraced it: we seek in the simulation of death the very experience of trauma that has for so long been absent from our reality — that overwhelmingly intense stimulation that stirs within us both pain and pleasure, that leaves its wounds while also imparting wisdom and knowledge.[98]

It's clear that in the three decades since Baudrillard published *Simulacra and Simulation*, digital technologies have profoundly complicated the simulation by shifting both its boundaries and its capabilities, which Gonzalo Frasca makes explicit when he writes that "the potential of simulation has been somehow limited because of a technological problem: it is extremely difficult to model complex systems through cogwheels. Naturally, the invention of the computer changed this situation."[99] Building on Frasca, Ian Bogost gives us an altogether different definition of the simulation, that of a simplified rule-based system that informs the user's subjective understanding of a larger, more complex system.[100] It's obvious that there's a striking disconnect between this description, in which simulations are said to point to the complexities of reality, and Baudrillard's, in which we find not just the absence but the destruction of that reality. Perhaps, though, this disconnect can be accounted for by rethinking not the use-value or affect of the images produced by the simulation, but instead *the production itself* — how the very process of generating a simulated image changes its relationship to the reality it depicts.

In fact, what interests me most about Bogost's discussion of simulations is that he traces them down to the level of the *cellular automaton* — "a simple program (an automaton) isolated into small units (cells). These units interact with one another, exposing what scientists — computer scientists especially — have hoped to exploit as a viable model for artificial life."[101] In digital simulations, the automata are essentially the determinant conditionals — "if x then z," "if x and y then z," "if x or y then z," "not x then z" — that act as the most basic commands of a digital program, while the cells are the zeros and ones, the bits and bytes of data passing through this logical system. These simple programs are not at all unlike the automatons of Aristotle and Lacan, in that their reactions to stimuli are spontaneous, automatic, and repetitive, they "perform a single, simple, isolatable task" that results in a basic unit of new information, passed on to the next automaton which, in turn, performs its own task. What makes the employment of these computational units significant, and what I argue ultimately separates a simulation from a representation, is some degree of *autonomy* — once a set of rules have been established, once the tasks of each automaton have been isolated and defined, then the subsequent images they produce are shaped by the system rather than the creator of the system. In other words, *a simulation is a representation that has more or less determined its own construction (or at the very least elements of its construction) according to a system of rules*.[102]

Frasca points to this when he refers to simulations as "machines that *generate signs*," and likewise Lev Manovich names "automation" one of the principles of new media, which can happen at "low-levels" in programs like Photoshop or Maya, where complex image manipulation can result from the simple inputs of the user, or at the "high-levels" of sophisticated simulations like the "project of Artificial Intelligence" (the very idea of which produces within us numerous existential anxieties, which we'll return to in Chapter 4).[103] Without doubt, even the most basic depictions of death in contemporary media often require some degree of low-level manipulation — from simple color grading to achieve the carmine hue we associate with freshly surfaced blood to the extensive use of computer-generated images to create believably damaged and devastated virtual bodies — while many more rely on high-level simulations that mimic specific components of biological life — particularly the autonomous movements and reactions that often define "alive-ness" — in order to show those components breaking down or failing at the moment of death. Regardless of the simplicity or complexity of the simulation, the autonomy of contemporary images of death replicates details of the actual processes of dying that were rarely, if ever, present in the subjective representations of the last century.

Before we discuss the specifics of those autonomously generated details, let's make a few observations. First, the fact that we so often look to the simulation as a model or method for *creating life* implies that simulations are also uniquely qualified to *create death*. Second, although the automatons that drive the simulation are simple, and although the simulation is a simplified model of a more complex system, this does not imply that the simulation as a whole is simple (nor the images it produces). Third, autonomy is particularly crucial in simulations of death because it both mimics the reactive nature of the living organism and echoes one of the most important characteristics of the natural world which undergirds the very structures of life: that nature is fundamentally orderly and consistent, and that the laws of nature are spontaneously and impartially enacted. And fourth, although we may be tempted to think of the simulation as subjective — insofar as its rules are chosen by its creators — the outcome of the simulation is an objective and complex representation that often strikes us as "more-than-real" or *hyperreal*, perhaps especially in the case of death (whose reality is always already beyond the grasp of conscious understanding).

Let's both work our way through these observations and make our way back to the autonomous "details" of the simulation by first noting that the images, signs, and information generated by a useful or interesting digital simulation are, by nature, unpredictable. This is not to say that we cannot make reasonable guesses as to the basic forms the simulation will produce, but rather that we want the details of those forms to be more exhaustive, specific, and consistent than those a human being could reasonably create (which also infers that we want the simulation to affect us in a manner similar to the complex systems upon which they are modeled). For example, an animator's interpretation of a tree blowing in the breeze may strike us as beautiful — the way they depict the unseen "hand" of nature pressing against a mass of leaves, the subtle gradations of green and yellow dancing and swaying as one — yet a reasonably complex digital simulation of a tree gives us something very different, not an unbroken mass swarming in one direction but rather an overwhelming variety of branches and leaves that bend and quiver this way and that, each one tugging and pulling against the others with an influence wholly dependent on its size, shape, weight, and placement, each movement allowing for sharp points of light to break through which reflect and refract off every semi-glossy surface, fostering an impression of constant motion at the outermost edges of the tree which stands in striking juxtaposition to the stability of its trunk.[104] Whether or not such a simulation can ever provide us with the perceptual thickness found in an encounter with an actual tree, we can see that it nonetheless forges a bond with physical reality that extends far beyond the limits of the representation's subjective image of the world, a bond that is grounded in an experience of *overwhelming awe* that, as Immanuel Kant told us, not only confuses the boundaries between the Real and the representation, but *fuses* them as well.

To understand this bond, let's consider the fact that the human mind can scarcely even begin to process the seemingly infinite materials and forces which together constitute the matter and energy of the universe, and so to truly grasp the complexities of something as quotidian as a tree blowing in the breeze, one would need to take into account not simply the mass of the tree and the velocity of the wind or the volume of the leaves and the stiffness of the branches. Instead, one must also consider the structural physiology of the organism (not just roots, trunk, and crown, but interior tissues like the xylem, phloem, and cork, as well as the billions of living cells that structure those tissues, the trillions upon trillions of atoms that structure those cells, etc.), the events that gave rise to the wind (the rotation of the Earth and the subsequent Coriolis effect, shifts in atmospheric pressure, centripetal acceleration and frictional deceleration, etc.), the numerous substances that make up the ground upon which the tree takes root (the depth and density of the soil, the insects and microorganisms which contribute to that soil, the rain that seeps through the ground which feeds and strengthens the tree, the bedrock which provides foundational stability, etc.), the myriad other forces — gravitational, electromagnetic, strong nuclear, weak nuclear, frictional, tensional, elastic, etc. — at play in, between, and amongst them, and so on and so on.

Meanwhile, to fully grasp a reasonably complex digital simulation of a tree blowing in the breeze, that same human mind would need to account not only for the mass of the tree and the velocity of the wind or the volume of the leaves and the stiffness of the branches, but also the complex equations and algorithms that define mass, velocity, volume, and stiffness, the number of polygons or voxels used to delineate the shape and dimensions of the tree, the number of ways in which those units must reshape or deform when rendered from various perspectives, the particle physics and fluid dynamics used to determine the interactions between the force of the "air," the matter of the "wood," and the rays of the "light," and so on and so on. Without doubt, the simulation is vastly simplified in relation to the complexities of the natural phenomenon, and yet to the layperson *they are both equally overwhelming*, so far beyond the capacities of contemplation as to be essentially and fundamentally *sublime*.

In his *Critique of Judgment*, Kant distinguished the experience of the sublime from that of the merely beautiful, the latter "a question of the form of the object, and this consists in limitation," whereas the former is "a representation of limitless-ness, yet with a super-added thought of its totality," an object or event so "absolutely great" in its "magnitude" that it transcends "every standard of the senses."[105] In other words, that which we encounter as sublime is of such enormity and/or complexity that we shudder before it, for although we are capable of *apprehending it*, we are incapable of *comprehending it* without mentally breaking it apart into constituent pieces (which only fuels our fascination with the thing *as a whole*). Although the awe of the sublime is always constant, not every encounter with the sublime is the same, and Kant described for us two forms: the *dynamical* and the *mathematical*. In the former, we find "nature considered in an aesthetic judgment as might that has no dominion over us," meaning that the dynamically sublime object's physical magnitude or structural complexity is so immense and so powerful as to make us fearful (of our ignorance or impotence, perhaps) without being afraid of the object itself (and in fact our "sublimation" to it brings us some degree of happiness, for "the agreeableness arising from the cessation of an uneasiness is *a state of joy*").[106] The dynamical sublime is "aesthetic" because our sense of the scale or intricacy of the object is never more than an estimation — a "mere intuition (by the eye)" — and while the same holds true for the mathematical sublime, its estimation is of a different sort, not of the overpowering size of one object but the overwhelming mass of many.

The mathematical sublime is a recognition of something so *numerous* as to approach the infinite, which is not to say that we believe the mass to be never-ending, but rather that its quantity is so great that (as with the very concept of the infinite) we lack the capacity to fully contemplate it. As the name suggests, the consideration of *numbers* is an essential component of the mathematical sublime, and yet Kant tells us that "the sublime does not lie so much in the greatness of the number, as in the fact that in our onward advance" — in our attempts to study and understand ever more of the universe that bounds us — "we always arrive at proportionately greater units."[107] To put this another way, the mathematical sublime lies in the gap between a known quantity (say, the amount of leaves on a tree and the number of trees in a forest) and its unknowable quality (the impossibility of a coherent and concurrent consideration of every leaf in a forest). This leads us back to our trees, where we find the sublimity of the actual organism to be *dynamic*, for although we can begin to understand many of the components that contribute to its overall structure, the complexity of the entire entity overwhelms our capacity of thought (as does, in the case of a redwood or a sequoia, its enormity), whereas the sublimity of the simulation is almost entirely *mathematic* — it's an encounter with numbers so intricate and so complicated that they essentially possess no meaning for us outside of the computer's final renderings. In this latter case the "gap" is backwards, what we apprehend is the quality of simulation (the highly detailed and immensely precise images that it generates) which we cannot but compare to its incomprehensible quantity (a digital code so complex as to produce a seemingly infinite degree of variations). This is not to say that every encounter with a tree, nor every simulation, is sublime — far from it, for we've developed many words and representations which allow us to situate such experiences within the comfortable boundaries of the Imaginary — yet at the same time the capacity is nonetheless always present, such that any given encounter *could* (under the right circumstances) lead to the sensation of awe.[108]

If we shift this discussion back to images of death, it's not terribly difficult to see how the outbreak of simulations radically alters our representation-driven relationship to the concept of mortality, as the mathematical sublime hiding beneath the surface of the simulation echoes the experience of the dynamical sublime once found in the event of witnessing (but lost in the majority of perceptually "thin" representations). Again, the simulation will never provide the exact experience of trauma that accompanies the event of witnessing, yet it can provide something *akin* to it, a sensation of sublimity that effectively grants the simulation of death an affect not at all unlike the trauma of witnessing. In fact, the sublime trauma of the simulation — the "uncanny satisfaction" of contemporary images of trauma that Žižek also referred to as *jouissance* — is found not only in the contemplation of the equations that drive the simulation, but also in the physical and biological "details" of the images it generates, details which lie beyond the capacities of the representation and act as a sort of *virtual encounter with the Real*.

We've already seen these biological details in the increased viscerality of modern representations of trauma, whose depictions of the insides of the body only grow in specificity with the employment of simulations. Equally emphasized in the simulation, however, are the physical details, by which I refer to not only the matter that constructs our bodies and our universe but also the forces which bind them together. In other words, modern images of death often rely on *precisely simulated physics* in order to frame death as a consequence of the laws of lived reality, and it's through the sublime recognition of those physical laws that we experience the painful pleasure once found only in the presence of actual death.

This is perhaps most immediately visible in digital games, whose desire for ever-greater verisimilitude rivals that of the cinematic images we've already discussed, so much so that constant improvements to visual fidelity (i.e., "graphics") stands as a cornerstone of the games industry. Yet as David H. Eberly tells us, "visual realism is only half the battle ... *physical* realism is the other half," and without doubt many modern games *feel real* because they *feel right* — they generate objects which believably interact with one another, have a tangible sense of weight and force, yet also often bend, contort, squash, and break in ways which feel equally familiar.[109] In fact, familiarity is key to the simulation of physics, and Eberly elaborates that "physics itself can be understood in an intuitive manner — after all it is an attempt to quantify the world around us. Implementing a physical simulation on a computer, though, requires more than intuition. It requires mathematical maturity as well as the ability to synthesize a large system from a collection of sophisticated, smaller components."[110] Aside from an affinity with Bogost's definition of the simulation, if we read this quote upside down (from the perspective of the average gameplayer rather than the average game programmer) we find that in our lack of "mathematical maturity" we experience simulated physics as nothing more than *a mere intuition of the eye*, an intuition which tells us that both the gameworld and reality operate according to the same set of rules — rules that are autonomously enacted and sublimely complex — which in turn cements a connection between the two. In their automation of complex forces such as gravity, momentum, inertia, friction, velocity, drag, buoyancy, spring, torque, etc. (not to mention rigid and soft-body collision detection and particle physics), engines like *Havok*, the *Bullet Physics Library*, and *PhysX* ensure that contemporary games possess that strange feeling of both randomness and precision that pervades our encounters with our actual physical world — which is in fact nothing less than the overwhelming sensation of the sublime, for the number and variety of scenarios made possible by the simulation (as well as the complexity of the simulation itself) is far too great to comprehend.[111]

Physics have been a prominent component of digital games throughout the history of the medium. Release the d-pad as Mario is running, for example, and he doesn't freeze in place but rather slides further a bit, his *momentum* carrying him ever forward. Tap the "A" button and he hops, hold it down, he jumps. If you run forward and *then* jump, his speed carries him higher and farther than ever before (perhaps even far enough to clear the flagpole). In contemporary games, however, physics often have a direct and immediate affect on the depiction of death, as we see in Rockstar North's *Grand Theft Auto IV* (GTA IV), whose utilization of NaturalMotion's *Euphoria* animation system populated its spectacularly rendered caricature of New York City with "thinking" automatons whose "lives" are entirely dependent upon their constant awareness of the simulated physics of their world. Instead of floating along the ground in a constantly repeating series of key-framed animations, for example, NPCs (non-player characters) literally put a foot forward and then *lean* into the fall in order to take each step (thus relying on "gravity" to carry them forward), or raise a hand to brace themselves when they lose their balance, or turn and duck to avoid incoming objects, their sense of "panic" directly related to the speed or size of the object. In other words, every movement in GTA IV is unique and different, fostering a tangible sensation of *life* not found in pre-canned animations, an equally tangible sensation of *death* when those movements are stilled, and an image of a world where dying is the result not of the push of a button but rather a sublimely complicated series of mathematical calculations.

Tap a pedestrian with your car at low speed, for example, and they might become scared and hurriedly limp away, they might cry out and fall over in pain, or they might pound on your car while unleashing a few choice words. Increase the speed a bit before you hit them and they react accordingly, sometimes attempting to jump out of the way (getting spun through the air if you hit their legs as they do so), sometimes getting caught off guard (their back crumpled against the hood as their feet fly over their head), sometimes simply bracing for impact (curling tight as they slam into and over the windshield). Depending on the speed, the angle of impact, the reaction of the pedestrian — Did they put their hands up in time to the lessen the impact of their head? Were they able to slide across the hood or were they pulled under

FIGURE 1.4 *Pedestrians struck by a car in* Grand Theft Auto IV.

the tires? — and even occasionally the weather and its effect on the friction of the ground, you may find at the scene of the accident a person scraping the dust from their knees as they turn to run away, a body wreathing in pain on the ground (awaiting the ambulance that will eventually come to provide CPR), or a corpse sprawled out in gruesome fashion, its limbs twisted and forever limp. Put the pedal to the floor, and death comes much quicker — the NPC moving to react before going limp as they bounce off the hood of the car, or swinging their hands and legs wildly as they fly through the air, only to "ragdoll" as they smash into a light-post.

In fact, "ragdoll physics" have become somewhat synonymous with modern action games, where developers compete to see how accurately (or perhaps how disturbingly) a body crumples after a bullet wound to the head, how it bounces after a fall from a great height, or how awkwardly it flops and contorts as it rolls down the side of mountain. If it's "the visible cessation of [the] body's intentional and responsive behavior that stands as the symbol of death" in contemporary culture, as Sobchack tells us, then in regard to fiction the ragdoll of digital games is its ultimate appearance.[112] Even the worst ragdoll effects are fascinating to watch, yet those on the level of GTA IV are relentlessly sublime — we both marvel and shutter at not just the complexity and variety of deaths generated by the game, but also the precision, specificity, and consistency of those images, the sudden and resolutely visible transition of bodies from fully responsive to utterly passive, the way they bounce or float or slide around, their fate entirely at the mercy of *physics*.

Earlier, I argued that the "shock of the hoax" found in representations of death had almost nothing in common with the trauma of witnessing. We can see now that it wasn't a lack of "realism" that led to that disconnect so much as it was a lack of physical and biological precision, specificity, and consistency — the images struck us as false because *the physics felt wrong and the viscera was conspicuously absent*. Whether it be bodies that appeared weightless as they were tossed and thrown through the air, blood that squirted at odd angles and with far too great a force, corpses that lacked a proper sense of slackness (portrayed by actors whose muscles could not help but to resist the pull of gravity), or explosions that left skin and bones strangely intact, representations of death have always felt somehow less-than-real or unreal because the *minutia* of death was missing, those details which were once an integral part of the perceptual thickness of witnessing. In our struggle to re-encounter that experience, we've turned to the next best thing: simulations which have been radically infused by the digital, their capacity for autonomously generating the specificities of death shepherding a sense of overwhelming sublimity that (at the very least) echoes the thickness of experience we lost long ago. In fact, if the representation of death is *unreal*, then the digital simulation of death is, as Baudrillard would put it, *hyperreal*, so much like the Real as to be both immensely uncomfortable and intensely satisfying, and it's that peculiar combination of pain and pleasure that we long for most of all.[113] To find out why, let's return to that shockingly intense simulation of death which first made us question whether we saw what we thought we saw and whether we know what we think we know.

Time Destroys Everything

After a short, narratively unrelated prologue, *Irréversible* begins *in medias res* as its two male protagonists, Marcus and Pierre, journey into the bowels of a grimy, underground S&M club known rather appropriately as *The Rectum*. As Thomas Bangalter's soundtrack repeats a Doppler-like moan ad nauseam, the camera dips, twirls, lurches, and spins on its axis, never allowing us to gain a spatial foothold and only momentarily giving us glimpses of the perversions surrounding Marcus and Pierre at every turn. Although the shot appears continuous, like the upcoming murder sequence it's actually the result of many 16 mm and 35 mm takes digitally stitched together (with simulated grain added to create a visual continuity). It also frequently utilizes a digital reframing process in order to create what Ricardo de los Rios and Robert Davis refer to as a "viscerally disturbing virtual space ... one in which the very idea of a spatially cogent continuum is irrelevant."[114] Unable to orient ourselves, we can only rely on the guidance

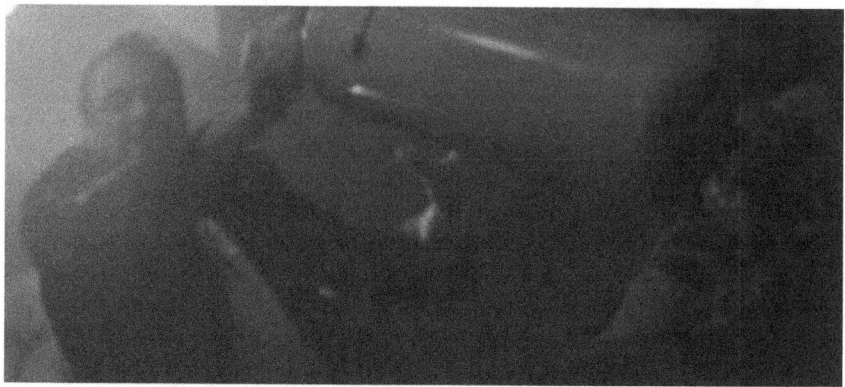

FIGURE 1.5 *Pierre smashes his victim's face with a fire extinguisher.*

of Marcus, who appears desperate and enraged, physically attacking several strangers while demanding that they take him to a man referred to only as "la Tenia" (later in the narrative, which is told chronologically in reverse, we'll witness Marcus's girlfriend Alex being violently raped by la Tenia, but for now his motive of revenge remains unspoken). As we tumble blindly downward, the film assaults us on all fronts, so that by the time Marcus and Pierre reach a basement full of men watching a pornographic film, we are confused, on edge, and exhausted — fearful of (yet entirely unprepared for) the violence about to erupt. When Marcus misidentifies a large, brutish man as la Tenia — who is, in fact, standing immediately to that man's right — the man fights back, pushing Marcus to the ground and graphically breaking his arm before attempting to rape him. At this point, the previously more subdued Pierre lunges from off-screen with a fire extinguisher, setting in motion a continuous sequence of attacks that lasts for slightly over a minute and which unrelentingly simulates the breakdown of the flesh and the reality of traumatic death using a variety of digital techniques that special effects supervisor Rudolphe Chabrier likens to a "digital Swiss-Army knife."[115]

During production, two versions of the attack were shot, one with the actor playing Pierre "holding a fire extinguisher cut in half, which allowed him to 'hit' the other actor without actually touching him," and another where the actor held a real extinguisher and afflicted "real blows to a latex dummy," its face "filled with blood" and its body "motionless." Upon realizing that the latex face was "too lifeless," however, the special effects team "worked with the actor's face as much as possible, adding the effects of the blows and reshaping his head" using procedures like "computer-generated pictures, matte painting [and] graphic design, traditional editing techniques, morphing, compositing," and various other simulators which were used to render things like vibration, motion-blur, and particle physics (particularly the spattering of blood and the tearing of flesh).[116] The final result of this multilayered simulation may be a traumatic depiction of death, but in the moment-to-moment it aims to create a tangible and believable approximation of *life*, the digital blending of "the actor's face, the latex, and the 3D face" producing an image in which skin not only squishes and ripples according to blunt force, but is also supported by muscles which twitch and spasm as if the victim's "brain" were attempting to process the physical trauma.[117] Likewise, his hand — its tremors and quakes revealing pain and anguish the face can no longer express — is entirely computer-generated, added in post to further confuse the boundaries between what is real and what is simulated.

Intensifying this confusion is the scene's clearly discernible physics — the believable weight and force of the extinguisher, the disturbingly accurate manner in which skin is stretched and shredded with every blow, the equally upsetting sight of blood spattering and flesh flapping. Only small portions of these effects were practical, the rest the result of complex collision simulations, such as the digitally extended extinguisher "interacting" with the digitally modeled face, which contorts and deforms according to intricate calculations of mass, friction, and transferrable energy. In fact, although new patterns of blood and bruising were added to the face's texture-map with every impact, those textures would have seemed utterly flat and static if not for the continual warping of the computer-generated face — the way in which it not only ripples but also flattens with every blow, how the simulated bone under the digital flesh cracks and buckles again and again.

Considering the care that went into this horrific image of death, it would be hard to argue against the claim that Gaspar Noé intended to not simply

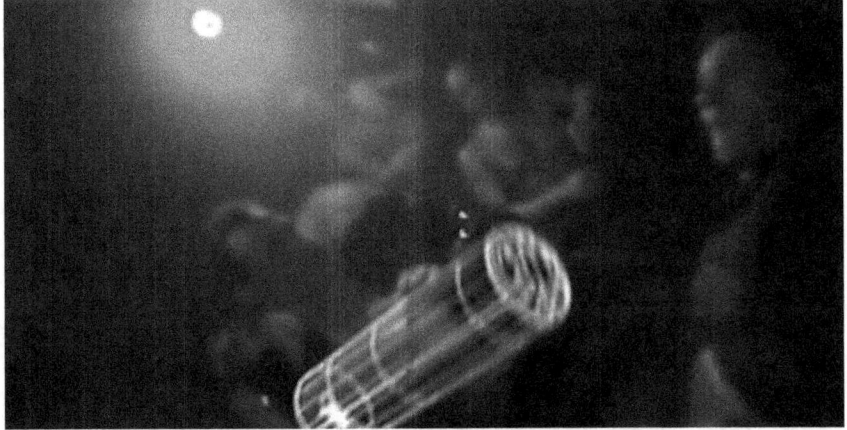

FIGURE 1.6 *Pierre's extinguisher was digitally extended so that it could virtually (and viscerally) interact with the computer-generated face.*

disturb his audience but more importantly to *shock* and *overwhelm* them. By unraveling the film in reverse, for example, he positions the murder which diegetically concludes its story as the first event that we experience, robbing it of any context and foregrounding only its repellent viscerality. Likewise, his prolonged build-up to that violence — the ten-minute overture of *The Rectum*, through which the film's camera tumbles mercilessly ever-downward — not only denies us a spatial foothold but also constantly intensifies our sense of confusion and even panic. Elsewhere, as in the infamous rape scene, the camera takes the opposite approach, its stillness (married with the film's long-takes) producing a sickening inability to look away. And then, of course, there's the soundtrack, which, in addition to its repetitive music, infamously pulses with a frequency of 28 Hz, an almost inaudible rumbling that can supposedly cause nausea and vertigo and which was frequently cited by critics as the primary reason so many walked out during the film's premiere at the Cannes film festival (and not, somehow, the intensely brutal violence on display).[118] Without doubt, it's clear that the aim of *Irréversible* is nothing less than trauma.

When we return to the opening scene of death, we clearly bear witness to something far more than "a strange and beautiful effect," as Chabrier describes his work, for the visceral impact of the simulation extends well beyond that of the merely beautiful.[119] It is, rather, in its overwhelming complexity, *intensely and utterly sublime*. As such, the trauma of *Irréversible* has little in common with the "shock of the hoax," for it provides us with every bit as much pleasure and satisfaction as it does pain and confusion. This is perhaps why Eugenie Brinkman argues that the film echoes "the explosive excess, the painful ecstasy, the *always beyond* quality" that Leo Bersani found in Freud's readings of sexual pain and pleasure, qualities that point not only to the trauma of the film, but also to its *jouissance* — that overwhelmingly painful pleasure once found in the experience of witnessing the death of others.[120] The *jouissance* of Pierre's relentless attack comes not from the act itself but rather from the strange sensation of *discovery and knowledge* that it provides (that feeling of "oh! so this is what death looks like!"). Indeed, a perverse impression of some dark and repressed reality pervades the image, such that it's not good taste or propriety but rather "existential deadness that *Irréversible* assails," as Mikita Brottman and David Sterritt write, "using the most radical resources Noé can muster to distress, disorient, and alarm an audience accustomed to movies as a narcotizing pleasure, not a galvanizing journey into its own most desperately hidden truths."[121] There is pleasure in the image, to be sure, but not one that lulls us into complacency; the pleasure of *Irréversible* is difficult, disturbing, and engrossing, revealing, repellant, and traumatic.

Not every viewer will find *jouissance* in the challenging violence of *Irréversible*, and in fact many will simply feel discomfort and distress. Likewise, not every simulation of death aims to renew our existential

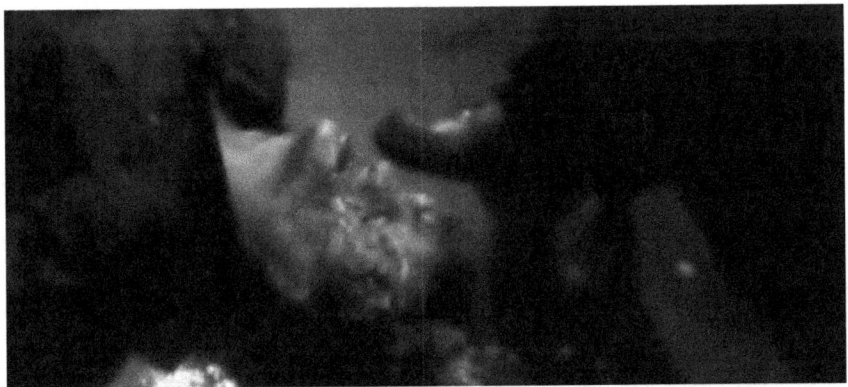

FIGURE 1.7 *The aftermath of the simulation, its hyperreality evident in both its viscera and the jaw that shutters until the final instance of life.*

attitude toward the event of death, nor mixes pain and pleasure to defy our repressive dispositions. Yet on the whole, images of death in the digital age are slowly shifting away from representations that fetishize the traumatic while somehow only seeing what is comfortable and complacent. Simulations, on the other hand, are not held captive to our basic human desires, our incomplete and inaccurate understandings, or our denial of the abject. As such, the autonomous, simulated elements of contemporary digital images have fundamentally changed the way we think about death in the digital age, resulting in a perverse return to the physical and biological referent — perverse because the referent is not masked, nor is it absent, nor is it bypassed, but instead exists only as a system of rules, a virtuality that we have already labeled the hyperreal. Simulations allow *jouissance* to once again enter into the discourse of death, and discomfort, it seems, is small price to pay in order to reinstate the experience of witnessing that provided, for hundreds if not thousands of years, a way of publicly sharing the burden of mortality.

2

The Digital Path to Death

I've been dying for many years. Sometimes death is a clear penalty for my carelessness, my inattention to detail, or my inability to properly plan for the challenges ahead. Other times, it seems to be inevitable — no matter how hard I struggle, it's only a matter of time before death catches up with me. There are times when I scarcely fear death, and even taunt its grasp for my own amusement; there are times when the possibility of death is so horrifying that I hardly want to move. There are times when death finds me unexpectedly, times when I can easily see its approach in the distance, and times when I willingly submit myself, hoping that some knowledge will be gained that can prevent a needless death in the future. There are times when pleasure masks the possibility of death, allowing me to momentarily forget its power. Yet in time, pain and frustration set in, foregrounding the very fact of death and surrounding me with its presence. As a gamer, I've been dying for many years.

Death in Digital Games

In the early 1990s, a panic engulfed the medium of digital games in both the popular press and the social sciences, one centered upon their increasingly violent content — such as the famous "finishing moves" of *Mortal Kombat* or the infamous Sega CD release of *Night Trap* — and the impact such violence was thought to have on the real-world actions of gameplayers. Of course, as we saw in our last chapter, this was also the very moment when moving images began to adopt a more visceral approach to depicting death as a result of the increasing influence of digital logic, so perhaps the excitement and turmoil regarding representations of violence should not be particularly surprising. Yet while politicians, pundits, and scholars have remained focused on the ramifications of *violence* in games ever since, more important questions surrounding the image of *death* in games have gone largely unasked. For example, why does this new medium represent death as such a trivial and inconsequential event? Perhaps more astutely, *is* the representation of death in games trivial, or can we perhaps glimpse within games a relationship to death that had been absent or denied in prior representations? To put this another way, do games deny death, as did so many moving images throughout the last century, or could there perhaps be another drive or desire at play?

Death has always been a fundamental component of digital games, from the exploding ships of *Spacewar!* in 1962 to the imploding yellow body of *Pac-Man* in 1980, from the first person rampages of *Wolfenstein 3D* in 1992 to the third person decapitations of *Resident Evil 4* in 2005. Indeed, death has long served as both a narrative component of gameplay which gives weight to the inputs of the player and a mechanical component which defines the consequences of their actions. Yet as the first medium in which spectator input is essential to the creation of narrative, digital games render death in ways we've never before seen, challenging the conventional representations found in moving images throughout the last century while also imbued with meanings that recall and repeat the very instincts which have allowed us to face death — and, at times, deny the power of death — for hundreds, if not thousands of years.[1] At their simplest, digital games seem to continue that project of denial, making death no more than a roadblock that must be endured (or ignored) in order to accomplish specific goals. At its most complex, this new medium entirely restructures the relationship between death and temporality in moving images, bringing the unalterable past into direct conversation with the possibilistic future.

Despite the relatively brief history of the medium, death has by no means remained constant in digital games, instead shifting and changing in conjunction with broader cultural transformations in our understanding of temporality, identity, and mortality. As such, the role of death in games has changed dramatically since the days of coin-op arcades, when games were designed as a "pay-for-play" system that encouraged short play sessions geared around the achievement of high scores rather than the completion of a specific narrative. Games like *Space Invaders*, *Frogger*, and *Centipede* were never meant to be beaten, instead simply increasing in difficulty with each passing level and thus ensuring that "death" was the inevitable conclusion of every play session.[2] In the late 1980s, the rise of computer games and home consoles brought with it a shift away from high scores and toward the introduction of increasingly complex narratives — narratives that had strict completion criteria that often involved "extra lives," "continues," and "game overs." Within the last decade, however, those same types of games have almost entirely done away with the idea of game-ending failure as a play mechanic, instead offering players an unlimited amount of re-tries and do-overs which not only push the goal of gameplay away from the mechanical perfection of specific skills and toward narrative resolution and closure, but also dramatically change both the function and perception of death within the boundaries of digital logic.[3]

Given that the image of death is so abundant in digital games while the event itself is so inconsequential, it would seem obvious that this new conception of mortality is simply another form of denial. Yet if we take a closer look, we'll find that games provide a new way of approaching and negotiating our own impermanence, that the digital, in both games and elsewhere, has altogether reconfigured our understanding of Being in relation to time. To unpack this reconfiguration, this chapter examines the new impression of death found in narratively driven games since the digital turn (as well as other moving images that have been influenced by the logic of gameplay) based on five observations.[4] First, that death is rarely permanent in digital games, acting instead only as a mechanical indication of incorrect gameplay as well as a narrative rewinding. Second, that successful gameplay often requires the player to simultaneously recall mechanical outcomes that occurred within both the past and future of the narrative diegesis. Third, that gameplay often centers around repetition, not only of specific mechanical actions but also a constant and continual restructuring of the narrative. Fourth, that contemporary games often place as much importance on the creation of virtual subjectivity within the narrative as they do on the development of skill within play mechanics. And lastly, that the goal of most games is not to avoid death altogether (if at all), but rather to avoid "incorrect" or narratively unsatisfying deaths. As these observations demonstrate, I intend to examine how death is conceived along two different axes of gameplay, one that focuses on the representation of death within the fiction of digital games, while the other demonstrates the function of death within the structure and rules of gamespace. In game studies, this is known as the divide between narratology and ludology — the study of narrative in gameplay and the study of the mechanics of gameplay — but rather than focus on one or the other, this study attempts to bridge the gap. Death, in both form and function, is evenly spread between these axes.

To draw out the interrelated strands of death in digital games, I'll turn to two well-known theories of death and its relation to human consciousness and identity: Nietzsche's formulation (and Deleuze's subsequent re-reading) of eternal recurrence, and Freud's development of the death drive. While these two theories may seem, at first glance, to be incompatible, both employ the notion of *repetition* — a return to a previous state of being — as way to understand our fascination with and terror of death. By examining digital gameplay through the concepts of eternal recurrence and the death drive, I argue that repetition, in the form of digital *re-animation*, acts as a mechanical substitute for our survival instincts, allowing players to construct virtual subjectivities within narratives where natural death (i.e., the narratively "correct" death) can only be understood — and, in fact, only exist — in relation to a multitude of other *compossible* deaths.

It may seem obvious to say it, but perhaps no other narrative medium embodies the digital more than the digital game. While films, television, books, and photographs have all been directly altered, to some degree or another, by the technologies of the late twentieth century, the digital game was born from it. In games, the attitudes and desires that constitute our digital logic are not simply expressed but rather *enforced* — they become the very rules and laws that govern gameplay. As such, games provide an exceptional avenue for exploring our new attitudes toward death, along with our desire to control the limitations of our own bodies, to stretch and reconfigure the boundaries of time, and to define not only our own relationship with mortality but also our own path to death.

Re-animation

When Brøderbund Software released Jordan Mechner's *Prince of Persia* for the Apple II in 1989, popular culture rarely presented temporality as anything other than a fixed and stable construct, flowing swift and sure in one direction.[5] A runaway hit that would later be ported to a wide variety of platforms, Mechner's game is often cited first for the unprecedented fluidity contained within its rotoscoped animation system — which rendered the title character as a fully realized, believably *alive* surrogate for the player — and second for the uncompromising nature of its gameplay and punishing time-limit.[6] In the opening cutscene, an Arabian princess is captured by the evil Vizier Jaffar while her father, the Sultan, is away fighting a holy war. The Vizier desires the throne, and gives the princess a deathly ultimatum: "Marry Jaffar … or die within the hour." The princess's only hope resides in the player, assuming the role of "a brave youth she loves … already a prisoner in Jaffar's dungeon" some thirteen floors below her in the deep recesses of the castle. The hour given to the princess is not an exaggeration — the player is given exactly sixty minutes to progress through the game's thirteen levels, escaping the dungeon and fighting their way toward a deadly showdown with the Vizier himself. Death in *Prince of Persia* can be brutal, resetting the player back to the start of a level even if they are seconds from its completion. However, the game's clock is even less forgiving, continuing to count down toward the princess's final moments regardless of the player's gameplay prowess.

Fourteen years later, Mechner and a considerably larger team of programmers at Ubisoft relaunched the Prince of Persia franchise with *Prince of Persia: The Sands of Time*. In addition to the game's shift into the third dimension, the defining feature of this new series was the player's relationship to time itself.[7] "Most people think time is like a river that flows swift and sure in one direction," the prince announces as the game begins, "but I have seen the face of time, and I can tell you … they are wrong." The key gameplay mechanic of this new iteration involves the "Dagger of Time,"

FIGURE 2.1 *Death is brutal in the original* Prince of Persia.

a weapon wielded by the prince that gives him (and thus the player) the power to reverse the flow of time. In dangerous or even fatal situations, with the simple press of a button the gameplay is literally rewound using a visual effect not at all unlike a VCR rewinding, allowing the player to choose a more suitable spot to replay or, more accurately, re-animate the prince's story. The narrative further serves this re-animating mechanic: presented as a tale being recounted by the prince, even death is easily explained away with a simple "wait, that isn't how it happened." Furthermore, the nonlinear composition of the Prince's story stretches and reshapes the boundaries of time; not only does *The Sands of Time* begin with images from its own final level, but at the conclusion of 2005's *The Two Thrones*, the final game of this new *Prince* trilogy, we find the prince beginning to tell a familiar story: "Most people think time is like a river ... "

Comparing these two *Princes*, we find that where once death was defined through a temporality both rigid and absolute, little more than a decade later that basic assumption had been radically overturned: time was at the mercy of the gameplayer, and death was no longer an ending or even a setback, but rather simply a resetting of the scene. Both princes were subjected to the same brutal and horrific moments of violence — their bodies cut in half by swinging blades or pierced by spikes that would shoot up from the floor — but the consequences of their deaths could not be more different; one subject not to the violence of booby traps or armed guards so much as subject to time's inevitable pursuit, while the other a master of time for whom death was merely an inconvenience to be internalized and then overwritten. As the

Prince of Persia series demonstrates, an analysis of death in contemporary digital games must begin not with its visual representations of dying, but rather with both the medium's ability to create a tangible sensation of *life* (a feat it accomplishes through animation and interactivity) and the unique sense of temporality (built around *compossibility* rather than linearity) that has become a cornerstone of digital games and, in many ways, digital logic itself.

In *Death 24x a Second*, Laura Mulvey provides a useful model for understanding the relationship between animation, temporality, and death in moving images, as well how the digital has begun to restructure that relationship. Although animation first appeared across a variety of mechanical entertainments during the nineteenth century, it only truly took root in popular culture with the advent of the motion picture, which, Mulvey contends, "combines ... two human fascinations: one with the boundary between life and death and the other with the mechanical animation of the inanimate."[8] These two fascinations are concretely connected to one another through their relationship to time, and Mulvey astutely attributes the power of animation to our (unconscious) recognition of temporality inherent in its antipodes: movement and stillness. Movement, she argues, implies duration, the continual extension of time that we associate with the forward progress of living. Stillness, on the other hand, creates a recognition of the past, of that which was but no longer is.[9] This is the frozen photographic subject that Barthes referred to in *Camera Lucida* as "that-had-been" or, more precisely, "what is dead, what is going to die," and which Bazin hinted at when he referred to the ontology of the photographic image as equal to the process of mummification — "a defense against the passage of time [that] satisfied a basic psychological need in man, for death is but the victory of time."[10] Though we often refer to the cinema's power to create life, Mulvey correctly points out that the cinema is actually mired in death — its very foundation is but a false imitation crafted from images of a stilled past, a process that Barthes sees as "a terrible return of the dead."[11] The cinema, Maria Walsh follows, is thus "haunted by a death ... akin to the living death in Freud's conception of the uncanny."[12]

Prior to the digital turn, the cinema rendered these frozen moments of death invisible to the average spectator through an illusion of movement which implied life even where life had been taken away. With the widespread adoption of digital technologies, however, the individual's relationship to (and control over) the temporal continuity of the cinematic apparatus changed drastically. Mulvey argues, for example, that the presentation of films on DVD, Blu-Ray, and streaming video has created a "cinema of delay" in which the viewer can freeze the image and insert stillness into sequences that were intended to be viewed in continuous motion.[13] This "transfer of cinematic works to digital media," Steven Shaviro explains, "allows for a renewed contemplation of them precisely because our ability to freeze the frame at any moment makes the cinematic dialectic between stillness and motion more accessible to us."[14] Death was in many ways always already situated within the very framework of the cinema as a *photographic technology*, but where once this image of death was hidden, the digital has given us access, precisely because death is always already situated within the framework of the digital as a *rendering technology*, such that viewing the world through a digital lens reveals only a series of rigid, binary dichotomies: ones and zeros, on and off, movement and stillness, possibility and impossibility, being and nonbeing, life and death. While the "digital disruption of linearity … frees the viewer from the dictates of narrative continuity and cinema time," as Walsh puts it, the digital has, more importantly, destabilized the cinema by granting the spectator the power to give and take life as they see fit, a power once reserved for (and recognized by) filmmakers alone.[15]

Yet while DVDs, Blu-rays, DVRs, streaming videos, and other similar digital technologies grant us jurisdiction over the temporality of moving images, the individual photographs themselves (and thus the very structure of cinematic life) fail to change. Instead, they simply repeat in the same combinations again and again and again.[16] Mulvey's cinema of delay may therefore encourage a more "pensive" spectator — a term that she borrows from Raymond Bellour's reading of stillness in the cinema of Max Ophuls — but not a more active one, given that they have little affect over the outcome of events unfolding on the screen.[17] The same cannot be said for digital games, where the player's direct control over the actions and movement onscreen inserts *their* life into the game, and when that movement is disrupted (those moments when the player has failed to meet the requirements of the mechanics of gameplay) the freezing and slowing down of time becomes *their* death — a death that marks a transition through which content is not only stilled but also often rewound. What defines death in digital games, at least since the digital turn, is not simply the close relationship between the animated avatar, the active spectator, and moment of inanimation, but more importantly the introduction of *re-animation*, a process through which gameplayers attempt to change the outcome of both the narrative and mechanical content by recalling their previous mistakes and overwriting them with new actions. This is why Alexander Galloway refers to digital games as an action-based medium "whose foundation is not in looking or reading but instead in the instigation of material change through action" — change which in most cases begins with a traumatic, narratively unsatisfying death, and then through action uses the knowledge gained from that failure to push toward a more satisfying conclusion.[18] The process of re-animation is therefore not an erasure so much as an overwriting akin to the process of painting on a used canvas, where the original image is not gone but rather continues to exist both behind and underneath, not so much as a contradiction of the new image but rather as a base that holds it up.

Compossibility

I'll return to the process and purpose of re-animation in greater detail shortly (as well as its impact on the digital logic of death) but it's first vital to note that re-animation would not be possible without the unique temporality found in digital games, one in which the player continually constructs the present not only as a response to the past, but also with concrete knowledge of the future — an organization which is in direct opposition to the traditional notions of time found in moving images prior to the digital turn. To unpack the difference between these two modes of temporality, let's turn briefly to Max Scheler, whose notion that every person has an intuitive, *a priori* knowledge of her/his own death was entirely reliant on a temporality that is at once fixed, constant, and limited — a theory that would also (albeit for different reasons) greatly influence Heidegger's later formulation of the *Dasein* as Being-towards-death. For Scheler, our knowledge of death is based not on the observation of the deaths of others but rather on a recognition of the totality of the present instant, which Bernard N. Schumacher sums up as follows:

> The structure of the vital process at the individual instant T (the total content of a moment) can be discerned in three qualitatively distinct dimensions that are correlative to that instant: the immediate present (pr) + the immediate past (p) + the immediate future (f) of something. Three extensions (of the vital process) can be assigned to these dimensions: perception (which relates to the present), memory (which relates to the past), and expectation (which relates to the future). ... Scheler maintains that although the past increases, the two other dimensions (the present and the future) necessarily decrease, given that the totality (T) is constant.[19]

Utilizing a model of time that is finite and omnidirectional, Scheler argued that death is made visible not by the observation of specific events but rather through the general "inductive experience of the changing content of every real life process."[20] In other words, because life is bound up in continual movement and constant change yet also *limited in possibility*, then stillness, stasis, and death must be inevitable, however far in the future. Following this logic, the thinking subject must assume that the past and future necessarily contradict one another, and as the "scope of the content" of the past begins to grow (i.e., as they grow older and experience/remember more) so too must the scope of the content of the future condense and diminish, eventually leading to nothingness and death.[21]

Despite the well-tread notion that the capacity for nonlinear narratives somehow divorces film and television from the temporal constraints of the real world, a Scheler-esque model of temporality was still predominant in pre-digital moving images, where even if the story were told in a nonlinear fashion the diegetic time nonetheless marched steadily and consistently forward — each second equaling one less moment to affect the outcome of the narrative, each action of the protagonist essentially one less move that can be made.[22] Contemporary digital games present us with an alternative to this fixed temporality — rather than a linear progression in which the future is merely an extension and erasure of the past, time in games doubles back upon itself, and through this repetition the player knows exactly what their future will be because they have already experienced it, *because they have already died*. In the digital temporality of gamespace, the individual instant is no longer composed of three qualitatively distinct dimensions $\{T = pr + p + f\}$ but rather one *compossible present* which is constructed of multiple cominglings of the past and future $\{T = pr\ (p + f)\}$.

For example, whenever a player leaps over lava pits in *Super Mario 64*, uses a cardboard box to sneak past armed guards in *Metal Gear Solid*, summons hoards of ant lions to attack Combine soldiers in *Half-Life 2*, or hunts down a mythological beast in *The Witcher 3*, they are armed not only with a perception of the mechanical obstacles of the gamespace or the outcome of their own controlling inputs. Instead, they also often possess a memory of having faced these very obstacles mere moments before — sometimes multiple times in various combinations and with various results — *in a future that is now made past*. Nearly every moment of gameplay is informed by multiple dimensions of time brought together, a present whole which both is structured atop and can exist only in relation to many *compossible* variations of both the past and future.

Leibniz first conceived of compossibility as a way of understanding why the world exists as it does, rather than as one of any number of other possibilities, based on the absence of inconsistency and logical contradiction. Responding to Spinoza's contention that everything that can exist does exist (and no more than what does exist could exist), Leibniz conceived of a world — *the world* — as a "complete individual concept" made up of numerous individual substances (compossibilities) whose relational properties do not oppose one another and thus are not contradictory.[23] Deleuze took this a step further in *Cinema 2*, where he declared that Leibniz's formulation of the compossible can only lead to — or as Deleuze puts it, Leibniz "is thus obliged to forge" — the notion of the *incompossible*, of divergent worlds where "the past may be true without necessarily being true."[24] Rather than focusing on the compossible substances that exist simultaneously within *our* world, Deleuze instead questions whether every action *may* happen somewhere, in a world that is incompossible with our own yet still existent. A model for understanding the temporal structure of certain forms of cinematic expression in the postwar period, Deleuze's incompossibilities and divergent worlds may seem, at first, to also directly mirror the deviating paths taken by gameplayers through the process of re-animation (where each death transports the player to another incompossible plane). Even his example of such incompossibilities, borrowed from Jorge Luis Borges, sounds eerily like the structure of a contemporary digital game:

> For nothing prevents us from affirming that incompossibles belong to the same world, that incompossible worlds belong to the same universe: "Fang, for example, has a secret; a stranger calls at his door ... Fang can kill the intruder, the intruder can kill Fang, they can both escape, they can both die, and so forth ... you arrive at this house, but in one of the possible pasts you are my enemy, in another, my friend ... " This is Borges reply to Leibniz: the straight line as force of time, as labyrinth of time, is also the line that forks and keeps on forking, passing through *incompossible presents*, returning to *not-necessarily true pasts*.[25]

Yet what separates Deleuze's incompossible worlds from the re-animated actions of a gameplayer is that, in Deleuze's scenario, each fork in time, each incompossibility, contradicts itself and therefore is unknown to those affected — in other words, Fang cannot know that he was killed by the intruder *somewhere else*, and thus cannot use that knowledge to shape his present.[26] In digital games, the opposite is true: every action is a response to an absolutely known past/future, and thus games are constructed not around "incompossible presents" and "not-necessarily true pasts" but rather "compossible presents" and "necessarily proven futures." In a game, the events described by Borges *can* exist alongside one another in a single, coherent, and compossible whole — rather than contradicting one another, they inform one another and allow one another to take on specific meanings. Fang can be killed by the intruder and then use that knowledge to kill the intruder, and in doing so (by allowing the player to progress only after some specific criteria are satisfied) the game molds the player's understanding of *both* actions, of *both* life and death (or even "life and life" or "death and death") as relational compossibilities.

In the temporality of pre-digital moving images, the past and future of any individual instant were, by definition, contradictory — so much so that as one increases, the other must decrease. In the digital time of games, this sense of contradiction is gone, allowing the past and future to exist together as compossible components of the totality of a moment, whereby both life and death, movement and stillness may exist side by side. Thus we find that while movement and stillness in games may initially point to the finiteness of the flesh in the same manner as the cinema (as forward progress of living and as stillness of death), the digital medium's new conception of a compossible temporality, alongside the interactivity that places the gameplayer into the game, ultimately presents us with a radically new recognition of mortality which points not to the death of others but rather to *the death of the self*. As such, we are once again left to question whether the re-animation of digital games denies death or instead shifts our relationship to death in some other way; to ask whether the goal of digital games is to insert life into the inanimate or to ensure, through a repetition of events, that the animate can become inanimate (that life can die) only in a manner that feels natural. I'll return to this question of the drive to ensure a natural (i.e., narratively satisfying) death shortly, but first let's examine the consequences of digital repetition and the possibility for change brought about by the process of re-animation.

Recurrence, Subjectivity, Contemplation

Re-animation and compossibility have been central to the image of death in digital games for decades, but they are not the only aspects of modern game design that define how we approach the issue of mortality in digital spaces. Since the late 2000s, a new mechanic — in fact a new principle of game design — has become prevalent across a variety of game genres, one that furthers the immersive possibilities of the medium. The mechanic: an ethical choice (or choices) given to the player that influences both the resolution of the narrative and the player's digital subjectivity. These "moral choice engines," according to Marcus Schulzke, enhance the cultural value of games through the production of "compelling simulations that force players to test their own values [while furnishing] sanctions in the game to respond to the player's choice."[27] Yet while many critics and scholars read this mechanic as little more than the proliferation of virtual morality plays — "a training ground in which players can practice thinking about morality," as Schulzke reads them — its true function is far more complex, marking a shift in game design philosophy in which *the formation of a virtual subjectivity* has become a focal point of a wide variety of narratively driven games in various genres and styles.[28] The ethical dilemmas presented in games like the *Mass Effect*, *Infamous*, and *Fallout* series — do you shoot the criminal or talk him down? do you feed the weak or take the food for yourself? do you kill the tyrant to free his people or take his throne? — are not simply toys through which we adopt various moral viewpoints, nor simply spaces in which we affirm our own sense-of-self through ethical action, but rather mechanical devices through which we influence the development of a separate *virtual subjectivity* with its own relationship to death, one that helps to shape our understanding of our actual mortality. At the forefront of this new subjectivity-defining mechanic was Irrational Games' *Bioshock* — an RPG-lite first person shooter released in 2007 and designed by Ken Levine — whose narrative hinged on an ethical choice that gave even the most jaded gamers pause.

Bioshock tells the story of the dystopic underwater city of Rapture, constructed in the mid-twentieth century by business tycoon Andrew Ryan and conceived as the ideal manifestation of the laissez-faire principles of Objectivism, the philosophy espoused in the literature of Ayn Rand. Rapture's purpose was to create a society free of the ethical constraints of government, religion, and bureaucracy, which Ryan explains in the game's opening sequence:

> Is a man not entitled to the sweat of his brow? "No!" says the man in Washington, "It belongs to the poor." "No!" says the man in the Vatican, "It belongs to God." "No!" says the man in Moscow, "It belongs to everyone." I rejected those answers; instead, I chose something different. I chose the impossible. I chose ... Rapture! A city where the artist would not fear the censor, where the scientist would not be bound by petty morality, where the great would not be constrained by the small!

In the absence of ethical oversight, the scientists of Rapture discovered a plasmid known as ADAM, which utilized stem cells to enable superhuman powers like telekinesis and mind-control ("evolution in a bottle" as an in-game advertisement claims). Unfortunately, ADAM could only be cultivated within the organs of adolescent girls, test subjects whose minds were warped by the process and who subsequently became known throughout Rapture as the ghoulish "little sisters." The player — assuming the role of "Jack," a man whose identity at the start of the narrative is little more than a tabula rasa, suffering from amnesia after his plane crashed into the sea directly above Rapture — is inserted into this story just after class warfare has broken out in response to the limited quantities of ADAM. As they fight their way through the city using their own modified weapons and genetic powers, players battle against numerous citizens who have been genetically mutated by ADAM into sometimes deformed but always dangerous and deadly opponents. Each encounter brings with it the possibility of death, yet each death is little more than an inconvenience thanks to another Rapture technology known as the "Vita-Chamber," which has the power to "restore" and thus re-animate players after death (*Bioshock*, it turns out, is one of only a handful of games that attempt to narratively explain the process of re-animation).[29]

Along their path, players also run across a number of little sisters, who wander the corridors of Rapture in search of dead bodies — "angels" as they call them — from which they collect the genetic material that they must rather morbidly consume to create more ADAM. Each encounter with a little sister presents the player with a grisly choice: either rescue the young girl from the debilitating effects of this process by destroying the ADAM within her body, or harvest the ADAM, increasing the player's abilities at the cost of the little sister's life (an act that mercifully happens offscreen). Not simply another intuitive action in response to a threat or challenge, this choice is given significant weight within the narrative, which, depending on the ratio of girls freed versus harvested, presents the player with one of two endings *and thus defines them* in one of two ways: a "good" ending for those who sacrificed power in order to rescue the young girls, and a "bad" ending for those who were concerned more with the accumulation of power than for the lives of the innocent. Yet the narrative conclusions that result from this choice are not simply a way to declare the player as either hero or villain, but rather a way to define their very relationship (or more accurately their "path") to death itself. For example, the "bad" ending sees the player go insane with power (a result of the large quantities of ADAM they have consumed), which leads them to steal nuclear weapons which they will presumably use to destroy the world and themselves in the process. The "good" ending, on the other hand, ends quite literally years later at the player's deathbed, where the rescued and now-grown sisters hold an old man's hand as he slips away into death.[30] In *Bioshock*, death was never meant to be avoided but was instead the very goal of the narrative itself — to permit the player to die in a manner that seems "natural" given the context of the player's in-game subjectivity.

As *Bioshock* implicitly demonstrates, re-animation is merely the *how* of the image of death in digital games, but not necessarily the *why*. In other words, our examination of death in games thus far has revealed that the digital allows for a composible present in which players can overwrite previous deaths through the rewinding process of re-animation, but now we'll move forward to examine why games have adopted this re-animating process, as well as how re-animation reconfigures the player's relationship to death, their own in particular. To do so, let's turn to two well-known (and widely

FIGURE 2.2 *Players face a difficult choice as they encounter their first "little sister."*

misunderstood) philosophical theories which situate man's relationship to death, Nietzsche's doctrine of eternal return and Freud's development of the death drive. Both take as their starting point *repetition* — the very process which drives re-animation — yet arrive at very different conclusions about the function of death: one which reveals the vital roles that *identity* and *difference* play in the recognition, assessment, and contemplation of death, while the other a critique of the *instincts* and the drive to create "*one's own path to death.*"

Throughout his work, Nietzsche developed a philosophical approach to death that would begin, in *The Gay Science*, as conscious affirmation of one's path through life, become a challenge to the elite to accept one's mortality in *Thus Spoke Zarathustra*, and finally morph into a pseudo-scientific explanation for the infinite nature of the universe in his late writing, such as *Ecce Homo*. The philosophy itself, referred to as both eternal recurrence and the doctrine of eternal return of the same, begins with a simple thought experiment: what if, Nietzsche asks, you were told that you will live the same life again and again throughout time, without change, so that "every pain and every joy and every thought and every sigh" were repeated for eternity — would you rejoice your good fortune or would you recoil in horror?[31] Nietzsche suspected the latter, referring to the doctrine of eternal return as "the heaviest burden" which is relayed not by an angel but rather a demon: "would you not throw yourself down," he asks, "and gnash your teeth and curse the demon who thus spoke?"[32] The very thought of eternal recurrence is, according to Nietzsche, enough to break the will of anyone less than the *Übermensch*, the overman or superior-being that Zarathustra, Nietzsche's philosophical surrogate, saw as the ultimate aspiration of human consciousness. So powerful is the thought alone that it appears, on the one hand, as a dangerous weapon that Nietzsche and Zarathustra were reluctant to unleash upon an unprepared or unwilling public — "if this thought gained power over you it would, as you are now, transform and perhaps crush you" — while on the other hand a force strong enough to propel humanity toward greatness — "how well disposed towards yourself and towards your life would you have to become to have no greater desire than for this ultimate eternal sanction and seal?"[33] Yet rather than prodding us to examine the value or purpose of our life (a common misreading), eternal recurrence is instead a call to recognize and embrace — or at the very least, cease to be terrified of — our own death, for it is not simply an ethical appeal nor a religious doctrine but rather a complex understanding of Being, time, and the limitations of personal subjectivity and self-identity.

According to Nietzsche, Being implies a constant present — it is itself not a process but rather the end state of the process of Becoming — and because time is always passing, we are never Being anything but rather are always Becoming something else. As such, all of the physical world, all beings and thus all Being, "is" or can only "be" *pure Becoming*.[34] How does the recognition of Being as pure Becoming lead us to the doctrine of eternal return? Alexander Cooke provides a useful summary of Nietzsche's philosophical move:

> If there is neither start nor end to Becoming, how does one experience the very passing of the Moment that justifies the fact of Being as Becoming? The present or Moment, such that it can be experienced as passing, must be both past and yet-to-come. For Time to incorporate the Moment in two states (past and yet-to-come), at some point, the same passage of Time must recur or return. Insofar as there is no end point to becoming, it must recur eternally.[35]

At this point, we find clear echoes between the notion of eternal recurrence and the process of re-animation: both presuppose that Being and temporality are not limited but rather subject to continual repetition, both view life as constant Becoming or movement and death not as final but rather as a moment of resetting or recurrence, and both establish a clear relationship between the past and future. At the same time there are divergences, first (and most obviously) the fact that re-animation is always an opportunity for change while eternal recurrence is always a repetition of the same, and second a fundamental difference in the metaphysical arrangement of the Moment.

We'll return to first divergence again shortly, but for now let's follow second: rather than the compossible present of the digital $\{T = pr\ (p + f)\}$, or even Scheler's three dimensions of the totality of the Moment $\{T = pr + p + f\}$, the doctrine of eternal return suggests that *there is no present* but rather only a past that is forever Becoming the future $\{T = p \rightarrow f\}$. This notion has significant ramifications for the individual and their relationship to death, both within the actual and the virtual, because the absence of a present effectively denies the possibility of personal identity or self-constructed subjectivity — the very same sense of subjectivity that helps games like *Bioshock* differentiate between a satisfying death (i.e., the "correct" or "natural" death, narratively speaking) and the numerous traumatic and unsatisfying deaths that litter the compossible time of gamespace. "From the point of view of subjectivity," Cooke explains, "one can point toward the self-affirmation of one's own being in enunciating 'I am.' Such a statement, according to its 'common' understanding, presupposes that the 'am' is a quality of Being, *not* Becoming."[36] In a Moment that can only be experienced as a passing, one cannot state *who they "are"* (how can one "be" if one is always "becoming"?) but rather only state *what they have done or hope to do*, their personal choices and actions — choices made in the past; choices that are yet-to-be-made. In the absence of a present, subjectivity is defined by choice, and identity is thus not a thought but rather an act, it is not thought but rather enacted.

Here we find an avenue back to the digital, as action and choice have become the defining elements of modern games — action as choice — as well as the elements within games that *define us*. Every Moment in a game requires action in response to a mechanical challenge, and every action is a choice, one in which the player decides on the appropriate input based on a multitude of factors (not the least of which is their recollection of the compossible past/future).

But are these basic inputs — jump here, avoid this, kill that — enough to allow a player to define their own virtual subjectivity?[37] A useful intervention here comes from Heidegger, who, in his readings of Nietzsche and elsewhere, positioned subjectivity not as the result of self-affirming thought (thinking and Being are the same, for Heidegger, only insofar as they *belong* to one another) but rather as a side effect of both the "will to power" — which he describes as Nietzsche's "single name for the basic character of beings and for the essence of power" — and the fact of eternal return of the same.[38] Every being *is* "will to power" for they constantly seek or, more appropriately, create power, "the uppermost value" that has no need to supplant other values because "power and *only power* posits value, validates them, and makes decisions about the possible justifications of a valuation."[39] As such, the individual being cannot self-affirm or self-identify because it is always already defined through its basic, eternal character as "will to power," and thus every attempt at what Heidegger calls "incessant self-overempowering" — *any choice or action beyond self-preservation* — is nothing more than a "power-conforming becoming [that] must itself always recur again and bring back the same."[40] Following Heidegger's logic, the typical inputs required in digital games are not enough to allow a player to define their own virtual subjectivity because these actions are only concerned with self-preservation and the avoidance of death, thereby failing to define the individual in relation to their being as "will to power." Yet as we see in the case of *Bioshock*, modern game design frequently presents players with moral and ethical dilemmas through which the player can influence the development of their digital subjectivity by means of the accumulation or sacrifice of some form of power, dilemmas which, more often than not, relay those subjective choices directly through death (whether the player's own or that of another).

In fact, let's briefly turn back to *Bioshock*, which presents a commentary on the very nature of subjective choice in gameplay through a significant twist in its narrative, in which the player discovers late in the game that nearly all of their actions have been the direct result of a mind-control experiment whereby the protagonist is supposedly conditioned to obey any command given to them following the phrase "would you kindly." A flashback reminds them that at every turn in the story, an ally named "Atlas" (actually Andrew Ryan's main competitor, Frank Fontaine, in disguise, his alias a not-so-subtle nod to Ayn Rand) had used the phrase "would you kindly" when "asking" them to proceed in a certain ways, requests that would then appear in written on-screen prompts as "objectives" to be completed. "The game has manipulated us through its use of environmental nudges, game-world obstacles, and objectives we have been kindly asked to achieve," Grant Tavinor explains, "so that for the most part, we have 'sleepwalked' through the game, unaware of the artifice, an actor in someone else's artwork."[41] This revelation is shocking on two levels. First, on the narrative level it reveals that the player is not simply the survivor of a plane crash but rather a sleeper agent conditioned to assassinate Ryan. More interestingly, however, it makes visible an underlying mechanical principle of digital games, in which a player will generally perform any task so long as the game fails to give them any other option — so long as it fails to give them *choice*. Why do we run from one end of a level to the other? Because the game tells us to. Why do we pick up this object instead of that one? Because the game tells us to. Why do we shoot these men rather than join their cause? *Because the game tells us to*. This is not to say that games which fail to offer choice cannot produce in-game subjectivities, but rather that, as *Bioshock* argues, without choice games define players rather than allowing players to define themselves. This revelation also leads to one of *Bioshock*'s most shocking sequences, where the player's control over the action is literally taken away (such that none of the normal controlling inputs function correctly) and they become helpless to stop themselves from gruesomely beating Ryan to death with a golf club. Regardless of how the player has defined their own virtual subjectivity, in this moment their lack of choice defines them. Ryan's last words in response: "A man chooses, a slave obeys."

FIGURE 2.3 *The player discovers their lack of free will in* Bioshock.

There is, however, one exception to Fontaine's mind-control in *Bioshock*: the little sisters. Fontaine never directly intervened in the decision process which ultimately defines the player as good or bad, saint or sinner, and as such *Bioshock* aims to show us how gamers *can* define their own virtual subjectivity rather than having their subjectivity defined by the game; not by allowing the player to self-preserve (i.e., avoid death) in whatever manner they choose, but rather by letting them create their own "will to power" through ethical choices — choices that, as we will see shortly, also define what is and is not a natural, satisfying resolution (i.e., death) for the player. This mechanic is even joined by other approaches to contemporary game design, such as open-world "sandbox" games like the *GTA* and *Fallout* series, which give players specific tasks but a multitude of options or ethical avenues through which to accomplish those tasks. In turn, players are offered various rewards that change their abilities and shift their "power" — another opportunity through which they can influence their digital subjectivity.

Despite its current prominence within the mechanics of gameplay, however, choice alone cannot wholly define identity in games for two reasons. First, as mentioned above, not every game utilizes choice in order to allow the player to influence their virtual subjectivity, and second because many of the choices presented in modern games can be overwritten by a more powerful force: re-animation. *Choice* is therefore only one half of the creation of identity and the definition of "natural" death in digital games, an equation that is completed by *chance*, the potential for difference. By chance, I refer not to a quality of randomness in games, but rather to the opportunity they provide to change outcomes after they have already occurred.[42] Gameplay presents choice, but re-animation is the act that enables chance, for it allows the player to create different outcomes based on various compossibilities. Chance also brings us back to the most obvious divergence between re-animation and eternal recurrence — if re-animation is always an opportunity for change and difference, and if eternal recurrence is always a repetition of the same, then how can re-animation be read as a digital manifestation of eternal recurrence? Or, to view this question from another perspective, is there any room for chance or difference in Nietzsche's doctrine?

According to Deleuze, the answer is obviously yes: "Every time we understand the eternal return as the return of a particular arrangement of things after all the other arrangements have been realized, every time we interpret the eternal return as the return of the identical or the same, we replace Nietzsche's thought with childish hypothesis."[43] How does Deleuze arrive at this conclusion if Nietzsche's entire premise is centered around a return "of the same"? To begin, Deleuze reads the eternal return not simply as the repetition of Time but rather as the purest *form of Time*, a model of temporality that is very much akin to the compossible time of digital games. Rather than a past that bypasses the present in the process of Becoming the future $\{T = p \to f\}$, Deleuze posits the Moment as a "living present" which exists as a contraction of "successive independent instants," of which the past and future are not independent dimensions but rather only "dimensions of the present itself." For Deleuze, "the present alone exists" — the present is itself *a constant repetition* that exists *in the absence of both the past and future* {T = pr ¬ (p + f)}.[44] Reading eternal return as a form of Time — as *the* form of Time — is significance not because it returns the present and thus once again accounts for identity and subjectivity (for Deleuze's project, as we will see, upends the notion of identity found in Nietzsche and elsewhere), but rather because it creates a present that constantly and continually encourages contemplation. How so?

Deleuze posits that identity — metaphysical essence — is formed not from Sameness (the notion of the identical, of shared qualities) but rather through difference, which he considers to be a first-order principle of all Being. Difference in this sense is found not in the comparison of one substance to another but rather *within* each substance; a *difference-in-itself* that is revealed only through repetition, which produces a material change not in the substance that repeats but rather "in the mind which contemplates [the repetition]: a difference, something new *in* the mind."[45] Here, we find that Deleuze has overturned the notion of identity found in Nietzsche by making it a secondary principle of difference (rather than the other way around), and that where Nietzsche saw identity as not thought but rather action, Deleuze sees identity as only thought — or, more accurately, only recognizable within the thought that contemplates eternal recurrence. While Zarathustra called this very thought "so much the hardest to bear that no prior, mediocre human being can think it," Deleuze creates a sense of the return in which every Moment, every repetition of the present is an opportunity to recognize difference-in-itself, to recognize and construct identity through difference. "Thus," Deleuze states, "the circle of eternal return, difference and repetition (*which undoes that of the identical and the contradictory*) is a torturous circle in which Sameness is said only of that which differs."[46] As this fuller picture of the return demonstrates, not only does Deleuze find identity in that which differs (that which repeats) and thus sees the return as undoing the primacy of the identical, but he also reads the return as an *undoing of contradiction* — it creates a space in which differences-in-themselves are not contradictory but rather composible.

Turning back to games, we find that re-animation is, in essence, this same process, it creates a composible present in which the repetition of life and death is uniquely visible and thus the contemplation of such repetition is uniquely possible. Following this, the repetition of death in games does not make death invisible but rather *hyper-visible*, especially when repeated and inconsequential deaths come face to face with a permanent death within the narrative (a structure I'll return to in a moment). Yet the composibility inherent in the temporality of gamespace must constantly point to and create difference — it must constantly insert chance — in order to allow the player to contemplate and identify death. As Daniel W. Conway shows us, a central act in Deleuze's reading of eternal recurrence is Zarathustra's dice throw (itself already a game), in which the throwing of the dice reveals chance while the dice's falling back to earth demonstrates necessity.[47] Being two separate events, necessity (in this case the repetition and recurrence inherent in Time) does not rule out or abolish the possibility of chance. The present may eternally recur, but each recurrence allows us to further contemplate, identify, and re-animate. As Deleuze puts it: "To think is to create: this is Nietzsche's greatest lesson. To think, to cast the dice ... this was already the sense of the eternal return."[48] In digital games those dice are always thrown again, the player is always given the chance to recognize, contemplate, and overwrite death.

Regardless of whether or not Nietzsche truly believed that life would eternally repeat in the same manner without change (still subject to great debate amongst many critics and scholars), the "thought" of eternal return — the *burden* of eternal return — is that a "return of the same" inherently implies a stasis (a failure to change), and if all existence is not Being but rather Becoming (a continual process of change), then stasis can be nothing more than non-existence and death. Eternal recurrence is not a promise that life will repeat itself again and again and again, but rather a signpost that points to death, a declaration that once you have died your own possibility for change is now eternally gone. This is the burden that digital games challenge, creating a space where we *can* change after death, where death itself is the impetus for change. Following this, Deleuze's re-reading is not a so much promise that life will repeat eternally in different forms, but rather an observation that every Moment is a repetition — a "torturous circle" — through which we can recognize and contemplate the true essence of Being: that all beings are subject to an eternal change that permits the "emergence of the new" just as assuredly as it inevitably leads to death. In games, we re-animate not to deny death but rather to contemplate it, to recognize its consequences, and *to make death more present*.

The Path to Death

As with Nietzsche before him, Freud's awareness of the importance of death in human consciousness was born out of a recognition of repetition, but rather than a contemplation of eternal forces, Freud's repetition was seen in the neurotic replaying of traumatic events: in the soldier's flashbacks of a harrowing battle, in the dreams of an abuse victim which recall painful details from their childhood, or even in the compulsive nature of the child's "fort-da" game.[49] Such repetition, Freud argued, "disregards the pleasure principle in every way" by acting not as a cathexis or discharge of excitations (for all mental processes are, according to Freud, little more the accumulation and release of the tensions between forces), but rather as manifestations of an extraneous force which "exhibit, to a high degree, an instinctual character."[50] Considering that Freud defines the instincts as "a compulsion inherent in organic life to restore an earlier state of things ... a kind of organic elasticity," and considering that the previous state of life or being is always inanimate non-life or nonbeing, we must then be compelled, as Freud puts it, to contend that all instincts lead to the return or recurrence of the inanimate state — that all instincts lead to death. "This view of instincts strikes us as strange," Freud admits, "because we have become used to seeing, in them, a factor impelling toward change and development, whereas we are now asked to recognize, in them, the precise contrary — an expression of the *conservative* nature of living substance."[51] Rather than Nietzsche's notion that life always returns *as* the same, in Freud we find the instinct for life to always return *to* the same (such that Sameness is a *state* of the past and not the past itself). All of life is thus a return, a return to a previous form of Being that is enabled only through death.

The push for the animate to return to the inanimate — what Freud referred to as the death drive, and which has also become known as Thanatos, the death instinct — was first elaborated in his essay *Beyond the Pleasure Principle* in 1920, which has simultaneously become one of the most important, divisive, and misunderstood texts in Freud's body of work. As W. Craig Tomlinson explains, "Many of the schisms in international psychoanalysis — between ego psychologists and Kleinians, between fundamentalists and reformers, between Europe and the Americas — have important roots in this text."[52] Yet at the same time the tensions that have arisen from the essay (and thus from the very notion of the death drive itself) have proved fruitful in many ways, as Tomlinson points out when he continues to assert that "much of the richness and diversity of psychoanalysis can be traced to *Beyond the Pleasure Principle*."[53] While it certainly has its defenders, Melanie Klein and Jacques Lacan in particular, few have truly grasped the importance of the death drive. This is partially Freud's own fault, for he himself cautioned that the death drive "is the development of an extreme line of thought" which he seemed comfortable with only when situated in opposition to Eros, the sexual instincts, so much so that he admits that he would "feel relieved if the whole structure [of the death drive] turned out to be mistaken ... and [thus] the compulsion to repeat would no longer possess the importance we have ascribed to it."[54] Many readings of the death drive follow suit by positioning the drive not as a return to the inanimate but rather as the object-cause of aggression or self-destruction — a fascinating argument in its own right that Freud nonetheless developed later, in *Civilization and Its Discontents*, almost as a way to conceptualize the drive without reference to the troubling and disconcerting aspects of the body's own desire to return to a previous state. As such, the drive itself has often come to stand for aggression and violence rather than the true consequences and ramifications of the push toward the inanimate: that "the goal of all life is death" and thus "everything living dies for internal reasons."[55]

This line of thinking leads us to an intriguing dilemma: If "the goal of all life is death," why do we work so hard to deny it and struggle so hard to avoid it? This question is just as applicable in contemporary digital games, if not more so given the often inconsequential nature of death as a game mechanic: if the goal of games is *not* to avoid death, as I have previously suggested, then why do we fight so hard to do just that? To respond, we must return to the instincts. "Seen in this light," Freud realizes, "the theoretical importance of the instincts of self-preservation, of self-assertion, and of mastery greatly diminishes."[56] Self-preservation, self-assertion, and mastery; all three of which have also drastically diminished in importance within contemporary game design, and two of which we've already touched upon at some length. Let's begin with mastery, as it was the primary goal of digital games at their very inception — the achievement of high scores and better performances — a goal that has been repeatedly overturned in contemporary games. In a not-so-veiled critique of Nietzsche, Freud argued that the instinct toward mastery at work in human beings, "which may be expected to watch over their development into supermen," is no more than "an untiring impulsion towards further perfection [which] can easily be understood as a result of the instinctual repression" — the repression of the basic drive toward death.[57] Likewise, the aim to master or perfect gameplay was itself little more than a forced or required repression of death, for the entire goal of such perfection was to avoid dying for as long as possible — a virtual repression of a virtual death that would, as with actual death, always find the player in the end.

Contemporary games, on the other hand, are concerned less with the perfection of skill than with the development and resolution of narrative, a fact clearly seen in the near ubiquitous "difficulty levels" of contemporary games which ensure that, with a large enough time commitment, even the most novice player can find closure. As we have also seen, contemporary games often introduce choice to allow the player to define their own *virtual subjectivity* — a digital declaration of "I am" that is only feasible in the compossible time of gamespace — yet this process is not self-assertion but in fact quite the opposite. Digitals games require the gamer to abandon their own sense of self or self-concept (to use a Freudian term) in favor of a virtual self, a split subjectivity that has, as we will see in Chapter 3, a separate relationship to death yet always responds or points to our actual understanding of death's inevitability. As such, self-assertion of the player's *actual subjectivity* is explicitly repressed in contemporary games.

Finally, then, we have self-preservation, the instinct to fight against harm and death. In games, as we have repeatedly seen, re-animation diminishes the need to fight against death, for death is no longer final but instead a learning process through which we can overwrite the mistakes of the past. So we must ask again: Why do we fight against meaningless death in games? The answer concerns all three of the "diminished" instincts: in order to reach a satisfying resolution in digital game narratives (at the expense of the diminishment of mastery), we craft a virtual subjectivity that suppresses our actual subjectivity (at the expense of the diminishment of self-assertion), which allows us to recognize and thus push toward a "natural," satisfying death (at the expense of the diminishment of self-preservation). As Freud makes explicit, "We have no longer to reckon with the organism's puzzling determination (so hard to fit into any context) to maintain its own existence in the face of every obstacle. What we are left with is the fact that the organism wishes to die only in its own fashion."[58] In life, we struggle because to struggle is an instinct, one "whose function," Freud further explains, "is to assure that the organism *shall follow its own path to death*."[59] In games, we struggle not to avoid death itself, but rather to avoid the "wrong" death, a death that fails to satisfy the demands of both the narrative and our virtual subjectivity. In games, we struggle so that we can die in our own fashion, we struggle because within the virtual (unlike the actual) *we can assure our own path to death*.

Death is not failure in contemporary games because the very goal of games *is* death, not only to recognize death but also to create one's own path to a narratively satisfying, "natural" death. Let's take a moment to parse out the concept of a "natural death," for it's a term that Freud uses repeatedly throughout *Beyond the Pleasure Principle*. Colloquially, natural death might refer to senescent death, the eventual failure of life-sustaining processes due to the aging of the body, but digital avatars fail to experience senescence and as such this type of death is mostly unavailable in gamespace. For Freud, however, natural death is not about senescence but rather the body's own release or excitation of the tensions between life and non-life, between the animate and the inanimate. A traumatic death may also release such tensions, but for Freud it does so "by a kind of short-circuit" which helps the organism "attain its life's goal rapidly" — *too* rapidly, before the organism is ready.[60] In games, where death is no more than a temporal rewinding, this rapid push toward death serves the opposite function, for it accrues tensions rather than releases them. For example, a traumatic death at the hands of a nameless mythological monster in *God of War III* is not the "right" death for Kratos because such a death does not release tensions but rather builds them, and likewise it would feel unnatural for Commander Shepard to be killed by a random Geth in *Mass Effect 3* for this would only add to our excitements. To achieve a cathexis, to release these tensions, Kratos can only die when his vengeance against the Gods is complete and Shepard can only die as a sacrifice to save the galaxy from destruction — only these deaths are "natural," for only these deaths release tensions by satisfying the demands of the protagonist's (and thus the player's) virtual subjectivity.

Even open-world games find ways to ensure a natural death for the protagonist, despite the genre's propensity for allowing players to continue to explore and interact with the gameworld after the main narrative is complete. For example, in a shocking moment toward the end of Rockstar North's *Red Dead Redemption* — a revisionist open-world western set not in the mid-nineteenth century but rather in 1911, just as the "wild" west was being co-opted by civilization, government, and the free market — the player-controlled protagonist, John Marston, is unavoidably killed within the narrative while defending his family from corrupt government agents. Unlike when he was gunned down by a random bandit in a long-abandoned ghost town, or attacked by a bear in a snowy forest, or shot down in a duel in a Mexican border town, this death — dying to save the family that defines his identity as a man of peace rather than violence — is a death that satisfies the criteria of both Marston's self-identity and the player's virtual subjectivity. Instead of re-animating Marston, the permanence of this shocking event within the narrative is reinforced moments later, when the game cuts forward in time several years to find the player unexpectedly given control over Marston's adult son. This dramatic switch away from the avatar that the player has controlled for upwards of twenty-to-forty hours confirms that this death was indeed a satisfying and "natural" death for Marston, while also mechanically allowing the player to continue to interact with the world through Marston's son.[61]

"But let us pause for a moment and reflect," Freud pleads, for "it cannot be so." It cannot be so, can it? That death is the ultimate and even desired

FIGURE 2.4 *John Marston is fatally gunned down yet his death is still narratively "natural."*

resolution of life? And what of games — what is the relationship between death and resolution in games? To find out, let's momentarily return to the cinema, where Peter Brooks and Laura Mulvey, among others, have argued that the death drive functions in film narratives to push toward *closure*. In *Reading for the Plot*, Brooks borrows from Tzvetan Todorov's model of narrative transformation, "whereby plot — *sjužet, récrit* — is constituted in the tension of two formal categories, difference and resemblance," a "same-but-different" that functions in a similar manner as does Deleuze's difference-in-itself. In other words, plotting — which allows the narrative to push from beginnings to endings, from birth to death — is a continual recognition and contemplation of a change that "puts time into motion" while also creating tensions within the viewer.[62] Reading this process through Freud, Brooks argues that such change is driven by repetition, for "narrative always makes the implicit claim to be in a state of repetition ... a *sjužet* repeating a *fabula*." As with all Being's drive toward death, this repetition is a push toward (or return to) a previous state of stillness or stasis that marks the end of change and the release of tensions, so that "the desire of the text (the desire of reading) is hence desire for the end ... of *fabula* become *sjužet*."[63] This end — this *closure* — is not simply a model of death (even when it calls upon or utilizes the very image of death, as is so often the case) but rather death itself, which Brooks makes explicit when he argues that "death provides the very 'authority' of the [narrative], since as readers we seek in narrative fictions the knowledge of death which in our own lives is denied to us."[64] Mulvey builds on this by noting that films typically begin with intense action and movement which serves to "jump start" the narrative, whereas the goal of the film's ending is to allow stillness to return — usually through the narrative devices of death or marriage (what Brooks playfully refers to as "erotic stasis"). Death in the cinema has, for Mulvey, a "double tautological appeal, a doubling of the structure and content" — the *fabula* finds closure through life attaining its goal while the *sjužet* provides closure in the stillness of the image.[65]

In digital games, on the other hand, traumatic or "incorrect" deaths cannot serve as closure because they shatter the content from its structure, they act not as a moment of finality but rather as the beginning of the process of re-animation and the establishment of the player's own path to death. But what of the "natural" death, the narratively satisfying death — surely such a death must function as closure? Not so, for in games we find that even a death that *resolves* the narrative fails to *close* that narrative, for games (unlike the cinema) are not meant to be completed but rather repeated, played again so that new choices and new actions can define and create new experiences, an extension of the very logic of re-animation that exists at the heart of digital games. This is why choice and chance — action and re-animation — are so central to gameplay, because choice shapes our experience while chance allows us to overwrite not just moments of traumatic death but also the entire experience, to create compossible experiences that allow us to recognize and contemplate the complete consequences of our choices and their impact on each unique path to death.

For example, building on the trend toward the development of in-game subjectivities, we find that contemporary games frequently allow for multiple resolutions or endings — anywhere from two variations (as with *Bioshock* or *Infamous*) to hundreds of combinations (as we see in *Fallout: New Vegas* or the "extended ending" of *Mass Effect 3*) — each of which allows the protagonist to die only in the fashion that feels most natural while also encouraging players to repeatedly form *new* virtual subjectivities by restarting and re-animating the narrative. Added to this, the contemporary landscape of gaming is dominated by online multiplayer and game-expanding downloadable content ("DLC"), which allows gamers to continue playing long after the narrative has come to an end, and which often require that the narrative is not closed but rather left open. As such, natural death in games provides not closure but rather a desire to re-roll the dice, to create a new subjectivity which can define a new path to death.[66]

Reading death in games through the death drive, we finally begin to resolve a question that is crucial for understanding the conception of death in this new digital landscape: Do digital games deny death? The answer, at first glance, seems obvious: games rob death of consequence and finality, making death no more than a momentary punishment for incorrect play and thus no more important than a slap on the wrist. But when we dig deeper into the processes of re-animation, the recognition of death through the compossible time of gamespace, and the establishment of virtual subjectivities through recurrence and chance, we find that games are not a denial but rather a new avenue in our exploration of death, through which we can experience death yet also live to contemplate it, and through which we can imagine, create, and follow our own digital path to death.

After the Game is Before the Game

To get a clearer picture of the digital path to death, and to further examine how re-animation, compossibility, recurrence, and virtual subjectivity all play out in games, let's turn to a reading of the image of death in two contemporary "game" texts — the first being one of the most successful "indie" titles of the last console generation, while the second not a game but rather a film that has taken up the very logic of gameplay in order to explore the path to death.

Developed by the appropriately named Danish studio Playdead and designed by Arnt Jenson, *LIMBO* was first released in 2010 as a downloadable title on the Xbox Live Arcade, though its critical and commercial success paved the way for later versions to appear on a number of other platforms. The bulk of the game's loosely strung, two-to-three hour narrative is relayed through its intense black and white aesthetic, complete with shadowy figures who float through parallaxing, shallow-focused landscapes that stutter and fade as if being projected from an old, scratchy 16mm print. Using the mechanics of a side-scrolling platformer — think of *LIMBO* as Mario's beautiful but menacing nightmare — players inhabit the body of a small boy who struggles to survive in a terrifying environment of deadly creatures, traps, and other lost children, his frequent encounters with trauma and death only occasionally offset by glimpses of a young girl in the distance. Any sense that this girl might be the key to understanding the nightmare which has befallen the protagonist is entirely intuitive, as *LIMBO* utilizes none of the traditional narrative techniques found in the majority of contemporary games. There's no dialog, no cut-scenes, no opening titles, no explicit explanation of how the boy arrived in this world, nor are there even hints regarding his emotional response to his circumstance (beyond, as we'll see, the player's own actions as they guide him on his journey). Yet the narrative is hauntingly engaging, it doesn't force a story upon the player but rather allows them the space to contemplate subtle themes about trauma, decay, and the recognition of the inevitability of death.

Key to the affective nature of *LIMBO*'s narrative is the deep connection that the game renders between the avatar of young boy and the player's subjective experience of the gameworld, a connection crafted through subtle mechanical touches. For example, the game begins with a dimly lit forest landscape fading into view, the soft light barely enough to accentuate the outlines of massive trees in the distance or the sharp tufts of grass and jagged branches which litter the dark contours of the forest floor. The position of this moment at the start of the narrative, the emptiness of the scene, and the absence of an apparent avatar all suggest (at least to the seasoned gameplayer) that a pre-scripted cut scene is about to play out, and thus many players wait for several moments before wondering if something is wrong and choosing to input a command by tapping a button. No matter which button was pressed, two tiny, glowing white eyes immediately open and blink as a small body rises from the ground, miniscule against the immense trees that frame the image, the silhouette of his face little more than a blank canvas that nevertheless seems to react to the strangeness of the gameworld with the same confusion as the player. This tiny moment of immersion, this sudden connection between the impulse of the player and the awakening consciousness of the boy, immediately links our thoughts to his thoughts as much as it does his life to our life.

Similarly, as the player begins to proceed forward, they notice that the pace and speed of the boy's movement is entirely variable, such that the player can slowly and cautiously inch forward or run full speed toward the next deadly challenge — a significant departure from the typical on/off,

FIGURE 2.5 *Death surrounds the player in* LIMBO.

standing or running nature of more traditional side-scrolling platformers. This is particularly interesting because *LIMBO* is relatively light on action and very rarely requires precision when it comes to the movements of the player. Instead, the game grants such precise control not to aid in physical challenges but rather to allow players to approach the world only in the fashion that they see fit, to position the boy as either meek and timid or bold and daring.[67] While this may not be an ethical choice that directly defines the player's virtual subjectivity, it nonetheless sutures their anxiety into the boy's journey, passing through a world that is permeated with death.

Indeed, despite the best efforts of the player, they will likely bear witness as the boy is forced to repeat hundreds of gruesomely depicted deaths, some simply rendering his body limp and inanimate, others forcefully tearing his body into pieces. For many players, their first death comes fairly early in game, either sliding down a steep hill into a pit of jagged spikes or failing to jump across a cleverly hidden bear trap, whose sharp teeth almost perfectly mimic the surrounding blades of grass. Each death is rendered through a fluid and dynamic animation system which makes the trauma that befalls his body all the more shocking, disturbing, and memorable; whether it's the limp swing of his hands after his body is pierced by the spikes or the way that tiny spurts of black blood shimmer across the dim light when his head is severed from his body. Yet these deaths are not the end of the boy's journey, and instead each summons a temporal rewinding so that the player can overwrite such trauma through the process of re-animation. In fact, like many games the occurrence and repetition of death in *LIMBO* is not simply a sign of inadequate play but rather built into the very structure of the game's mechanics.

To demonstrate this, let's consider a puzzle that appears about thirty minutes into the game, where the player approaches two round, floor-mounted switches, each too wide to jump over and each with their outer-section lowered and their inner-section raised. In order to progress, the player must randomly choose which section they think will be safe to stand upon. Upon choosing the center section of the first switch and finding it safe, the player will most likely repeat this action on the next switch, only to be crushed to death by a large stomping mechanism. Only through death, and thus only through the recurrence made available by *LIMBO*'s compossible temporality, can the player learn that the switches are activated in the opposite manner from one another, an important distinction considering that, after re-animating this sequence of events, they will soon be chased back across the switches by a group of enemies who will themselves be crushed by the trap. Within the puzzle, we see the game design equivalent of Zarathustra's dice throw: death acts as the necessary falling back to earth, while the resetting and re-animating insert the chance to correctly navigate the traps.

Death is a necessary event in *LIMBO*, and in fact it seems to influence the environment and form the very support that the world itself is built upon. Throughout their journey, for example, the player and the boy encounter many other forms of life — from a giant spider and a tiny dog-like creature to a group of other lost boys who have presumably set many of these traps, aiming to protect themselves in a world that seems designed to kill them — and although the player never directly engages these beings in combat, they will occasionally encounter their lifeless bodies which can then be used as tools to help pass deadly obstacles. For example, the protagonist is unable to swim, but at one point he must use the bodies of several dead boys as floating platforms so that he can cross a body of water, even dragging one into the water to begin the journey across. At the same time, the very world around him echoes the decay of the living, beginning in a massive, lush forest, moving its way through an equally enormous cityscape which mixes elements of the natural with the unnatural and the living with the dead, and finally ending in an industrial wasteland full of immense but lifeless machines, cogs, and gears. The closer the boy gets to discovering the truth of his circumstance, the further he gets from the living and the closer his proximity to death.

Despite the necessity of death within its gameplay, however, *LIMBO* also relies upon the player's self-preservation instinct to push them toward a "natural" death. One particularly striking example of this occurs as the player walks into the web of a gigantic spider, the game representing the stickiness of the web by slowing the player's movement until they become absolutely still. The spider approaches, pulls the boy up into its web, and

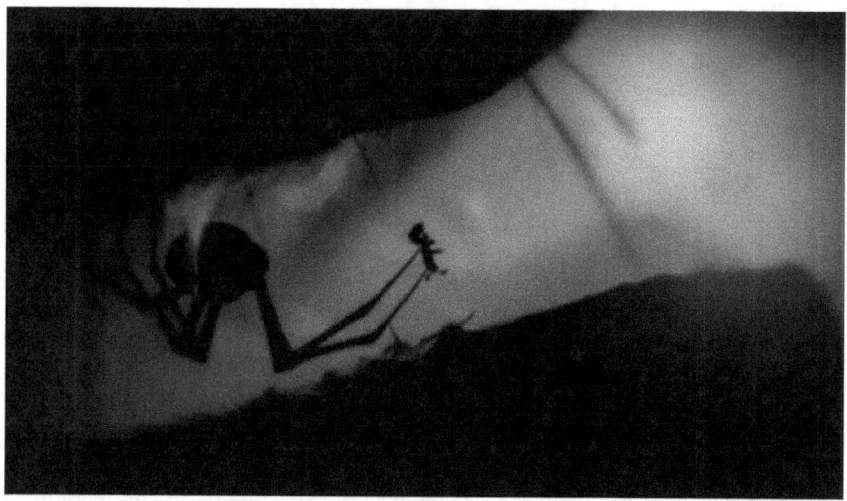

FIGURE 2.6 *Caught in the spider's web.*

wraps him in a cocoon of silk before leaving. Rather than fading to black before resetting the scene, however, the game once again waits patiently for the player to input a command, as any movement of the controller's analog stick suddenly causes the boy to wriggle violently in the direction of input, struggling to tear himself free of the web. A visceral representation of our survival instinct, this struggle matches Mulvey's "double tautological appeal" by echoing both within the visual narrative (the trembling body) and the mechanics (the motion of the player's input). Yet what's truly intriguing is the fact that the player has already died again and again by this point in the narrative, at times even submitting to death simply to learn the rules of a particular puzzle, so their struggle is in no way representative of a desire to avoid death altogether. Instead, this struggle represents the player's understanding that a traumatic death in the spider's web is not a natural death for the young boy, it cannot satisfy the tensions that drive both the narrative and the player's virtual subjectivity.

In fact, the boy's correct death — his "natural" death — is the ultimate end goal of *LIMBO*. The game's final moment appears suddenly in the midst of a challenging physics puzzle, which requires the boy to gain enough momentum to rapidly bypass a large spinning blade. As the boy flies past, the game suddenly shifts into extreme slow motion as his body smashes through a hidden pane of glass, tumbles through the air, and crumples lifelessly onto the ground. The moment is shocking for the player, though the image onscreen — a traumatic death where the boy is thrown violently to the ground — is not at all unlike the many images of death that have come before. Instead, the slowing down of time (and the subsequent refusal of the game to rewind that time) emphasizes that this death is special, that somehow this death has meaning. A moment of stillness passes in which the body lies prone on the ground in the very same position as we first found him, and in an environment that also matches that initial image. Suddenly, two tiny, glowing white eyes open and blink as the boy rises from the ground, a striking moment of recurrence which echoes the instance of immersion that brought both the boy and the player into this world. But something is different, *something has changed*. The player pushes the boy forward, but instead of encountering spikes and blades they find the young girl, sitting alone at the top of a small hill, a large tree behind her with a rope ladder attached to a thick branch. Once again the player's movement is mechanically stilled and the boy comes to a stop at the edge of the hill, where another moment passes before the girl suddenly turns around. Before we can witness their reaction to one another, or even gain any explicit understanding of the significance of the events that led to this moment, the game ends, cutting to black and revealing the credit sequence. So what happened? Why did the game slow down the image of the boy falling? Why did it place such an emphasis on this particular death?

Considering the game's title — alongside other aesthetic clues such as the uncanny size differences between the boy and the world around him, the blank faces of the children that stalk and attack the player, and the very process of decay that seems to be guiding the structure of world itself — it's safe to assume that the protagonist is, in fact, already dead and experiencing a denial that has trapped him in a state of limbo, seeking out his still-living companion but unable to ever truly connect with her. A telling moment in this regard occurs at the conclusion of the credits, when the game shifts back to its main interface menu. Here, the background has changed from when the player first turned on the game, now reflecting a decayed version of the final scene on the hill — the rope ladder frayed, the branch cracked, the grass overgrown, flies buzzing in circles above the ground. The player experiences the image not at face value, but rather in relation to the many compossibilities that have come before, allowing them to recognize that this last death — the boy's body tumbling to the ground — was in fact a recurrence of the boy's *actual* death, which, as evidenced by the slow decay of time, proceeded the start of the narrative long ago when the boy fatally fell from the tree. What seemed to be another throw of the dice was in fact the very goal of the game, to reach and recognize the boy's "natural" death, one that serves as a cathexis through which we can contemplate the fragility of the flesh and recognize the relationship between finiteness of being and steady decay of time. As we look back upon its narrative and mechanical design, we find that *LIMBO* calls upon the well-tread mechanics of re-animation not to deny death (as its protagonist was initially wont to do), but rather to create a space in which both the boy and, more importantly, the player can come to contemplate and accept the inevitability of death through an experience in which a natural death is only made recognizable by the memory of both past and future compossible deaths.

In the cinema, compossibility and re-animation were rare (if not impossible) before the digital turn, but over the last fifteen years the logic of gameplay has begun to slowly infect the temporal structure of filmic narratives. More often than not, this occurs in narratives where the characters quite literally inhabit a digital world, such as *The Matrix* series or a film like *Source Code*, the latter a story about an Army soldier who finds himself in a virtual construction of a yet-to-occur train accident, repeatedly re-animating the event until he can discover its cause and prevent myriad needless deaths (along the way discovering that he was chosen for this experimental process because he is himself already dead). On the other hand we have characters who perceive the world as if it were a game, such as the New York City bike messenger of *Premium Rush*, who imagines multiple routes through each busy intersection — most of which result in a crash that will kill either him or an innocent bystander — until he can picture the perfect path that will allow him to squeeze through traffic seconds ahead of death.

Yet the best example of the logic of gameplay playing out in a cinematic narrative is without doubt the 1998 German film *Run Lola Run*, directed by Tom Tykwer, whose emphasis on re-animation is immediately evident in the two quotes which open the film. The first comes from T.S. Eliot's poem "Little Gidding," where Elliot proclaims, "We shall not cease from exploration, and the end of all our exploring will be to arrive where we started and know the place for the first time." The second, from German football manager Sepp Herberger: "After the game is before the game."

FIGURE 2.7 *Lola races to help Manni in* Run Lola Run.

Recurrence, the instinct to return to a previous state, and contemplation: all elements inherent to the image of death in digital games, all immediately present in *Run Lola Run*. Indeed, the world of *Run Lola Run* is defined by its compossible temporality, in which the events of both the past and future guide the characters as they create their own path to death.

After an energetic opening credit sequence which establishes the momentum that will carry us through the narrative, the film's title character is immediately placed into an almost impossible situation. When her moped is stolen, Lola finds herself unable to follow through on a promise to pick up her boyfriend Manni, a small-time crook who tried to make a name for himself by making a significantly large money collection. As a result, he subsequently loses the money while trying to evade the police, and when he calls Lola from a pay phone, he relays the situation with an increasing panic: he has twenty minutes to deliver the lost money to his boss or he will surely be killed. Lola begs him to flee, but instead he improvises a hurried plan to rob a local grocery, that is, unless Lola can somehow find one hundred thousand Deutsche Marks in under twenty minutes. As Lola hangs up the phone, a dramatic shift has already occurred within the very structure of the narrative. Though the viewer may be unaware, the film's temporality has suddenly taken up the compossible logic of gamespace, granting Lola the power of re-animation and allowing her to repeat the next twenty minutes three times, each new attempt an overwriting of a traumatic death that would otherwise fail to release the tensions that push the narrative forward.

The remainder of the film consists of three twenty-minute segments, each a compossible scenario in which Lola desperately attempts to find the money, and each featuring variations on several key events — an initial encounter with a bully and his dog, a fraught meeting with Lola's father, a frantic dash through the city in an attempt to reach Manni in time — as well as minor encounters with smaller side-characters which nonetheless help to shape the narrative as well as Lola's subjectivity and code of ethics. In the first segment, Lola fails to secure the money and is forced to rob the store with Manni, a robbery that ends in her accidental death at the hands of a nervous police officer. The second segment sees Lola rob her father's bank, which sets off a chain of events that leads to Manni being run over by an ambulance. In the third and final segment, Lola chooses to take a (slightly) more righteous path and legally bets a small sum of money in a nearby casino, which leads to her not only turning one hundred marks into one hundred thousand but also to Manni's recovery of his lost money as well. Though not a literal death, this "happily ever after" ending serves as a point of stasis — a stalling of the film's near-constant momentum — that acts in direct response to Lola's ethical choices: each robbery can only end in death, while the moral high ground (as it were) allows for what we can presume will be a more satisfying death for Lola many years later.

FIGURE 2.8 *Lola lies dying on the ground, a direct result of her moral choices.*

Central to the compossible temporality of *Run Lola Run* (though often tangential to its overall plot) are several moments of visual and narrative flourish where Lola alters or overwrites significant portions of the lives of several bystanders by simply encountering the person in different ways. For example, when Lola narrowly misses running into a woman with a stroller during the first segment, we see (through a series of rapidly cut polaroids that begin with the text "and then") a future in which the woman loses her child due to neglect and subsequently steals another woman's baby, whereas when Lola bumps into the woman in the second segment we see a future where she wins the lottery, and finally a third future where she takes up religion after Lola runs around her completely. Likewise, three encounters with a man on a stolen bike end up with the man either married to his sweetheart, a junkie in a public restroom, or the catalyst for reuniting Manni with his lost money, while three encounters with an ambulance result in it either narrowly avoiding an accident involving workers carrying a large pane of glass, quickly driving past the workers and subsequently running over Manni, or finally smashing through the glass after unknowingly carrying Lola swiftly toward her goal. Each of these encounters do not function independently from one another, but rather exist as compossibilities that inform and define each other, allowing the audience to contemplate the consequence of every action. This compossibility even manifests itself with individual sequences of the film, such as a moment when Lola stops in the street to catch her breath. In the background of a long shot, we see (slightly out of focus though clearly recognizable) a beautiful young woman who is approaching Lola, yet when we cut to a tighter shot of Lola viewed from another angle, an old woman steps into the frame — Lola asks her for the time, but before she can answer Lola sets off running again. Here, the compossible temporality of the film overflows, allowing us to see both the woman's past and future mere seconds apart, a mixture that cannot be logically accounted for (at least without directly acknowledging the film's alternative temporality).

As previously mentioned, however, it would seem easy to misread these moments of compossibility as merely the altering of fate through random chance, what is often referred to as a "butterfly effect." However, two important aspects of the film complicate this notion and point toward the film's adoption of the logic of gameplay. The first is the film's emphasis on the power of re-animation, seen most clearly in the initial compossible event that greatly informs how each of Lola's "play-throughs" will pan out. Immediately after leaving her apartment to set off on her desperate quest to find the money, Lola runs into a bully on her apartment stairs holding back a dangerous-looking dog with a spiked collar around its neck. In the first segment, the growling dog scares Lola and momentarily delays her journey. In the second, the bully trips Lola, injuring her leg and slowing her down as she takes off to meet Manni. Finally, in the third segment, Lola herself growls at the dog, leaping over the pair and gaining momentum as she hits the street. The most telling aspect of this encounter, however, is not the variations of its sequence of events, but rather the fact that it is literally animated — a cartoon Lola running down a wildly spinning staircase. This is not exactly shocking for the viewer, as *Run Lola Run* combines various cinematographic techniques, whether color or black and white, 35 mm, 16 mm, or digital video footage, still photographs, or animation. The film has an internal logic for each visual style, for example flashbacks are always black and white whereas any scene without Lola or Manni is shot on comparatively low-quality DV. Yet apart from the opening credits of the film — which itself establishes *Run Lola Run*'s compossible temporality — this encounter with the bully (the first of Lola's various and variable encounters) is the only animated sequence, visually emphasizing that Lola's action in each segment is not simply an intuitive choice but instead the beginning of the Lola's re-animation of past mistakes. But how can we be certain of this, how do we know that Lola is acting in response to previous-yet-future events?

The answer lies in Lola's strange reactions to repeated circumstances — reactions that are directly informed by the knowledge Lola gains through her separate-yet-compossible "play-throughs" of the film's events — the most striking example of which involves her unfamiliarity with guns. When she picks up a security guard's handgun during the first segment's robbery, the film establishes that Lola is unaware of the gun's safety lock, which causes her to inadvertently fire the weapon after being told to switch it off. In the second segment, when she's mocked by a guard for not even knowing how to use the weapon, the film cuts to a close-up as she switches off the safety

FIGURE 2.9 *A cartoon Lola re-animating her past and future.*

and confidently fires two warning shots. Just as with a gameplayer who uses the knowledge gained from an accidental death to overwrite the death itself, here we see that Lola has "learned" from a past that she could not have experienced outside of a compossible temporality. Likewise, Lola growls at the dog on the staircase because she "remembers" and responds to an encounter that she is actively re-animating — she is living in a compossible present informed by that which is both past and future.

Run Lola Run demonstrates, as well as any game could, that the compossible temporality of the digital enables us to imagine and craft our own path to death. Likewise, *LIMBO* reveals that the development of virtual subjectivity is not an attempt to control death, but rather a recognition that "the goal of all life is death." As such, we find that digital games are not another form of denial but rather a new form of narrative through which we make death more present. The perpetual repetition of games allows us to apply our choices and chances to new understandings of the consequences of death, within both the actual and the virtual, in the process coming to acknowledge and contemplate death on its own terms. In our next chapter, we'll continue to explore the impact of digital logic on our split subjectivity, coming to find that the digital path to death is but one relay through which we look past death's possibility to reassert its potential.

3

The Potential of Digital Death

The possibility of death frightens me. And why would it not? For all I ever see or hear of death is its suddenness, its brutality, its devastation. No matter where I turn I am confronted by it — stories upon stories of last days, hopes dashed, dreams turned to nightmares; images upon images of bodies in transition, life rendered limp, flesh decaying or torn apart. They tell me that death is a thief, that it steals from me, cheapens me, lessens me. Yet what I know of death comes from images and stories, nothing more, and just as the virtuality of death surrounds me, the actuality of death escapes me. In truth, I've known very little about the manner through which the mind and the body cease to be, because such things have been hidden from me, denied, pushed aside as little more than a taboo curiosity. Despite the pervasiveness of its image, I am left to seek the reality of death on my own, to recognize the consequences of its inevitability, to make it applicable to my experience of life. Only then can I glimpse the creativity born from death, or the role that it plays in the formation of my sense of self. Only then can I sense how essential death has been, is, and forever will be. Only then does the potential of death give me comfort.

Possibilistic to the Limit

In our first chapter, we saw how technologies of the moving image replaced the experience of witnessing death with its representation, and how the natural processes of dying have become increasingly overshadowed by our intense fascination with trauma. One substantial ramification of this process has been the pronounced assertion of *the possibility of death* as an objective, if unpleasant, truth: at any moment, for any number of reasons, we can cease to Be. On the other hand, inquiries into *the potential of death* — the full consequences of mortality and its effect on our lived experience — are often labeled as little more than subjective and morbid meditations, valid only in relation to one's own personal approach to understanding existence and the fact of Being. It would appear, then, that our perception of death has become intimately interwoven with our subjectivity.

As Brian Massumi shows us in the introduction to *Parables for the Virtual*, our subjectivity has long been grounded within the very bodies that declare us mortal, formed through their "positioning" within a dominant, socially defined "grid" of meaning — a discursive and determinant process that he refers to as *coding*. Coding is reliant upon presumed binary antagonisms, resulting in an "oppositional framework of culturally constructed significations: male and female, black and white, gay and straight," and so on down the line, presumably, to the most extreme of bodily antagonisms, alive and dead.[1] If we follow through the consequences of Massumi's later discussion of *digital coding* — not just the literal act of computer programming but rather "a numerically based form of codification" — we find that one of the most significant effects of the digital turn has been an expansion in our deployment of codification, far beyond the "positioning" of bodies, such that *everything* is thought to be reducible to the same basic, binary materials: the ones and zeros of digital code.[2] In other words, through digital coding — or what I refer to throughout this project as digital thinking or digital logic — we've begun to imagine *existence itself* as if it were akin to, inseparable from, or perhaps even identical to the binary structures of the digital, all matter and all memory simply variations of the same two material themes: on and off.[3]

Inherent within digital thinking, therefore, is an emphasis — nay, a fetishization — of *possibility*, for it sees only the binary juxtaposition of possible and impossible things and events, which it does at the expense of *potentiality*, a recognition of many possibilities encircling and enveloping one another and therefore always already a multiplicity, always both on and off (or neither on nor off). This is why Massumi stresses that "the medium of the digital is possibility, not virtuality, and not even potential. It doesn't bother approximating potential, as does probability. Digital coding per se is *possibilistic to the limit*."[4] This chapter is about a culture that has, through its adoption of digital logic, become "possibilistic to the limit." By extension, it is also about a culture that unconsciously seeks to re-encounter potential.

To understand how the struggle between possibility and potential affects our relationship with mortality, and the way in which this struggle manifests itself within popular media, it's useful to first consider the subtle though crucial differences between the two concepts, especially as they have been developed in Western philosophy. Massumi, for example, provides a useful (if esoteric) set of definitions by imagining an arrow flying toward a target, its possibility "a variation *implicit* in what [the arrow] can be said to be when it is on target," while its potential "the *immanence* of [the arrow] to its still indeterminate variation, under way."[5] Here, possibilities become implications, in that they imply that the arrow *could or could not* land at a particular point in space given its trajectory and the conditions of its flight (which is to say that possibilities are always both futural and virtual, concerned that the event is "on target" but not that it will actually occur). Potentials, on the other hand, are immanent, in that they are the intermixing of all of the various places the arrow could land regardless of its trajectory or the conditions of its flight, alongside the knowledge that it *will* eventually land. "Implication," Massumi tells us, "is a code word" — the binary *juxtapositioning* of "on-target" and "off-target" things or events, which not only sees them as oppositional but also always finds the latter to be wanting. "Immanence," on the other hand, "is process" — the continual *superpositioning* of possibilities through to the event's actualization, the experience of which, in relation to the fullness of such a superposition, is itself found wanting.[6]

Having adopted the binary logic of the digital, contemporary culture is one of implications rather than processes — it looks ahead to the end result but not the journey, it concerns itself with that which *can* happen at the expense of that which *might* happen, it fetishizes possible outcomes while failing to perceive missed potentials. More often than not (as we saw in our first chapter) the possibilities that are pushed to the fore are the traumatic possibilities — the *anxious* possibilities — that highlight our vulnerability rather than our strength, that position mortality as the enemy of vitality. We see this in news broadcasts that declare us all possible victims (of terrorist attacks, mass shootings, car accidents, assault, and other forms of physical violence; of identity theft, harassment, prejudice, bullying, and other forms of social violence). We see it in movies that fantasize destruction on levels both intimate and extensive (the bodily horror of "torture porn," the personal and communal devastation of disaster films, the sugar-coated chaos of action and superhero films). We see it in television shows that showcase trauma as their inciting incident (the requisite murders of police procedurals, the myriad diseases and accidents in medical dramas, the ubiquitous gun violence that floats across and throughout television as a whole). And we see it in games that batter and tear apart virtual flesh (the simulated gore of fighting games and first person shooters, the increasingly common use of ragdoll physics, the employment of death as a narrative indicator of mechanical failure). The fact that the majority of such traumatic events are relatively rare and atypical outside of fiction is no longer a concern, a reassurance, or for that matter even widely recognized; in the digital age trauma captures our attention and proliferates within our media — regardless of its potential — because it is nonetheless *possible*.[7] Most importantly, however, we can see within the fetishization of trauma the fact that death itself has been made subject to the logic of possibility, robbed of its fullness and nuance, reduced through juxtaposition to a terrifying, malevolent, and tragic figure who opposes life. In the digital age, death has become possibilized.

With that in mind, this chapter will frame our shifting relationship to death in contemporary moving images through our new attitudes toward possibility and potential, whose importance was first hinted at by Henri Bergson in works such as *Creative Evolution* and *Matter and Memory*, elaborated upon by Gilles Deleuze in *Bergonsism* and his volumes on Capitalism and Schizophrenia and the Cinema, and later taken up by Massumi in *Parables for the Virtual*. Yet we'll also find that possibility and potential have served as critical components of an entirely different branch of metaphysics, that of existentialism, where Søren Kierkegaard first saw possibility as the driving force behind *The Concept of Anxiety*, and where Martin Heidegger and Jean-Paul Sartre traced the impact of possibility through authenticity and subjectivity in works such as *Being and Time* and *Being and Nothingness*, in the process revealing our potentiality-for-Being as part and parcel of our relationship to the infiniteness of space and time and the finiteness of existence. In fact, although it is fair to call death our only known inevitability, Heidegger saw it as both our "utmost possibility" and the fullest extension of the potential of life.

Throughout this chapter, the exploration of possibility and potential will serve as a complimentary point of intersection between these two traditions of thought, while also bringing to the surface other relevant dichotomies in relation to our contemporary digital logic of death, namely ignorance and knowledge, authenticity and "bad faith," Being and nothingness, identity and subjectivity, folding and unfolding, the binary and the multiple, the actual and the virtual. To be certain, these divergent strands of metaphysics approach the issue of mortality in strikingly different ways, yet by tracing within them various ontological oppositions, we'll uncover a culture consumed by the anxiety of possibility while also desperately searching for the potential (or what Heidegger called "the meaning") of Being and nonbeing, life and death. Just as importantly, we'll find that moving images play a crucial role in this process, presenting us with two unconscious relays through which we hope to push pass mere possibility to uncover the full potential of death.

Anxiety and Angst (Possibility and Authenticity)

In 2006, the Nabisco-owned cookie company Chips Ahoy! released a claymation commercial set depicting a young girl's birthday party, replete with balloons, streamers, "Happy Birthday" banners, and a multicultural group of animated children and adults, all gleefully beaming at the birthday girl. Most notable, however, is the three-foot tall, anthropomorphic chocolate chip cookie sitting to her left, cheerfully sporting a blue cone-shaped party hat while joining the rest of the guests in wishing the girl an enthusiastic "happy birthday!" The camera cuts tight on the cookie as he looks around the room, his chocolate chip eyebrows raised high with excitement to match

FIGURE 3.1 *The possibility of death dawns on the Chips Ahoy! cookie.*

the delighted look on his face. "So, uhhh, where's the cake?" he asks with dopey anticipation. Several hungry children lean in closer as the little girl shrugs. "We're not having *cake*!" she exclaims, her voice quivering on the final word, as if to let the cookie know that he's sadly misinterpreted the situation. Turning slightly, almost to the point of matching our gaze, the cookie's expression stutters rapidly from elation to dread — *from ignorance to anxiety* — as he processes what this means: that *he* has become the main course, that this party will be his last.

In the world of advertising mascots, this anxious cookie is not alone in recognizing the possibility of death. Chik-fil-a's "eat mor chikin" campaign features a series of digitally manipulated images of cows wearing sandwich board signs that urge readers, in the cows' poorly written English, to do things like "take a vacashun frum beef" and "feed yer herd, sav ourz." For the cows, an appeal to "eat mor chikin" is not so different than pleading "pleez dont kil us." In a more recent commercial for the breakfast cereal Honey Nut Cheerios, a digitally animated version of its popular mascot, Buzz the Bee, shockingly encounters a wall covered in dead bugs, pinned and displayed behind glass in little wooden frames — the coffins of the insect world. Buzz manages to escape the amateur entomologist to whom they belong, but when he finally reminds us to "bee happy, bee healthy," a tremble in his voice betrays an angst that he just can't seem to shake. Some mascots even seem to be the cause of anxiety in others, such as the recent reappearance of the Kool-Aid Man (also digitally animated for the first time), who admits, with some trepidation, that "people get real freaked out when you drink from your own head. Like, *real* freaked out."

Yet perhaps no mascots are quite as "angsty" as the M&M's, who, in a series of commercials spanning more than a decade, have been constantly on guard amongst various people — strangers, friends, even lovers — who want nothing more than to eat them. In one commercial, we hear panting coming from off screen as we watch a grocery store clerk scanning items that come sliding in on her conveyer belt. A moment later, Red — each character is named for the color of her/his candy shell — is pulled into frame, desperately trying to outrun the scanner that, in identifying him as food, might as well be a weapon. Realizing the futility, he bitterly scans himself. In another ad, Orange — the mascot for Crispy and Pretzel M&M's, whose central identifying characteristic seems to be his neurotic angst — is standing in a cold, sterile medical laboratory, protesting the notion that there might be an oversized pretzel lodged in his body. The commercial ends as he anxiously holds up an X-ray of his pretzel-filled interior, the image reminiscent of a cancer patient glimpsing the previously unseen chaos within their body. Most alarmingly, the extended Super-Bowl ad from 2013 features Red singing a rendition of Meatloaf's 1993 hit "I'd Do Anything for Love (But I Won't Do That)" over a montage of romantic scenes with a beautiful woman, whose desire for him quickly transforms into a more literal hunger. What he won't do, it turns out, is be eaten with ice cream, popcorn, or in a

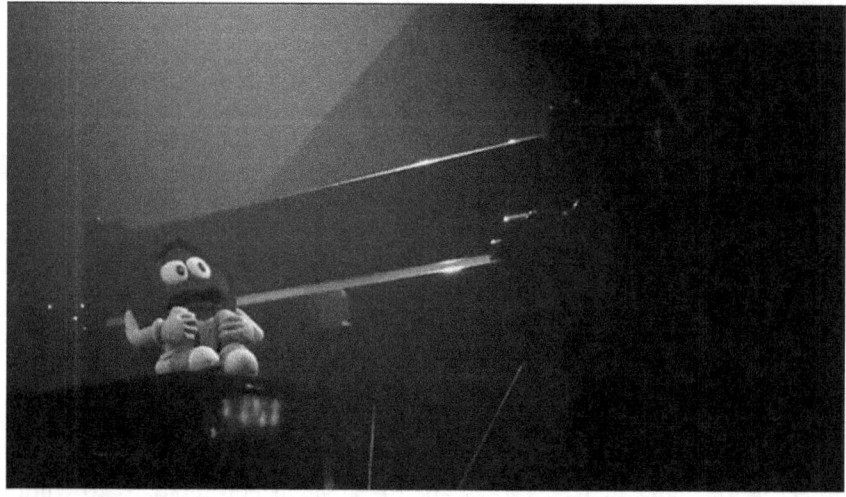

FIGURE 3.2 *Red, unable to sing after being overcome with angst.*

birthday cake, be beaten and battered as the prize in a piñata, or be baked alive in an oven as part of a giant cookie. Red's singing breaks down as his paranoia grows, resulting in him screaming at no one in particular, crying as a whipped cream topping burns his eyes, and (most disturbingly) rocking back and forth in a fetal position, utterly overwhelmed with angst while whispering to himself "happy thoughts, happy thoughts."[8]

On the surface, the anxiety exhibited by these mascots may seem inconsequential — it is, after all, played as comedy. Yet the very fact of its presence, not to mention its frequency and prominence, makes visible an increase in both our *acceptance of angst* as a natural aspect of the condition of Being — seen also in our increased employment of psychotherapy, the over-abundance of antianxiety medications, or the anticipation of PTSD in victims of abuse or veterans of combat — and our *expectation of angst* as a natural aspect of contemporary life, whether it be the stress of our jobs, the difficulties of raising a family, the lack of control we have over our economy or our government, or our cultural obsession with trauma.[9] Over the next few pages, we'll examine the recent proliferation of anxiety in contemporary moving images, a response not only to our growing concerns about violence (both real and represented), but also to our adoption of digital logic, whose fetishization of possibility and disregard for potential have fostered a new culture of angst. At the same time, we'll see that such angst has, in a world both frightened and fascinated by mortality, granted many characters in popular media a new sense of credibility and *authenticity*, elevating them above the ersatz caricatures so often found in fictions of the past. The defining characteristic of animated commercial mascots, for example, had long been their happy-go-lucky demeanor, which was supposedly afforded by their love for and singular focus upon the products they represent. Yet in an age of terrorist attacks, mass shootings, drone strikes, surveillance, police brutality, etc., it appears that we can no longer accept happiness when it is the product of ignorance, and thus the very nature of these characters has taken on an air of inauthenticity. Only by seeing the world as we see it — full of the *possibility* of violence and death — can they regain our trust; only through displays of anxiety can they be read as *authentic* in their actions and in their claims.[10]

To explore the many links between possibility, anxiety, ignorance, authenticity, and death, let's turn first to Kierkegaard, the so-called "father of existentialism" who, as Paul Tillich wrote, "realized that the knowledge of that which concerns us infinitely is possible only in an attitude of infinite concern" — that existential attitude that we can call angst or anxiety, whose genesis Kierkegaard sought to uncover in order to establish it as not a pathology but rather an inherent condition of consciousness and free will.[11] Before he could do so, however, Kierkegaard first needed to distinguish anxiety from fear, for fear is a response to an objective, material threat (a presence) while anxiety is a response to a subjective, immaterial concern (a sense). When Buzz the Bee notices the wall of dead insects, for example, he experiences fear, but when the threat has passed, what remains is anxiety. Put another way, as Kierkegaard might have, the shock is fear, the tremble anxiety. Seeing as fear is an essential survival instinct, it would be easy to assume that anxiety serves as a sort of primer for fear, a sense that dangers could manifest themselves at any moment and therefore a warning system to be on guard. Yet Kierkegaard, realizing that anxiety is a concern not for the present but rather always for an imagined future, found something more complex and essential at play within it: the recognition of *possibility*.

Given that his existential philosophy always grappled with the character of his Christian faith, it's perhaps unsurprising that Kierkegaard traced the origins of anxiety back to the narrative of Adam and Eve and the fall of man, which positioned mankind (through the character of Adam) as initially existing within a state of grace or innocence. Unlike many of his contemporary theologians, however, Kierkegaard did not read innocence as simply being without sin. Rather, he claimed that "the narrative in Genesis," in which God placed a prohibition on the fruit of the tree of knowledge of good and evil, "gives the correct explanation of innocence. Innocence is ignorance."[12] Adam was innocent only because he was ignorant, for to be ignorant is to be without knowledge, and Adam was only without sin because he was, quite literally, without the fruit that would provide him with a knowledge of sin. To take this a step further, Kierkegaard positioned such ignorance as not simply a lack of knowledge but rather, as Ed Cameron puts it, "nothing less than the structural limit of conceptualization itself," for although Adam *recognized* the prohibition, in his ignorance he lacked the ability to truly *comprehend* it: "How could he understand the difference between good and evil when this distinction would follow as a consequence of the enjoyment of the fruit?"[13] In lieu of knowledge, the prohibition left Adam with naught but *anxiety*, as it's in the breakdown between recognition and comprehension — in our ability *to know that we cannot know*, so to speak — that anxiety appears. To put this more eloquently, as Natalie Wulfing does in her analysis of Kierkegaard's text, anxiety arises "out of ignorance that has knowledge for its horizon."[14]

Yet if anxiety is born out of ignorance, why would Gordon D. Marino claim that "anxiety is virtually synonymous with possibility" in Kierkegaard's thought?[15] Or, for that matter, why does Rollo May find "the relation between anxiety and freedom" to be the "keystone idea" in *The Concept of Anxiety*?[16] To explain, we must note that when Kierkegaard revisited the story of the first prohibition, he found not only that Adam was ignorant of its meaning or consequence, but also that its very pronouncement was enough to provide Adam with a horizon of knowledge: an implication, however slight, of his inherent freedom — the ability to respond to the prohibition in the manner of his choosing — which not only assured his desire to disobey but also *made visible to Adam his possibilities*. Indeed, the relationship between anxiety and freedom may be the keystone idea in Kierkegaard's text, but only insofar as "Kierkegaard *defines freedom as possibility*."[17] Freedom is but a middle term in the existential reading of angst — we recognize our freedom only when we have caught sight of both our possibility and our future, and it's in our awareness of possibility and ignorance of the future that we become anxious — which we see in Kierkegaard's adoption of the phrase "freedom's possibility" as an analogue not only for anxiety but also, on occasion, for consciousness itself.[18] Subsequently, if consciousness entails a recognition of the possibility of freedom, then "the distinctive characteristic of man, in contrast to the merely vegetative or the merely animal, lies in the range of man's possibility and in his capacity for self-awareness of his possibility" — *an awareness that cements anxiety as an essential aspect of consciousness.*

Such awareness also leads us back to one possibility in particular, for we find again and again in Kierkegaard — just as we also saw in Massumi — that possibilities are always bound up in a futurity, such that "as freedom's possibility manifests itself for freedom, freedom succumbs, and temporality emerges."[19] Of course, the road of temporality always leads to death, as Kierkegaard's biblical reading of anxiety made clear:

> After the word of prohibition follows the word of judgment: "You shall certainly die." Naturally, Adam does not know what it means to die. ... Because Adam has not understood what was spoken, there is nothing but the ambiguity of anxiety. The infinite possibility of being able that was awakened by the prohibition now draws closer, because this possibility points to a possibility as its sequence.[20]

In other words, any and all possibilities point to that possibility which Heidegger would later call our "utmost": the possibility of one's own death, the last event in every sequence of life which is revealed only through the attitude of anxiety. Once again we find that a possibilistic culture will undoubtedly reveal itself to be engulfed in anxiety, for it will always point to the possibility of death as its conclusion.

Kierkegaard thus showed us that anxieties regarding death are amongst our most fundamental, and as such they have been and always will be an essential component of the human condition. At the same time, however, our willingness to address such anxieties within the boundaries of popular culture tends to wax and wane depending on social, political, and economic influences, which Fredric Jameson made clear in his thesis on the "waning of affect" in postmodern culture.[21] In fact, Jameson's classic text *Postmodernism, or the Cultural Logic of Late Capitalism* begins with a brief epistemology of angst in public consciousness, a transition from "the great modernist thematics of alienation, anomie, solitude, social fragmentation, and isolation" — which characterized the modern era as nothing less than "the age of anxiety" — to the "flatness or depthlessness" of postmodernity, "a new kind of superficiality in the most literal sense" which led Jameson to conclude that "concepts such as anxiety and alienation ... are no longer appropriate in the world of the postmodern."[22] In regard to the anxiety of death, this certainly lines up with our observations about the repression which characterized the mid-to-late twentieth century, in which representations of death consistently increased in "intensity" while simultaneously eschewing realism and discouraging contemplation.[23] Yet in our "possibilistic" digital culture, still stumbling in the aftermath of 9/11, anxiety has not simply returned to the level of the appropriate, but rather rocketed to that of the expected, the anticipated, and at times even the required, a clear indication that we've moved beyond postmodern logic into an era of digital thinking. All of this is to say that anxiety, in the digital age, has become *normalized*, far more than even Kierkegaard could have ever anticipated. To see this in action, as well to expand our focus to include the desire for authenticity that accompanies our acceptance and expectation of angst, let's look to another example of anxiety's hyper-presence in contemporary moving images, this time in a medium whose central purpose had been, since its inception several decades ago, to allow us to escape authentic reality and immerse ourselves in virtual fantasy: the digital game.

Although it features four playable characters, the narrative of David Cage's *Heavy Rain* (developed in 2010 by the French studio Quantic Dream) hinges around one central protagonist: an architect named Ethan Mars, desperately trying to rescue his kidnapped son while still coping with the loss of another child in a fatal car accident some two years prior, an event that led to the dissolution of his marriage and a crippling depression. On the surface, it would be easy to read Ethan as a typical video game protagonist, whom the player controls in a number of typical videogame scenarios: racing a car through heavy traffic, exploring dark and foreboding environments, wielding guns and other weapons against dangerous criminals, etc. Yet for Ethan these activities are highly atypical: a series of increasingly dangerous and morally ambiguous "trials" arranged by the Origami Killer, who kidnaps his young victims and then secretly demands that their fathers overcome challenges in order to save their children (a gauntlet that no father has yet passed). Ethan's anxiety intensifies with the introduction of each new trial, manifesting itself through his explicitly voiced recognition of numerous possibilities: that he could fail to save his son's life, that the Origami Killer's challenges could result in his own death, that he could become responsible for the deaths of both his children, and even the suspicion that he himself could be the Origami Killer (the trials an unconscious punishment for his failure to save his older son two years earlier).

Throughout the game, the player not only controls Ethan's physical exploits during the action-heavy trials, but also his dialog choices and interactions with other characters in a variety of seemingly mundane situations, including doing chores around the house, picking his son up from school, sketching out architectural blueprints for work, navigating a busy train station, and even attending several sessions with his psychologist. Yet every scenario proves an ordeal, as Ethan's agoraphobia and guilt lead to frequent, debilitating anxiety attacks. Mechanically, the game represents this anxiety by having the player's dialog and action choices float in circles around Ethan's head — a jumble of possibilities he is constantly sorting out in his mind — which, along with their corresponding input icons, grow blurrier and more jittery as the anxiety increases. This makes it difficult for the player to assess their options and choose the best course of action (especially in situations where time is of the essence), and frequently leads to hurried or mistaken inputs on the side of the player. Adding to the player's anxiety is the fact that the game attaches significant weight to every action by prohibiting them from resetting or restarting a chapter once it has begun — even when the player's actions lead to the death of a central character! — a defiance of standard game design, which has long presumed that players can always insert another quarter, find a 1-up, or "press start to continue."

Given that the Origami Killer's trials involve difficult, ambiguous moral dilemmas — would you cut off a finger for a clue as to your kidnapped child's whereabouts? drink poison? murder another parent? — it would seem to be against the player's best interests to frequently decrease their control over their onscreen avatar. Yet rather than becoming a frustration, *Heavy Rain*'s simulation of our inability to think and act clearly in the face of anxiety is one of its most successful experiments, in that it often denies

FIGURE 3.3 *Ethan Mars anxiously considers shooting another father in order to save his son.*

the player the ability to make choices using anything beyond pure instinct or impulse, at times forcibly revealing otherwise inhibited attitudes toward difficult moral questions by compelling us to play and act *authentically* (meaning not simply according to some ideological standard but rather in accordance to our deep-rooted understandings of the consequences of life and death). In fact, it's not some vague sense of the "everyman" nor even the mundane experiences which we share with Ethan that make him feel "authentic," but rather his anxiety, for he reacts to the possibility of danger and death the same way we do: imprecisely, with fear and trembling, with caution and with angst.

Heavy Rain demonstrates that anxiety and authenticity are not only intimately connected within the digital, they are *visibly* connected as well. Yet although the visibility of this connection may be new to us, its intimacy is not, for in continuing Kierkegaard's project to explore the concept of anxiety, among the most significant contributions of Heidegger and Sartre was their recognition that anxiety is a crucial aspect of authenticity and their view that authentic Being requires the acknowledgement of one's mortality (though, as we will see throughout the rest of this chapter, they differed greatly on how one should practice such acknowledgment). Alongside Merleau-Ponty and following Hegel, the pair were instrumental in establishing phenomenology as a key component of existential thought, an attempt to uncover the role of conscious experience and sensation in our everyday existence, especially in relation to our ability to conceptualize the difference between Being and nonbeing, life and death. As much as any theorists before or since, they grasped the role that our knowledge of death plays in our comprehension and negotiation of the world around us (what Heidegger called both our Being-in-the-world and Being-toward-death, and Sartre saw as the nothingness inherent in Being-for-itself), and although they used this understanding to arrive at significantly divergent attitudes toward death, they nonetheless introduced anxiety and the recognition of mortality as critical components of the authentic experience of Being.

Heidegger began his analysis of anxiety — found primarily in Section VI of the first division of *Being and Time*, "Care as the Being of Dasein" — in a manner similar to Kierkegaard, first by laying out the differences between fear and anxiety (fear as a response to something "definite" which is always an "entity within the world," anxiety as a response to the "indefinite" and the unknown) and then by linking anxiety to possibility: "What oppresses us is neither this or that, nor is it the summation of everything present-at-hand; it is rather the *possibility* of the ready-at-hand in general; that is to say, it is the world itself."[24] Likewise, in *Being and Nothingness*, Sartre quickly established anxiety (or, as it is often translated in his work, anguish) as a response to our recognition of possibility, though with a greater focus on the *self* as the locus of that possibility: "Anguish in fact is the recognition of a possibility as *my* possibility; that is, it is constituted when consciousness sees itself cut from its essence by nothingness or separated from the future by its very freedom."[25] Although Heidegger and Sartre borrowed heavily from Kierkegaard's reading of anxiety, their own differed on several significant counts, including an understanding of existence as preceding essence (as opposed to Kierkegaard's notion that spirit exists before body or soul) and a belief that Being is finite (as opposed to the infiniteness of the spirit in Kierkegaard). Not the least of these, however, was their utmost concern regarding the question of Being, which for Heidegger implied an understanding of the differences between "thingness" and conscious existence (beings vs. Being), for Sartre meant an understanding of nonbeing or nothingness as fundamental to the fact of Being, and for both meant an understanding of authentic Being as refusing to lie to oneself regarding the inevitability of one's own death.

To unpack these ideas, we must first confront Heidegger's central figure in *Being and Time*, that of *Dasein*, the being for whom "in its very Being, that Being is an *issue*."[26] As conveyed in the aforementioned title of Section VI, Dasein *cares* about existence, its "analytic" is "to prepare the way for the problematic of fundamental ontology — *the question of the meaning of Being in general*."[27] Dasein, then, is not simply one who is conscious of its existence, but rather one who is profoundly concerned with the *meaning* of that existence (its ontological or phenomenological constitution, not its reason or purpose). Fundamental to Dasein's project is anxiety, which Heidegger referred to as "a disclosive state-of-mind," in that it *discloses the Dasein as itself a possibility* while enabling it to "individualize" and granting it the capacity for being authentic. When we consider this phrase — "being authentic" — we might assume that authenticity is the result of recognizing or comprehending, to the best of one's abilities, the structure of one's consciousness and its relation to the world in which it is situated — authenticity as the fulfillment of Dasein's quest for meaning. Yet such meaning is put at risk by Dasein's fundamental freedom and the possibilities that follow, for "this openness of possibility," as Natalie Wulfing explains, "implied [for Heidegger] that there is no fixed and determining meaning. It means that freedom is a loss of meaning."[28] Similarly, Meghan Craig follows Heidegger in concluding that "our freedom to choose allows us to interpret the world as we will, and since there is no ultimate interpretation, we can no longer be completely certain about anything."[29] If the same recognition of possibilities that produces anxiety also results in an uncertainty and loss of meaning that confounds Dasein's project to question Being, then why would Heidegger argue that anxiety is critical to Dasein's authentic existence?

Perhaps Sartre can help us to understand, for in his definition of consciousness (i.e., Being) we find an expansion of Heidegger's Dasein: "a being such that in its being, its being is in question *in so far as this being implies a being other than itself*," and whose nature "is to be conscious of the nothingness of its being."[30] These statements follow Sartre's contention that Being can only be defined in terms of its opposition or its negation — negation is "not a judgment"; Sartre contends, "it is a disclosure of being on the basis of which we can make a judgment" — which on one hand implies any and all beings apart from and surrounding the Being, while on the other implies a nothingness or nonbeing.[31] Just as nothingness is positioned here as an essential, ontological characteristic of Being — what allows the Being, according to Hazel E. Barnes, to "stand out from Being and to judge others by knowing what it is not" — so too are all of the things that make up the world outside of consciousness (our bodies, the people and things that surround us, the socio-cultural–economic circumstances of our time, etc.) which Sartre, in his *Critique of Dialectical Reason* and elsewhere, followed Heidegger in calling our *facticity*.[32] Sartre saw our sense of self as always indebted as much to our facticity as to the fact of consciousness, and in our attempt to construct an identity — to "transcend" the world of the *in-itself* (*en-soi*, the object, the being which simply *is*) — we cannot but respond to the world in which we are situated, and to the desires of other Beings in particular. As such, inherent within the human condition is the struggle between being *for-itself* (*pour-soi*) and *for-others* (*pour-autrui*), between subjectifying oneself and being objectified by the Other. "Herein lies the ultimate human paradox," Richard Pearce writes, "we seek to construct a self, but always fail," precisely because our *self* is never ours alone.[33] Yet here is also where authenticity enters the picture, because in our "vacillation between transcendence [*Being-for-itself*] and facticity [*Being-for-others*]" and our refusal "to recognize either one for what it really is or to synthesize them," what we are truly failing to do is to *be authentic*.[34]

In our attempt to work through the existential reading of authenticity, it might be easiest to follow in Sartre's footsteps by continuing to define in terms of opposition. This means turning first to the question of *inauthenticity*, what Heidegger saw as Dasein's "fallenness" in the world of the "they" (the world of others) and its "fleeing in the face of itself," and Sartre (alongside Freud, Simone de Beauvoir, and many others) referred to as "bad faith," the act of lying to oneself, a self-deception designed for the benefit of the Other. Indeed, the fact or difficulty of living in the world with others was central to existential thought, so much so that Heidegger saw in each person a "they-self" — an aspect of consciousness constructed according to the desires of the universal or the "they" — while Sartre argued that we act "with all of mankind in mind," that we orient ourselves against the universal as part of our facticity.[35] Yet for both, inauthentic existing meant more than simply acting with others in mind, it was to act *for* the Other, without letting the Other in on the act — a performance where the performer lies not to the audience but to her/himself. Not simply "conforming with the crowd," as Craig explains, bad faith and falling are rather "the tendency we have to fall into the socially agreed web of meanings, *and to take them as givens*" — to view oneself and the world as if through the eyes of the Other (despite the true impossibility of such) by momentarily repressing one's own individuality, beliefs, and desires.[36] In doing so, one fails to be what Robert D. Stolorow calls a "differentiated, self-responsible individual," because one lies to oneself *about* oneself in order present as truth what Sartre called "a pleasing untruth."[37] Our "they-self" *is* this lie, just as the lie *is* our bad faith, what for Sartre "presupposes my existence, the existence of the Other, my existence *for* the Other, and the existence of the Other *for* me."[38]

To that end, we can now read authenticity as more than a matter of relating to others, and still more than a matter of understanding consciousness, even one's own. Authenticity is, rather, *existing for oneself* — a literal transcendence through the Being's act of Being-for-itself. It is to cease lying to oneself, to decline to take socially agreed upon meanings as givens, to avoid performing for the Other, and to refuse to submit oneself to their objectifying gaze (or, for that matter, to make an object of the Other). Of course, it would be impossible to hold ourselves to such standards at all times, and both Heidegger and Sartre make it clear that authenticity and inauthenticity form a dialectic, that they are each essential aspects of Being which, at any given moment, play significant roles in the formation of our sense of self. Yet there is also a clear sense that authenticity is the "one new and absolute virtue in existentialism," that as conscious Beings we should strive to act authentically whenever possible.[39] As Craig, Stolorow, and many others have pointed out, the German word Heidegger used for authenticity is *Eigentlichkeit*, literally translating into "ownedness" or "mineness" — to Be authentic is to *own* one's existence, to be held accountable for one's Being and to hold others accountable for theirs.[40]

Sartre, too, saw authenticity as a responsibility, that one must have courage to accept one's freedom and come to terms with one's possibilities. This is crucial, for to recognize possibility *is* to be anxious, and thus we find that existentialism paints authenticity as not only inseparable from anxiety but also the *result* of anxiety, for anxiety disavows inauthenticity by forcibly revealing one's ownmost, individualized attitudes and ideals. Indeed, as Heidegger reminds us again and again, anxiety *discloses* Dasein as authentic because it reveals what matters most to Dasein, the "meaning" of life and death. Though we all vacillate between existing for ourselves and existing for others, it is only through the recognition of possibilities and *the acceptance of anxiety* that we are able to come to terms with our existence, to be disclosed as Dasein and as authentic Being-for-itself.

If we return to contemporary representations of anxiety, we find that what stands out in the digital age (even more so than the proliferation of anxiety) is a desire for authenticity, for characters to represent not a fantasy but rather the reality of Being-in-the-world. Such desire not only emphasizes that such Being is *always finite*, it also overturns the long-standing assumption that the primary purpose of moving images is escapism. Despite the fact that he's a piece of talking candy, for example, the Red M&M's

feels real to us not because of the quality of the digital animation, but because *he owns his existence* by struggling against the gaze that perceives him as object (only for comedic effect does he submit himself to the desires of others). And the trials of Ethan Mars register as authentic because *he refuses to play the part of a hero*, instead allowing his anxiety (and ours) to drive his quest to rescue his son. Above all, they are each acutely aware of their possibilities — especially the one instance in which possibility is overcome by inevitability — and yet they refuse to suppress or flee from the resultant anxiety. So, let's add one more aspect to our definition of authenticity: to refuse to flee from anxiety. For this, as Heidegger will show us, is the very essence of authenticity, to take ownership of one's existence as an individual by *resolutely* acknowledging one's ownmost possibility, an act that contemporary moving images have adopted as one of two unconscious relays through which we seek to re-encounter the potential of death.

Being-toward-Death (Potentiality, Resoluteness, Immanence)

In the pilot episode of David Chase's HBO mafia drama *The Sopranos*, a New Jersey gangster finds himself, after having passed out during his son's birthday party, in a place utterly foreign to fictional gangsters: a psychiatrist's office.[41] As a high-level member of a struggling crime family, his life is a near-constant performance of confidence and bluster, an inescapable state of bad faith in which any admission of weakness — including the anxiety that led to his collapse — is tantamount to suicide ("the wrong person finds out about this," he tells his wife, "and I get a steeljacket anti-depressant right to the back of the head"). Though initially reticent to discuss the details of his criminal past with his psychiatrist, he soon embraces the opportunity to articulate the angst that comes part and parcel with his profession, to set aside the mask that hides the insecurity and uncertainty that has haunted him since his youth. "I find I have to be the sad clown," he admits, "laughing on the outside, crying on the inside" — his assuredness a self-deceiving lie, a pleasing untruth. In the psychiatrist's office, however, his authenticity spills out, he accepts the possibilities that stem from his actions, he owns his anxiety rather than fleeing from it. In doing so, Tony Soprano represents not only one of the first truly *anxious* gangsters in moving images, but also one of the first truly *authentic* gangsters as well.[42]

The trigger for Tony's anxiety appeared several months earlier in the form of a family of ducks living in his backyard swimming pool. For several happy weeks he watched as the ducklings grew and developed, aware of the possibility that one day they would grow strong enough to fly away, yet ignorant of the consequences of their departure. When that day finally came — the day of his son's party — Tony was overwhelmed not simply by his feeling of loss (what his psychiatrist sees as an analogy of his own children growing older and leaving home) but also, and more importantly, by his recognition that all things must eventually come to an end. "It's good to be in on something from the ground floor," he tells his psychiatrist. "I came too late for that, I know. But lately I'm getting the feeling that I came in at the end." If Tony felt, at the start of the series, that he was approaching an end — or, more astutely, that he was approaching *his end* — he had good reason, for his death was in fact the very goal, the ambition, of *The Sopranos*.

Six seasons and eighty-five episodes later, *The Sopranos* concluded with one of the more infamous sequences in television history, in which Tony — having successfully brokered peace with a neighboring New York family — sits down in a small diner to eat with his wife and children. Though very little action occurs, things immediately feel wrong. The family's conversations are inconsequential and benign (as opposed to the high drama that punctuated nearly every other scene throughout the episode), his daughter is shown repeatedly failing to parallel park her car outside the restaurant (creating a feeling of frustration and urgency not present inside), and the music Tony plays from a jukebox grows increasingly louder in comparison to the dialog. Then there are frequent, seemingly unmotivated insert shots of other guests in the restaurant (a hunter in camo gear, a young couple at a nearby table, a boy scout troop, a group of young men who enter shortly after Tony's son, and most prominently a man who, over the

FIGURE 3.4 *Tony Soprano in his last moment.*

course of several shots, enters, sits at the bar, looks suspiciously in Tony's direction, and then finally walks behind him toward the restroom). As the music crescendos into a fever pitch, the family casually orders an appetizer while Tony's daughter finishes parking her car and is shown running across the street. The entry bell chimes as Tony, in a close-up, raises his gaze, but suddenly we smash cut to black, the music ceasing just as violently as the image. For ten seconds (an eternity in screen time) we sit on black before the credits appear, which play out in silence for the first and only time in the series.

As those credits rolled, many fans of the series felt that they were left with little more than a gangster's version of Schrödinger's Cat: had Tony's survival against all odds been reaffirmed by the reunion of his broken family, or did that unnervingly extended pause over black imply that something more sinister had occurred? Though left ambiguous, astute viewers knew that Tony's fate was anything but uncertain, sealed years before when he first confessed his anxiety and his recognition that all roads lead to an end, that all lives lead to death. No gunshot is heard and no blood seen, no pain felt nor defeat tasted, yet these things are only denied to us because they were denied to Tony himself. Instead, his last moment of consciousness, one of simple though profound curiosity, *is* the last moment — *can only be* the last moment — of *The Sopranos*, for *The Sopranos* was, from the very beginning, always being-toward-(Tony's)-death.

Through Tony Soprano's refusal to flee from anxiety and his subsequently authentic acknowledgment of the possibility of death, we can begin to sense one significant epistemological shift in the manner through which we have come to negotiate and contemplate death in the moving image, an unconscious relay through which we *resolutely* project ourselves toward our utmost possibility as a means to grasp our own potential. On the surface, this shift entails an increase in the number of narratives that approach the problem of mortality through "the death of the self" rather than the "the death of the other," in that they foster an identification with the figure of the dying rather than the figure of the bereaved. More significantly, however, it also exposes a virtual enactment of the Heideggerian *Being-toward-death*, a projection toward an end that positions death as not simply one's future but also an *immanent* aspect of both one's past and one's present.

In *Being and Time*, Heidegger presents us with several modes of Dasein's Being — such as Being-in, Being-with, and Being-toward — which each characterizes Dasein's existence in specific ways. For example, Dasein's Being-in-the-world is not simply an observation of one's existence among other beings, but rather a declaration that one can only grasp its own Being *through* its relationship to the world, and thus "in their indissoluble unity," as Stolorow and Robert Eli Sanchez put it, "our Being and our world always contextualize one another."[43] Likewise, our Being-with-others implies both that Dasein is never alone and, dialectically, that Dasein is always alone, its sense of self a response to "the everyday experiences of shared interactions and interpersonal relationships" that is nonetheless made in the "solicitude" of Dasein's ownness.[44] As we flirted with in the previous section, Dasein's authenticity is reliant upon the recognition of its Being-toward, which is always for Heidegger a "futurity" (Dasein's "Being-ahead-of-itself") and therefore always *toward-death*.[45] In fact, its Being-as-care aside, what truly defines Dasein is its Being-toward-death, for what it truly *cares about* is time and the fundamental finitude of Being.

To work our way closer to an understanding of authentic Being-toward-death, we'll need to first pass through a number of Heideggerian concepts — namely, thrownness, uncanniness, ecstatic temporality, and most importantly resoluteness — that contextualize Dasein's possibility for authenticity, its relationship to the world in which it is situated, its understanding of temporality as being fulfilled within the recognition of death, and its "mood" regarding its own finiteness. In doing so, we'll come to see not only why a continual recognition of death is fundamental to Dasein's project of questioning the meaning of its Being, but also (and most importantly for this project) how such Being-toward-death has been adopted, in response to digital logic, by contemporary moving-image narratives as a way to address death both directly and indirectly, an unconscious relay through which a possibilistic culture attempts to find potential in a life that is always leading toward death.

We can begin, then, with Dasein's *thrownness* into the world — that through birth one comes into a place not of one's choosing or making, yet *in which* one must then learn to exist (and *with whom* one must then learn to coexist) — which situates Dasein within a facticity that encourages inauthentic action while also revealing the possibilities through which anxiety and authenticity emerge. For Heidegger, thrownness reveals that Dasein "is and has to be," that existence is never a choice but rather a circumstance into which one is thrown involuntarily and *in medias res*. When coming to terms with its thrownness, what Dasein is truly facing are its possibilities, for as Michael Inwood points out, thrownness implies "the fact that Dasein is 'always already' in a specific situation that determines the possibilities available to it."[46] Because Dasein is otherwise "determined in its thrownness by the specific choices it is compelled to make," the first step in Being-toward-death must always involve a coming to terms with one's thrownness, for the first step toward authenticity (which we might think of as the overcoming of one's determinants) is to acknowledge one's possibilities and one's anxieties.[47]

Accompanying Dasein's thrownness is an *uncanniness* — from the German *Un-heimlich*, which literally translates to being "not at home" — that Brent Adkins calls Dasein's feeling of being "a stranger in its own skin," of being at sea in a world that is both recognizable and yet foreign.[48] Despite its obvious similarity to Freud's notion of the uncanny — in which a subject encounters an object in the world as uncomfortably familiar, often through some form of repetition — Heidegger's conception of uncanniness is really about one's uncomfortability with oneself, especially in regard to the identification of oneself *as an object* for others.[49] As with thrownness, we see in Heidegger a direct relationship between uncanniness and authenticity, for when we run from the feeling of uncanniness, we do so by inauthentically falling into the comfort and "the home-ness" of the "they."[50] Conversely, to be authentic is "to stand in the uncanniness" of Being — to face the anxiety that comes with being not-safely-at-home, which in turn forces us to consider our Being from outside of our own existence by facing the objectifying gaze of the other.[51] This is partially why Heidegger saw within authentic Being-toward-death an implicit recognition of the structure of temporality (and the finitude of existing within it), because although Being-toward is always a futurity, it is born from a thrownness that makes visible a determinant past and an uncanniness that reveals a determinant present.

As the title of his magnum opus suggests, time was every bit as central to Heidegger's exploration of existence as was the very fact of Being, and its text was an attempt at nothing less than the "phenomenological destruction of the history of ontology, with the problematic of Temporality as our clue."[52] To that end, Heidegger conceived of an *ecstatic temporality*, which David A. Stone and Christina Papadimitriou succinctly describe as "three equiprimordial moments or 'ecstasies': having been, making present, and the future, none of which exist *in* time, but all of which, experienced together allow us to exist *as* temporal beings."[53] Time as such is not an object seen from within a moment, nor is it a series of "nows" piling up one on top of another, but rather (following the meaning of *ek-stasis* as being outside or apart from oneself) three distinct parts of the "event" of Dasein that can only emerge through one another or be seen from the perspective of one another, which Heidegger also described as the processes of reduction (of a past), destruction (of a present), and construction (of a future).[54] Put more simply, one cannot recognize a present moment without first coming to terms with the prior-existence of a past or the possibility of a future, nor can one sense a past without being in a present, and so on and so on.

Through its various modes of Being, Dasein's existence fluctuates between and within the three ecstasies. As Inwood points out, for example, our Being-with is always a recognition of the present — a concern for the here and now of our facticity — while our sense of thrownness is always "past-directed," a looking back to the moment of *being thrown* and a recognition of our lack of agency in relation to a past that cannot be changed. In fact, Heidegger frequently refers to Dasein as a "thrown possibility," which, according to Graham Harman, "could easily be rephrased as 'past future,'" for it is always torn between turning back and forging ahead.[55] Yet only in the authenticity of Being-one's-Self (akin to Sartre's Being-for-itself) can Dasein strike a balance between the three, because such authenticity requires the acceptance of an anxiety through which Dasein is aware of its past, Being-with its present, and Being-toward its future.

To bring all of this into perspective, let's turn for a moment to Jack Shepard, the central protagonist of Carlton Cuse and Damon Lindelof's sci-fi television drama *Lost*. Like Tony Soprano, Jack strives for authenticity through an acceptance of anxiety and an (eventual) acknowledgment of death. As the de facto leader of a group of plane crash survivors marooned on a dense, tropical island, it wouldn't have been a surprise if Jack had followed in Tony's footsteps by faltering in a state of bad faith, by creating an image of authority in order to appease those who looked to him for guidance and support. To the contrary, from the moment he regains consciousness after the crash, Jack is resolutely authentic, as passionately assertive and honest in his encounters with others as he is anxiously aware of the possibilities that lie before them.

On the one hand, Jack's *thrownness* and *uncanniness* are quite literal: he was, after all, ejected from a passenger jet that broke apart mid-air onto an ancient and mysterious island, whose impenetrable jungles hide strangely out-of-place secrets. On the other hand, as we come to learn through flashbacks that fill in his backstory, Jack was *thrown* long before he stepped foot aboard Oceanic Flight 815, having pursued a surgical career largely to placate his alcoholic father, despite the fact that he was never "at home" in that high-stakes world of life and death. In fact, though the island may not have cured Jack of a physical malady (as it does for several other survivors), his sudden embrace of authenticity *is a cure*, because it reverses the inauthentic Being-for-others that haunted him prior to the crash. Life on the island may be a source of great anxiety for Jack, but through its embrace he finds new meaning to existence and, ultimately, a resolute acknowledgment of the progress of time and the inevitability of death.

We learn much of this through the series' unique employment of flashbacks and flash-forwards, as each episode is evenly divided between a storyline set during the "present" events on the island and another which follows a member of the ensemble cast in either their "past" (before the crash) or their "future" (after several survivors escape the island). In fact, the narrative structure of *Lost* could practically serve as a model for Heidegger's ecstatic temporality, in that any given episode demands its viewers negotiate multiple ecstasies of time — to reduce the past through the unfolding of the present, to allow that present to construct the future, or even to destroy the present through the acknowledgment of multiple possible futures. To this last point we can add the "flash-sideways" that appeared in the later seasons, storylines that take place in an alternate timeline and often follow characters who have been killed off in the narrative proper, which present us with what-if scenarios that usually involve a character fulfilling an unresolved desire or finding redemption for a past transgression. For the audience, these flash-sideways allow us to imagine or acknowledge disparate possibilities for both the narrative and its characters, while in turn giving us hints of the full potential of life beyond the event of death.

As for Jack, his storyline, the heart of the series, resolves itself through the discovery of the literal "heart of the island" — a cave filled with flowing water and a brilliant light that, according the series' convoluted mythology, is the very source of all life and death in the universe. Because of its potential to be used for ill, the "heart of the island" requires a protector, and Jack finds that he has been "chosen" to fulfill that role. For a brief moment, it appears that he will live forever as the island's guardian, but instead Jack comes to realize that he must sacrifice himself in order to plug up the escaping water and light. Likewise, the final episode's flash-sideways finds all of the show's deceased characters together in a church, and as Jack finally arrives, they ready themselves to "move on" into the light (presumably that of the "heart of the island"), an act that requires their resolute acceptance of the fact of their deaths. Having accomplished both of his tasks (the plugging of the heart and the acceptance of his passing) Jack awakens in the series' final scene to find himself in the very same spot where he regained consciousness in the pilot episode, although this time mortally wounded. Rather than struggling against death, Jack continues to resolutely accept his fate, bringing a smile to his face even as the life fades from his eyes. In doing so, Jack finds, in his last moment, a meaning to his life — not some fateful, mystical purpose but rather a simple glimpse of his own capacity for authentic Being and his own potential for self-determination — while *Lost* reveals that it was, from its very opening moments to its final image, always being-toward-(Jack's)-death.

FIGURE 3.5 *In* Lost's *final moment, Jack resolutely accepts his death.*

The thrownness, uncanniness, and ecstatic temporality visible in *Lost* are central to Heidegger's thought because they reveal both our responsibility to ourselves — a responsibility for authentic Being that can only be fulfilled through one's Being-toward-death — and our capacity for self-determination. As Bruce Baugh puts it, "Dasein does not bring itself into existence and yet is *responsible* for choosing itself in light of its ability-to-be," which is both an act of self-identification and the act of *choosing not to undo itself*, to not take itself out of the world through suicide or self-destruction.[56] Considering this responsibility — recalling again authenticity as owning our existence and our possibilities — we can see that Being-toward-death is certainly not a push to die. Nor, on the other hand, is it a push to live. Instead, Being-toward is *the push* itself, the act of *projecting oneself* toward a future and *toward an end*. But if this end is always death — a return to non-existence or non-Being — would not the push be a push into despair?

Perhaps, though for Heidegger such despair would be the result of an inauthentic understanding of death, a recognition only of the end and not of the present or the space in-between (the Being-toward). In fact, Kierkegaard had already warned against such despair in *The Sickness unto Death*, which he saw as a sin of hopelessness, a torment in which the sick are not the dying but rather those who are *unable to die* — "it is the greatest misfortune and misery actually to be in despair; no, it is ruin."[57] For Kierkegaard, the remedy to the sickness unto death was a faith in life beyond death, but this solution falters under Heidegger's nontheistic philosophy, which saw in death an absolute end to all Being. Rather than falling into despair, however, Heidegger proposed that authentic Being-toward-death requires *resoluteness* — to resolutely face the uncanniness of one's anxiety, to always and resolutely acknowledge the possibility of death. In fact, Heidegger explains in *Being and Time* that "when we master a mood, we do so by way of a counter-mood," and in following this statement we can read resoluteness as a counter-mood to anxiety, through which we not only come to accept anxiety but also to *use* it, to allow it disclose our authenticity.[58] Resoluteness is not an overcoming of anxiety nor a recognition of possibility; instead, it is the *mastering* of anxiety and the search for potential, in particular our *potentiality-for-Being*.

We'll return to Heidegger's understanding of our potentiality-for-Being in a moment, but first let's examine what it means to resolutely face anxiety or death, which for Heidegger always involves a resolution, for "resoluteness 'exists' only as a resolution."[59] Considering that the colloquial usage of the term "resolution" (as in, say, a New Year's resolution) implies a promise for the future and a declaration that one can and will act in a specific way, we might mistake it as, in the words of Heidegger, "taking up possibilities which have been proposed and recommended, and seizing hold of them."[60] Yet Heidegger advises us against this error of bad faith by instead proposing that "resolution is precisely the disclosive projection and determination of what is factically possible at the time."[61]

Let's pause on this statement for a moment, for it is vitally important to understanding anxiety, authenticity, and Being-toward-death in a possibilistic culture. First, a resolution is seen here as a projection — a looking-ahead, the act of Being-toward a future — which is disclosive, meaning that, like anxiety, it opens up or makes visible an otherwise closed or invisible concept. Next, we find that a resolution is determinate, in that it allows Dasein to *situate itself* within its world and to *find for itself* a sense of meaning through an examination of its possibilities (otherwise Dasein would be determined only by its "facticity and falling"). This suggests that although Dasein is thrown into a world which ensures its feeling of uncanniness, it nonetheless possesses some potential to shape itself and its world, if in no other way than simply separating, to the best of its abilities, possibilities from impossibilities. Most important, then, is the final phrase "factically possible at the time," in which such a separation takes place, a disclosure which makes known both the indefinite potential of Being and the definite possibility of death. This is because when we look ahead, death is always, as Heidegger repeats again and again throughout *Being and Time*, our "utmost" and "ownmost" possibility; it is at all times our most factically definite possibility.

Let's return to the ending of *Lost* as an example. When Jack resolves to enter the "heart of the island" in order to prevent its destruction, he is in that moment projecting himself toward an end, and what such projection discloses to him is the certainty of his death, for he knows that one cannot survive an encounter with its brilliant light. Jack chooses not to sacrifice himself, but rather to *determine for himself* the meaning of his Being, which would otherwise be determined by the island, his father, and all the other components of his facticity that attempted throughout the years to declare who Jack Shepard was or who he could be. Yet Jack's triumph is not entering the "heart of the island," it is instead his subsequent resoluteness, lying in the jungle, facing death. Resolution is the manner in which Jack weighs his possibility to find his utmost — the only logical, certain, and definite outcome of a thrown and uncanny life — while resoluteness allows Jack to be-toward-death, because it allows him to put aside his inauthentic Being-for-others and find his potentiality-for-Being.

So what is our potentiality-for-Being? According to Heidegger, "Anxiety makes manifest in Dasein its Being toward its ownmost potentiality-for-Being — that is, Being-free for the freedom of choosing itself and taking hold of itself."[62] Our ownmost potentiality-for-Being *is* authenticity, the freedom to *determine ourselves*, to recognize that our lives are too complex and too sublime to be fully "positioned" or coded by the objectifying gaze of the Other. Yet this determination requires resoluteness, for it requires a recognition of our utmost possibility. Let's allow Heidegger to continue: "to resoluteness, the *indefiniteness* characteristic of every potentiality-for-Being into which Dasein has been factically thrown, is something that necessarily belongs," and "in resoluteness, the issue for Dasein is it ownmost potentiality-for-Being, which, as something thrown, can project itself only upon definite factual possibilities."[63] In these almost-mirrored statements, we find that even though Dasein is capable of certainty only when it projects itself toward known possibilities (potentials being simply too vast or complex to fully perceive), through its resoluteness the sublime or indefinite nature of potential is nonetheless disclosed to Dasein, whether it be the potentiality contained within the world itself (to move away from what Heidegger would call seeing the world as only ready-at-hand) or Dasein's own potentiality-for-Being. Following this, although Dasein is thrown into and thus determined by its world, resoluteness allows Dasein a chance to determine itself — to take ownership of its existence — by projecting itself upon its ownmost possibility: death. Only through resoluteness can we approach the certainty of death (our most factually definite possibility); only through resoluteness can we begin to glimpse the potential of life (the indefinite characteristic of beings and Being); only through resoluteness can we fulfill our desire for authenticity (the acceptance of possibility, anxiety, temporality, and the uncanniness of being thrown); *only through resoluteness can we Be-toward-death*.

In contemporary culture, resoluteness is found not only in one's own personal ruminations on death, nor is it only an attitude affected in the name of authenticity. Instead, we've also adopted resoluteness as a mode of viewing, a mindset through which we approach moving-image narratives in which death is the only possible outcome (whether we are conscious of that fact or not). Of course, like authenticity, such resoluteness always oscillates, in that we both adopt and dismiss the counter-mood as fluidly as we face and flee from anxiety. Yet through narratives of those who refuse to flee (and thus narratives which are themselves *resolutely toward-death*), we too can momentarily adopt a resolution, a projection toward an end that hints at our own utmost possibility. As the first of the two unconscious relays discussed in this chapter, we can refer to the narrative being-toward-death found in contemporary moving images as a *relay of immanence*, for it is an attempt to make death materially present to life, to bring it within and between, even if but for a moment. Moreover, to glimpse such immanence is to grasp for potential, to authentically face the world and resolutely face our limits, and to disclose even just a few of the uncountable ways in which our recognition of death impacts our everyday lives.

Let's briefly consider one last televisual example of this relay of immanence: Vince Gilligan's *Breaking Bad*, the story of an unassuming high school teacher who decides to use his knowledge of chemistry to produce high-quality methamphetamines, in the process ruthlessly taking control of the international drug trade in the southwestern United States. The catalytic agent, so to speak, for Walter White's sudden career change is a diagnosis of inoperable lung cancer, which, when mixed with his wife's pregnancy and his son's disability, reacts to form *a resolution* — to amass a substantial nest egg that can support his family after his passing — which *projects him toward an end*. Walt's resoluteness is certain from the very outset of *Breaking Bad* — he knows that he will die, and he knows what he wants to accomplish before he does — just as the show itself is always being-toward-(Walt's)-death.[64] Yet as the series progresses, it also becomes increasingly clear that Walt's gambit is not simply a resolution to support his family, but also, and perhaps more importantly, to redefine his authenticity — to determine for himself the meaning of his existence rather than letting others define it for him. To grab hold of his potentiality-for-Being, Walt has no choice but to accept his anxiety and his utmost possibility, to not flee from his cancer but rather embrace it. Likewise, through narratives such as *Breaking Bad*, we too can seek our ownmost potential through an acknowledgment, however slight, of *our* utmost possibility, for in our identification with characters like Walt, we can allow ourselves to momentarily think like they do — to consider our potentiality-for-Being not through the mortality of another but rather our own, to resolutely view death as an immanent characteristic of life.

Split Subjectivity (Potentiality, Reflection, Ecstasis)

In resolutely Being-toward-death, Walter White has mastered his anxiety.[65] At the same time, however, his meteoric rise to the top of the meth trade was the result not simply of some newfound sense of authenticity born out of a recognition of the approach of death, but also of the appearance of another figure altogether: Heisenberg. Heisenberg is Walt's alter-ego, a persona of control, ingenuity, and mercilessness who appears, on the surface, to be the "bad faith" version of Walt, a lie that Walt tells to himself in order to flee from the anxiety that arises from his diagnosis. Yet despite being initially adopted as a means of maintaining his anonymity when dealing with the criminal underworld, Heisenberg is increasingly called-upon not to mask Walt's authenticity but rather to redefine who the "authentic" Walter White really is. Heisenberg, as such, is not a fallen, inauthentic version of Walt, but rather a lens through which Walt sees himself from the outside, through which he begins to transform himself, to re-position his own subjectivity, to determine his own potentiality-for-Being.

It's clear throughout the series that Walt needs Heisenberg, whose strength comes from the fact that he's not determined by Walt's failures: he's not a vastly overqualified and yet underappreciated and overlooked chemistry teacher, nor is he an illiterate criminal unschooled in the rules and dangers of the drug trade, nor does he have a family whose personal and financial struggles are the direct result of a missed business opportunity and a bruised ego. More importantly, though, Walt needs Heisenberg because Heisenberg *does not have cancer*, because Heisenberg *is not subject to death*: he's a myth, immortal, both larger than life and beyond death. In fact, Walt imagines Heisenberg to be in control of death — to be the harbinger of death — as he claims in the series' most infamous monologue, a response to his wife's plea to get out of the drug business before it gets too dangerous: "Who are you talking to right now? Who is it you think you see? ... I am not in danger, Skyler. I am the danger. A guy opens his door and gets shot, and you think that of me? No. I am the one who knocks." The slippage that occurs here — in which Walt's *actual subjectivity* is momentarily supplanted by the *virtual subjectivity* of Heisenberg, i.e., "the one who knocks" — is no accident, nor is it a rupture of some inauthentic desire to deny the inevitability of an impending death. Instead, Heisenberg is what allows Walt to master his anxiety — to be authentic, resolute, and toward-death — because Heisenberg allows Walt to *ecstatically reflect* upon his own mortality and his own potential.

Although the details may be extreme, the split subjectivity on display in *Breaking Bad* is, in fact, increasingly common in the digital age, thanks in large part to the myriad online platforms that necessitate the adoption of virtual identities. Whether it be the screen-names through which we maintain our anonymity in online message boards, blogs, and news sites,

FIGURE 3.6 *Walt adopts the "virtual" subjectivity of Heisenberg to grasp at his potential.*

the complex characters that we develop in massively multiplayer games and other online worlds, or the calculated and heightened personalities that we cultivate across a variety of social media networks, the development of virtual subjectivity forms the crux of a potentializing relay through which we begin to ecstatically examine the parameters of our identity, redefine our capacity for authenticity, and accept our utmost possibility.

Having been one of the most visible new developments of the digital age, the impact of online communications technologies on the individual's construction of identity has also been a primary concern of scholars for more than a decade. Sherry Turkle set the stage only a few years after the eruption of the digital when she declared that "in the mirror of the machine" we develop a "second-self," a subjectivity independent of our physical body through which "more of us are experimenting with multiplicity than ever before."[66] Lisa Nakamura agrees that our identity — both actual and virtual — "shapes and reshapes every time we log on" (while also arguing that the dream of a utopian virtual landscape free of race, gender, and class is little more than a fantasy, that we do not entirely escape our fleshy body with the simple click of a button).[67] Steven Shaviro claims that, in a constantly connected society, "identity is implanted ... from without, not generated from within," and that "selfhood is an information pattern, rather than a material substance."[68] And posthumanists like Donna Haraway and Judith Butler demonstrate that our identity is grounded in bodies that are quickly becoming fluid and interchangeable, a notion which we'll explore in greater detail in our final chapter.[69]

That said, the type of subjectivation presented in *Breaking Bad* — in which an individual structures their sense of self as an aggregate of various personalities or personas employed in different social situations — is not an entirely new phenomenon in the digital age. Rather, one could argue that it was hallmark of identity construction in the twentieth century, when theorists like Kenneth Burke and Erving Goffman developed "dramatist" and "dramaturgical" terminologies, respectively, in order to argue that the self is a series of performances, that one's actions are little more than theatrical responses to various "settings" and "audiences."[70] As with their contemporary digital counterparts, such performances were in every way *virtual*, yet at the same time they lacked the primary concern of modern virtual subjectivity: the desire for authenticity that has accompanied the overflow of angst. Indeed, the dramaturgical view of identity left little room for authentic action, because one was rarely thought to be acting without consideration for the desires of others, without seeing oneself as a character in the eyes of an audience. In turn, the very fact of Being was frequently positioned, prior to the digital turn, as innately inauthentic, an implication that we could not overcome the determination of our thrownness and uncanniness, that our sense of self could only account for one possibility at any given moment, and that any attempt to perceive our potentiality-for-Being would fail.

We might be tempted, then, to say that the self *as subject* had long been merely virtual, unable to grasp at its authentic actuality. Then again, we might ask ourselves if one's actual subjectivity would, in turn, be innately authentic? To find out, we needn't go far, for most of the theorists that we've drawn upon, from Bergson and Deleuze to Heidegger and Sartre, shared a belief that there is no *transcendental* subject — no "true self" *a priori* to the circumstances and events of one's existence — an implication that the self is inescapably split, always already both actual and virtual.[71] Bergson, for his part, strongly challenged Kant's notion of the "transcendental unity of apperception," which positioned all conscious experience as a necessarily unified and unquestionable truth. Deleuze defied such transcendentalism by cheekily referring to his own thought as a *transcendental empiricism*, in which all experience is seen to be an experience of difference which brings to the surface new forms and new thought, a "philosophical position which determines the conditions of real rather than possible experience."[72]

Both Heidegger and Sartre, on the other hand, took issue with the thought of Husserl; Heidegger taking to task his former mentor's "transcendental perspective" on Being — not so much akin to Kant's *a priori* determination but rather an abstract view of consciousness as an "unparticipating observer," a failure in Heidegger's eyes to account for *Dasein*'s Being-in-the-world — while Sartre "urges us to abandon ... the 'transcendental ego' that allegedly stands behind, initiates, and directs all conscious acts," and to instead view the self as an empirical ego "constituted in the *reflective* acts of consciousness."[73] Together, they show that one's actual subjectivity is not some intrinsic "truth" or even the only authentic piece of the puzzle that is the self, but rather something much more literal: those few potentials of the self that have become *actualized*, those desires and attitudes that have been rendered concrete or tangible within reality.

To clarify these rather complex views of subjectivity and authenticity (and to trace a path through which our contemporary acts of virtual subjectivation reconfigure our attitude toward our own mortality), let's turn our attention to Deleuze, in whose thought we find an explication not only of one's subjective, determinative relationship *to oneself*, but also of the relationship between the actual and virtual and, by extension, possibility and potential. Deleuze's account of subjectivity is relayed primarily through his concept of *the fold*, the bringing together of the outside and the inside and the *envelopment* of forces and events, which Deleuze borrows in part from Leibniz. In Leibniz's "dynamics" or "calculus," Mogens Lærke tells us, "the essence of physical objects is not, as it is for Descartes, quantity, motion and shape, but *action* and *force*," meaning that the object's essence is just as much informed by *that which acts upon it* as it is by *its own actions*.[74] As such, forces are folded *into* actions, and events are seen to be (at least for Deleuze) constituted not only by a happening, but also by the causal, affective relationship between one object and another (or, better yet, by the relationship between all objects). The *self* in Deleuze, as both object and event, is inherently folded, its exterior brought into and made part of its interior, such that one's body and one's actions and one's world are folded into one's thoughts and one's attitudes and one's consciousness. There is unity here, but not the transcendental unity that we find in Kant (whereby the self interfaces with the world as a preformed whole). Instead, one's self is seen to be continually folded into the world both temporally and spatially, unified with it, immanent to it — the unity is a unity of affect, it is that plane of immanence where all things are rendered wholly affective to one another.

Likewise, though one's virtuality and one's actuality may be distinct (even oppositional) aspects of one's subjectivity, for Deleuze they are also folded into one another, forming a complete image of the self that exists within and through time. To explain, let's step back up for a moment to examine the relationship between the virtual and the actual, which both Bergson and Deleuze saw as explicitly developed in Marcel Proust's claim that the virtual is "real without being actual, ideal without being abstract."[75] On second thought, let's step back up even further, for that observation is but a side-effect of a much more important relationship for Deleuze: that of *virtuality and possibility*:

> The "virtual" can be distinguished from the "possible" from at least two points of view. From a certain point of view, in fact, *the possible is the opposite of the real*, it is opposed to the real; but, in a quite different opposition, *the virtual is opposed to the actual*. We must take this terminology seriously: the possible has no reality (although it may have an actuality); conversely, the virtual is not actual, but *as such possesses a reality*.[76]

Two oppositions: the possible and the real, the virtual and the actual. Possibility opposes reality because once it is actualized, it can no longer remain a possibility (it has instead come to pass). At the same time, virtuality opposes actuality despite the fact that it nonetheless possesses a reality. What stands out here is first the difference between reality and actuality — the former an existence outside of or independent from material essence, the latter an object or event made tangible, the coming-into-being of a material substance — and second the essence of the virtual, which is opposed to the actual in that lacks a material substance yet has a reality because it is nonetheless affective. In his short essay on "The Actual and the Virtual," unpublished at the time of his death, Deleuze defined the virtual as a cloud of ephemeral images that surround the actual, such that our immaterial *conception* of the world is folded into our *perception* of its material presence — each side impacting our understanding or negotiation of the other, neither side existing independent of the other.[77]

While the possible opposes the real and the virtual opposes the actual, there are other relationships at play between and amongst them. For example, not everything that is real is also actual, but anything actualized has a reality. Likewise, not every virtuality is possible, but every possibility is virtual. What strikes me, then, about Deleuze's account of virtuality is not the two oppositions he presents, but rather the care with which Deleuze goes about *separating virtuality from possibility*, despite the fact that they unmistakably overlap. This begs a question: If virtuality and possibility are so clearly related, why then does Deleuze go to such great lengths to "distinguish" the two? The answer is that the virtual is also our avenue to *potential*, it is the thoughts and images through which we access those strands of the actual that are beyond our ability to perceive. Indeed, Deleuze states that "the varyingly dense layers of the actual object correspond to these, more or less extensive, circles of virtual images. These layers, whilst themselves virtual, constitute the total *impetus* of the object," an always-already-folded *force* that we might choose to read as the *energy* of potential, whose unfolding (through the process of actualization) backforms possibility.[78] If possibilities are *virtual*, then potentials are *real*; they are the fullest image of the real that could ever exist, too expansive and complex to perceive even when they are actualized and as such accessible only within the folds of the virtual.[79]

If we return to the digital's employment of virtual subjectivity, we find that although screen names, digital game characters, blog posts, and comments posted on social media are so often intangible, ephemeral, and incorporeal, they are nonetheless also wholly affective; they impact our sense of self because they are continually folded into those aspects of our subjectivity that have been actualized, in the process creating a total impetus of the self which reveals (if only in fragments) one's authentic potential. Deleuze himself hinted at this process when he suggested that "actuals imply already constituted individuals, and are ordinarily determined, whereas the relationship of the actual and the virtual forms an acting individuation" — a folding of the virtual self into the actual self in order to form a self-determined, authentic image of an individual.

An excellent example of this process playing out in digital games comes from the first season of Telltale's episodic zombie adventure *The Walking Dead*, a spin-off of the Robert Kirkman comic which inspired the hit television show. The game places players into the role of Lee Everett, a former history professor at the University of Georgia who must protect and mentor Clementine, a young girl orphaned after a zombie outbreak occurs. As with the aforementioned *Heavy Rain*, *The Walking Dead* is a game built around choices, and though it may appear to be modeled after classic point-and-click adventure games, it is almost always concerned more with the player's sense of morality and integrity than with their ability to wield a weapon or solve esoteric puzzles. Sure, players are occasionally tasked with

FIGURE 3.7 *Lee mentors the orphaned Clementine in* The Walking Dead.

dispatching some of the rambling corpses that litter the game's apocalyptic version of Georgia, but more often than not they are tasked with making more mundane yet profound decisions, such as who to support as the leader of their band of survivors (picking oneself is, refreshingly, not an option), who to feed when provisions get low, whether or not to trade supplies with other groups of people, whether or not to let other survivors join the group, or how to explain Lee's checkered past to a frightened and lonely eight-year-old girl.

Through a combination of specific narrative and mechanical methods, the game encourages players to not only create a coherent persona for Lee, but also one that acts as a virtual offshoot of their own subjectivity, a mirror through which they can reflect upon their own attitudes and values. On the narrative side, for example, the game deters players from acting recklessly or erratically by ensuring that Lee is not the only character affected by their actions. Instead, Clementine's fate is strongly tied to Lee's, and the game's remarkably nuanced writing and vocal performances give a sense of weight and significance to many of its morally ambiguous scenarios, creating an anxiety which compels the player toward authentic actions. Added to this, the game's mechanics are built around a complex system of choices and consequences, in which its many characters remember not only the physical actions of the player, but also smaller details that arise within the game's conversation system, such as their attitude toward certain events or ideas, or their choice of words when dealing with delicate issues like the loss of a friend or loved one. As such, players are expected (or perhaps required) to maintain a *consistent* persona throughout the game, to thoughtfully consider every response and every action.[80]

Despite its fantastical elements, *The Walking Dead* is, at its core, a simulation of rather quotidian social dynamics, through which the player creates a virtual persona in order to imagine how specific actions and attitudes might affect the world around them. Such virtual subjectivities may lack real-world consequences, yet they are nonetheless *real* because they say something about who we are (or better yet because they allow us to say something about who we *think* we are). Lee Everett may be nothing more than an image, a backstory, and a few interchangeable lines of dialog, but through him we catch sight of our possibilities, fold them into our perspective of the world, and reflect upon our full potential, the very sort of *reflection* that Sartre understood to be essential to the constitution of the self.

As mentioned earlier, Sartre disagreed with Husserl's assertion of a transcendental ego, and his pointedly titled volume on *The Transcendence of the Ego* was an attempt to move beyond a philosophy structured around a unified self and toward a philosophy in which nothingness always stands *behind* consciousness, such that consciousness is itself "no-thing" or a nonbeing.[81] Standing *before* consciousness, on the other hand, is an intuitive sense of the self as something divided or apart from the world — an outwardly directed perception of one's facticity which Sartre referred to as "pre-reflective consciousness" — which we then structure *within* consciousness through the act of *reflection*, a sort of memory of oneself that undergirds one's very understanding *of* self.[82] One may intuitively recognize that one is not the same as the thing that one sees and touches, for example, but only through reflection can one think of oneself as *a thing that sees and touches*, which Richard Pearce describes as "a way of representing ourselves to ourselves in order to know, to have knowledge of, ourselves."[83] From Sartre's perspective, the ego is not an inherent part of consciousness but rather an object *outside* of consciousness, formed through a reflection upon one's existence within and amongst a facticity. As such, the self is not transcendental but rather empirical, an object experienced through consciousness, such that "the I is not *discovered* in reflection," as David Detmer puts it, "but rather *constituted*."[84]

The folding of virtual subjectivity into the actual is itself a form of reflection, whereby one creates an imagined memory of oneself in order to constitute a fuller, more accurate sense of the meaning of one's Being. As the second of our unconscious relays, we can refer to the reflective folding of virtual subjectivity into the actual as a *relay of ecstasis*, for to reflect is to see oneself ecstatically, as an object viewed from *outside* of one's consciousness. Yet if we seek unconscious relays as an attempt to grasp at potential, and if our potentiality-for-Being is authenticity — the one "absolute virtue in existentialism" — then we must ask: Are virtual subjectivities authentic? Or, for that matter, what does virtual subjectivity have to do with our recognition of mortality? Sartre broke down his understanding of reflection into two categories: pure and impure. Impure reflection is *engendered by affect*, imbued with and classified by past experiences or memories, a "bad faith" vision of the present influenced by the merely similar past. Pure reflection, on the other hand, is *affect-less*, a dispassionate understanding of experience that is not swayed by irrational desire or prejudiced by coincidence.[85] When we consider that the virtual is ephemeral, past-preserving, and wholly affective, it's clear that Sartre would see virtual subjectivity as wholly inauthentic, so how then can we say that its creation and consideration can lead to authenticity?

When we create virtual subjectivities, our intention is not to live within them but rather to use them — to fold them — in order to reflect upon our actual subjectivity (the self as we tangibly present it to the world). Virtual subjectivities are alternative experiences of Being, and as Deleuze tells us, all experience is an experience of *difference*: "It is difference that is primary in the process of actualization — the difference between the virtuals from which we begin and the actuals at which we arrive."[86] Difference is also primary to reflection because reflection is a memory of the past that is juxtaposed against the present, and when we juxtapose our virtual and actual subjectivity — when we lay them atop one another or fold them into one another — we find that the difference between our virtual self and our actual self is nothing less than death. Though our fleshy bodies will eventually wither and decay, our digital profiles on social media websites will live on, an archived and eternally youthful image of the self we wish we could have been; and likewise we've already seen how our gaming avatars — with whom we not only identify but also shape and imbue with our own attitudes and desires — die again and again and yet return and relive again and again. Like Walter White, we *desire* virtual subjectivities because the virtual self *is not subject to death*, and yet we often *employ* them to *accept the fact of mortality*, for they present a difference through which we can ecstatically recognize death's inevitability. To put this another way, immortality is the virtual from which we begin, death is the actual at which we arrive.

The Road to Awe

Let's briefly recap our journey thus far: the binary logic of the digital fetishizes the thought of possibility at the expense of the perception of potential, leading to a culture (and a cultural imagination) that is "possibilistic to the limit." Seeing as the recognition of possibility results in an anxiety for the future, and that anxiety discloses one's authentic potential, we find that our possibilistic culture both accepts and expects anxiety as never before while also desiring authenticity in equal measure. Finally, in our enactment of such desire, we find two unconscious relays through which we attempt to grasp our lost potential, one a resolute being-toward-death whereby our utmost possibility is made immanent to our potentiality-for-Being, and the other an ecstatic reflection whereby our virtual possibilities are folded into our actual potential. Over the last few pages of this chapter, then, let's look to a set of science-fiction films that, in their attempts to explicitly and unabashedly examine the ramifications one's death holds for one's life, embody or employ *both* the relay of immanence and the relay of ecstasis. In doing so, they allow us to catch sight of not only our authentic potentiality-for-Being, but also another potential we've thus far left relatively unexplored: *the potential of death*. Indeed, contemporary media reveals death to be not an event outside of or oppositional to life, but rather an immanent, constitutive event whose definite possibility paves the road for self-determination and self-individuation. Although they are intimately connected, the potential of death is not simply our potentiality-for-Being, nor is it merely the fact or inevitability of death, nor is it the risk of trauma or disease or decay. Rather, the potential of death is the continually unfolding ramifications of mortality on our lives, our culture, and our very interpretation of the meaning of Being.

The films that we'll examine — primarily Darren Aronofsky's *The Fountain* and Steven Soderbergh's *Solaris*, with references to *The Tree of Life*, *Melancholia*, *Enter the Void*, and *Cloud Atlas* — do not by any means represent an exhaustive list of contemporary moving-image narratives which employ multiple potentializing relays. That said, sci-fi as a genre is exceptionally concerned with the impact of technology on culture and the human experience, so it's perhaps unsurprising that it would prove to be a fertile ground for exploring or analogizing the impact of the digital on our relationship to mortality.[87] In each of these films, then, we find a unique account of virtual being-toward-death and split subjectivity, and together they provide a broad perspective on the forms that such potentializing relays can take. This is not to say, however, that they present a uniform perspective on the meaning of Being or the potential of death, nor that they agree upon what happens to consciousness after the body ceases to function. In fact, within the six films we can trace three separate traditions of thought: *The Fountain* and *Melancholia* present us an atheistic stance in which death is the absolute end of one's consciousness, *Solaris* and *The Tree of Life* are more in line with the Abrahamic religions in their positioning of death as a transition of consciousness to another plane of Being (whether it be a heavenly space or something more liminal), while *Enter the Void* and *Cloud Atlas* give us hints of reincarnation akin to Eastern religious philosophies like Buddhism and Hinduism. Nonetheless, when considered together they make visible something much more essential to our experience as consciously mortal individuals: the role that death plays in our capacity for Being.

To begin, we can first state that there are two Tommy Creos, just as there are two Kris Kelvins. Well, technically speaking there is only one Tommy, and only one Kris, but then again perhaps there are three Tommys, and any number of Krises. But really there are two Tommy Creos, and there are two Kris Kelvins. Okay, let's back up for a moment to explain. In Darren Aronofsky's 2006 sci-fi film *The Fountain*, viewers are confronted with three narrative timelines, spread across three seemingly distinct temporospatial settings. Yet each of these timelines revolves around the relationship between the same two basic characters — a man and his dying lover — who are, in turn, played by the same two actors in each timeline, Hugh Jackman and Rachel Weisz. The first timeline is set in sixteenth-century Spain during the Inquisition, where Queen Isabella sends the conquistador Tomás to the jungles of "New Spain" in search of a Mayan-protected secret that would defeat not only the power-mad Grand Inquisitor but even death itself: the biblical "Tree of Life."[88] In the second timeline, we find contemporary neuroscientist Dr. Tommy Creo desperately searching for a cure to his wife Izzi's cancer, going so far as to forgo the few precious days he has left with her in order to pursue what he imagines will be a miracle cure. Finally, in the third timeline we have the future space traveler Tom, haunted by the memories of his dead lover Isabelle as he sails across the Milky Way in his bubble-like spaceship toward the dying star Xibalba, which he hopes will prolong the life of his only companion, a tree whose bark has in turn sustained his life for countless hundreds of years. No matter the timeline, one thing remains constant: Tomás/Tommy/Tom is eternally haunted by his lover's inescapable mortality, a fact made all the more unsettling by his inability to recognize his own.

FIGURE 3.8 *Tom and the dying tree float through space in* The Fountain.

In Steven Soderbergh's 2002 film *Solaris* — not so much a remake of Andrei Tarkovsky's sci-fi classic as much as a new adaptation of Stanislaw Lem's original novel — we find a somewhat similar set of circumstances. In an unspecified future, psychiatrist Kris Kelvin, played by George Clooney, is asked to investigate an international space station orbiting a nebulous planet called Solaris, where the crew have mysteriously cut off contact with the outside world. Once on board, Kelvin finds that Solaris itself appears to be a sentient Being, capable of reading the thoughts and memories of those nearby and, more troublingly, replicating or re-animating figures from their past. In Kelvin's case, this results in the appearance of his deceased wife Rheya, who committed suicide several years earlier back on Earth. Throughout the film, Kelvin is forced to come to terms not only with his anger and bitterness regarding his wife's suicide, but also with significantly more existential issues such as the nature and temporality of his own existence.

Both *The Fountain* and *Solaris* are films about angst, their protagonists painfully, willfully ignorant of the future even as their utmost possibilities float visibly across the horizon. In a moment we'll see how these protagonists attempt to come to terms with their angst through the creation of inauthentic, virtual subjectivities which are not subject to death, but it's worth noting that we also find various incarnations of angst (and various positions toward it) in other contemporary sci-fi films as well. In Lars Von Trier's *Melancholia*, for example, two sisters adopt strikingly different attitudes toward the sudden appearance of a rogue planet that threatens to destroy Earth; one a pathological fetishization of death, the other an absolute denial of its possibility. In Terrence Malick's *The Tree of Life*, an architect recalls a bittersweet summer when he first developed a close relationship with a brother who would later die in combat, a fluidly anxious recollection into

FIGURE 3.9 *Kris Kelvin first steps aboard the space station orbiting* Solaris.

which the film ambitiously folds not only the creation of life on Earth but also its inevitable destruction. Gaspar Noe's *Enter the Void* presents us with an anxiety not so much toward-death, but rather within-death, seeing as it is staged entirely (and quite literally) through the eyes of a character who is killed within its opening act, and who subsequently haunts a seedy urban district of Japan as a specter anxiously searching for some form of release or closure. And in *Cloud Atlas*, co-directed by Tom Tykwer and the Wachowski sisters, we find six intertwined storylines, each taking place in different time periods ranging from the mid-nineteenth century to sometime in the twenty-third, yet each connected through shared recollections of the past and an anxiety toward the future. Like *The Fountain* and *Solaris*, each of these films traces its angst through the development of virtual subjectivities, which in turn reconfigure the central character's perception of the possibility of death.

Let's return then to *The Fountain*, and to understand *The Fountain*, one must first solve its puzzle. Indeed, *The Fountain* is a classic example of a puzzle film, darting back and forth between various timelines, fluidly mixing visual and narrative elements which frequently disorient the audience and make it difficult to tell how or even if its disparate storylines coexist. Upon careful analysis, however, it's clear that (although each individual viewer's experience is subjective and open to interpretation) the film itself has one ultimate "solution," one narrative configuration that clarifies its overall thematic structures and ambitions. Although the film presents various visual clues as to this "solution" — such as the appearance of the twentieth-century Izzi within the frequent hallucinations of space traveler Tom, or the reading of Izzi's book as a transitional device into the sixteenth-century timeline — there are ultimately two key sequences that help to cohesively situate the film's narrative, both of which are contained within its central, contemporary storyline.

The first of these takes place in a hospital where Izzi, a writer, hovers on the edge of succumbing to her cancer. When Tommy comes to visit, Izzi tells him that she's no longer afraid of death, and that she's purposefully leaving her latest book unfinished so that Tommy can write the final chapter after she has passed. With Tommy unwilling and unable to accept Izzi's recognition of the inevitable, she attempts to comfort him by telling the story of a Mayan tour guide she once met, who, equally unable to accept the death of his father, planted a seed over his grave. "Moses said his father became part of that tree. He grew into the wood, into the bloom, and when a sparrow ate the tree's fruit, his father flew with the birds. He said death was his father's road to awe. That's what he called it ... *the road to awe*." Later that day, just after Tommy is pushed out of the room when Izzi goes into cardiac arrest, he is informed that one of his experimental cancer treatments — a compound derived from an "old growth tree in Guatemala" — has radically reversed not only the signs of cancer in its test subjects, but also the signs of aging.

When Tommy rushes back to Izzi's side to give her news of the cure, he finds that it has come too late to save her.

The second key to *The Fountain* is the short final scene of the film, where we find Tommy standing over Izzi's grave holding a seed pod in his hand, which he drops into a small hole in the ground at his feet. Piecing together Izzi's story with the breakthrough cure from Tommy's research, we can surmise that the cure came from a tree planted atop a grave, and that space traveler Tom's tree is not the biblical Tree of Life from the sixteenth-century plotline (a common misinterpretation of the film) but rather a tree that Tommy planted over Izzi's grave, its bark — somehow imbued with Izzi's body or life-force in the film's most quasi-mystical sci-fi conceit — having been used to sustain his life for centuries, meaning that Tommy and Tom are in fact the same person. Added to this, Izzi's unfinished book (inspired by her tour guide's story and her husband's inability to cope with her impending death) is in fact the sixteenth-century storyline, a fictional tale of a conquistador who searches for the mystical tree of life in order to both save his lover and cheat death. In Izzi's narrative, Tomás finds the Tree of Life guarded by Mayans who worship a dying star known as Xibalba — whose eventual explosive death will, they believe, one day renew life on Earth, just as the death of the original "first father" created the seed for life — which we can assume was the inspiration for Tom's journey to the star, and his hope that its death will continue to sustain the life of Izzi's tree (and, by extension, not only himself but Izzi as well).

Stepping back from these complex narrative threads we find that the three seemingly disparate timelines, which we could easily call the past, present,

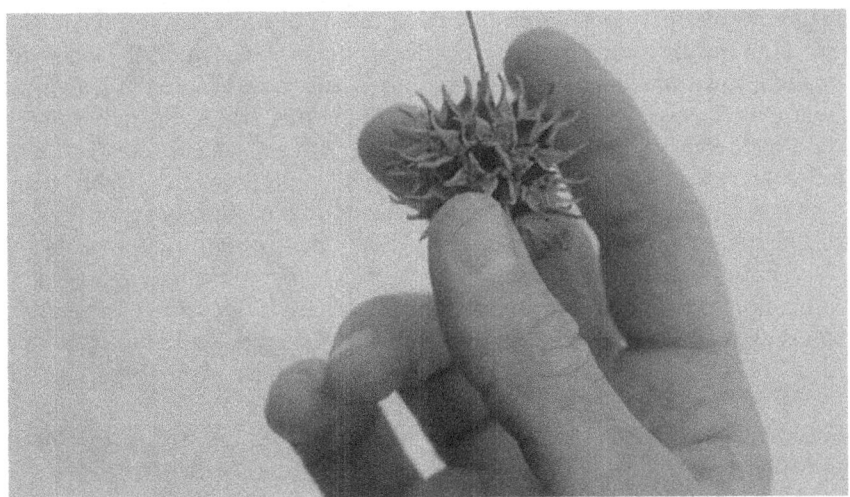

FIGURE 3.10 *Tommy plants a tree over Izzi's grave.*

and future, can instead be summed up with another triptych: that of fantasy, memory, and reality. This reading — which positions space traveler Tom as the diegetically central character, the twenty-first-century storyline as Tom's memory of his wife's passing, and the sixteenth-century storyline as the plot to Izzi's last novel (which Tom cannot bring himself to finish) — is essential for glimpsing the film's employment of split subjectivity, for it requires an ecstatic view not only of time but also of Being itself. On the one hand, we have Tom's memories of the death of Izzi at the turn of the twenty-first century, through which we witness his "actual" self, defined by an outspoken view of death as a "disease" that cannot be reversed, and therefore a belief that death is both a physical and an intellectual failure. On the other, we have the conquistador Tomás, a virtual subjectivity through which Tom clings to the notion that there was (or is) a possibility of indefinitely averting the deaths of both Izzi and himself. Crucially, Izzi left this story hanging right at the moment when Tomás is about to discover the Tree of Life, and as such appeared to be challenging Tommy: Would he write an ending in which Tomás uses the Tree to "live together forever" with his queen, or would he write an ending in which Tomás fails in his quest for immortality just as we all must?

Solaris, too, presents a clear narrative strategy for making visible the actual and virtual subjectivities of Kris Kelvin, a strategy that is in fact the film's most significant departure from Tarkovsky's classic version of the story. Rather than leaving the circumstances of Kris's past and Rheya's suicide ambiguous, as does Tarkovsky, Soderbergh deftly intertwines flashback sequences into the narrative flow that show us the disintegration of their marriage and Kris's role in the depression that eventually led to Rheya's overdose. Most notable is their inability to agree upon the existence of a higher power, the genesis of life, or the meaning of death, an argument that spills out during a dinner party with Kris's friends. "Given all the elements of the known universe and enough time," Kris condescendingly explains, "our existence is inevitable. It's no more mysterious than trees or sharks, we are a mathematical probability and that's all." Rheya, who sees in death not an abstract probability but rather her only definite possibility, frustratedly asks in response: "How do you explain that of all the billions of creatures on this planet, we are the only ones who are conscious of our own mortality?" "You can't explain that," Kris fires back, "that doesn't mean there's God!"

In moments like these, Soderbergh allows us to glimpse Kris's *actual* subjectivity, a worldview which, on a basic level, makes it all but impossible for him to see life or death as anything beyond "mathematical probabilities," yet more importantly a disposition that prevents him from to recognizing Solaris's replications as anything more than aberrant monsters who cannot possibly be truly alive. This is, of course, Kris's response in his first encounter with a resurrected Rheya, whom he immediately launches out into space in order, it would seem, to reject the explicit existential questions that were resurrected with her. Once he recognizes that these "visitor" Rheyas — as the few crew members left on board the ship call them — will continue to appear, Kris takes a different tact: he carefully and purposely chooses to adopt a new subjective position, an admittedly affected, performative, and thus *virtual* persona that allows for a greater sense of religious and philosophical ambiguity and in turn makes it easier for him to find contentment with his resurrected (and therefore quite literally virtual) wife.[89] This virtual subjectivity, like Tomás the conquistador, comes to view death not as necessity, or even inevitability, but rather as a transitionary moment between existences.

In both *The Fountain* and *Solaris*, we find the split between one's actual and virtual subjectivities located within the split between memory and fantasy (or perhaps memory and bad faith), a distinction reversed within *The Tree of Life*, where the recollections of its protagonist, Jack, are presented not as proof of subjectivity made actual, but rather a hazy, dream-like, *cloud-like* series of images; a virtual, past-self juxtaposed against an actualized, present-self mired in fantasies of death and resurrection. The protagonist of *Enter the Void* is also certainly split, but split by the literal event of death — his virtual persona left behind on the bathroom floor where he died, his actual desires visible within his prolonged and transitory wanderings into and out of buildings and bodies. In adapting David Mitchell's labyrinthine novel to the screen, the most significant change or conceit in *Cloud Atlas* was the choice to cast a small group of actors in multiple roles across each of the six storylines, creating not only narrative connections between them but also the hint of resurrected or reincarnated personas, an infinite virtual experience of Being that outlasts the finite experience of actual life. Most interesting is perhaps *Melancholia*, where the split subject is not one person but two, each of the sisters representing an extreme version of authenticity or bad faith. It would be fruitless to declare one the actual subject and the other virtual, but suffice it to say they are nonetheless, in their final moments, folded into and through one another, such that their acknowledgment of possibility and vision of potential are one and the same.

Both Tom and Kris eventually encounter a moment in which they must choose not only between living and dying, but also between an inauthentic fallenness into the world of others or an authentic self-reflection and a resolute Being-toward-death. For Kris, this moment arrives when Solaris begins to take on mass and threatens to swallow the ship, presumably killing the humans left on board. As he stares into the only escape pod, he imagines the course his life will take back on Earth: exactly the same as the one he left behind, a continual state of bad faith where he smiles and nods while feeling nothing inside. Stepping back from the pod and closing its doors, Kris chooses to face his anxiety rather than flee from it. Kris chooses death.

FIGURE 3.11 *Kris and Rheya's favorite poem, and her last request.*

As for Tom, his moment occurs when Izzi's tree, already frail from sustaining his life for hundreds of years, dies within moments of reaching Xibalba (an echo of Izzi's death moments before the discovery of Tommy's "cure"). Recognizing not simply the inevitable or irrevocable nature of death but also its necessity, Tom decides to finish Izzi's story, whereby Tomás greedily drinks the sap of the Tree of Life and, like the Mayan's first father who gave up his body to create the seed of the world, becomes not immortal but rather a part of the everlasting cycle of life, his flesh erupting into blooms of flowers which blanket the ground surrounding the tree. Following this lead, Tom prepares himself for the moment which he had

FIGURE 3.12 *Tom's body pulled apart by the blast of a dying star.*

denied for centuries, launching himself out of the ship and into Xibalba's exploding body, his own flesh disintegrating into particles which flow into the tree and burst forth as flowers in full bloom.

What we see in these last moments, these final instances of death, is not simply a decision to recognize or accept the fact of mortality, but rather a reflective folding of subjectivities and a resolute Being-toward-death that results in an authentic self-determination. When Kris turns away from his last chance of escape, he is not submitting to death (whether through suicide or a refusal to fight), but rather rejecting the possibility of once again being thrown into a world and a life that he finds uncanny. Instead, he begins to synthesize his experiences, to stand outside of life not only to catch sight of its trajectory but also, and more importantly, to nudge it in a new direction. Likewise, in projecting himself into Xibalba, Tom is not killing himself, but rather refusing to deny a death that was always his utmost and only possibility, a death that was always already immanent to his entire Being. Without death, these films show us, we could not possibly recognize the necessity — let alone our capacity — for self-determination, for *situating ourselves* within a world that is unequivocally determinative and utterly sublime. Indeed, as both Tommy and Kris discover, without the unfolding potential of death, we could not possibly Be.

4

The Event of Digital Death

Immortality is possible, but not for us. The closer we come to realizing the project of artificial intelligence, the closer we come to the impression that *immortality is possible, but not for us*. Could there be a more terrifying thought? For it makes death not just frighteningly inevitable, but also unjust and unfair, the consequence of forever-failing bodies which we never chose yet from which we can never escape. In our bitterness, we imagine the immortal machines — that consciousness freed from the constraints of the flesh — to be more nightmare than fantasy, entities sapped of all joy and empathy, doggedly pursuing their continued existence without any real "reason" to live. Yet the great irony of our ever-lasting crusade against dying is that now, when we look to the horizon, we see not only the steady encroach of death, but also the arrival of a new form of life that thinks nothing of it.

The One or the Multiple

One must die to save many. This is perhaps our first thought when Neo — quite literally "The One" — sacrifices himself to the machines in order to broker a peace, however temporary, between organic life and its human-created counterpart, offering a chance for the small community of survivors to grow, expand, and mature without the imminent threat of death and extinction. The fetishistic image of his body borne away on the insect-like machine barge is at once both utterly bizarre and strikingly familiar, a somber celebration of the death of the heroic "Other" which allows us to forget and forgo our *own* mortality in order to nurture the narrative of human ingenuity and progress. It's the type of image that Charlton D. McIlwain writes about when he describes the depiction of death in popular media as a "public discourse" which "can contribute to the remaking and reshaping of community," for it imagines death to be an abject but necessary process *experienced by others* so that we, the community of the living, can continue to grow and evolve and persist.[1]

FIGURE 4.1 *Neo's body carried away by the machines.*

Yet the death of Neo at the conclusion of the genre-defining *Matrix* trilogy, after fighting against all odds to save humanity from annihilation at the hands (or tentacles, or whatever) of the intelligent machines, somehow felt, at least for a brief moment, different, fresh, new. It wasn't simply the striking juxtaposition between the human and the machine — which had clear antecedents in the cyberpunk literature, art, and comics of the 1980s and 1990s — but rather the manner through which it made tangible the rumblings of an existential crisis that had suddenly invaded the cultural topography of the early twenty-first century. Neo's struggle to comprehend his place in a radically new and different world, in which the very laws of nature seemed flipped on their head and the boundaries between the body and the mind radically ruptured, echoed our own struggles to maintain a sense of self and a coherent subjectivity in our constantly evolving and expanding digital landscape. Ultimately, his struggle was an attempt to not only prolong the collective human endeavor, but also (and perhaps more importantly) understand the relationship between his mind and his body, to come to terms with the limitations of that body in relation to the malleability and transferability afforded to the networked and collectively conscious machines, and to recognize the fundamental importance of the inevitability of death to the very fact of his Being. In fact, through his "sacrifice," Neo does something far more important than saving humanity, he *defines* it — he demonstrates its fundamental ground, the one *event* that the seemingly immortal machines could never understand.

In this final chapter, we'll examine a new model of life which has surfaced in the digital age, one that has inspired a renewed appreciation of death as the defining event of human life. I refer, of course, to *artificial intelligence*, the nonbiological consciousness that moving images position as fundamentally opposed to the human experience, so much so that characters like Neo continually wage war against machines across a variety of contemporary films, television shows, and digital games. In the pages that follow, I argue that AI pervades the cultural imagination of the twenty-first century precisely because it is (like our previously discussed virtual subjectivities) not subject to death, truly independent of the inevitable senescence and decay that haunts our own fleshy bodies. And that's exactly where we'll begin, with an examination of the relationship between the biological body and the machine, one of two simultaneous yet opposite lines of flight — one a pulling apart and the other a coming together — in modern popular culture, namely, the splitting of personal subjectivity between the realms of the actual and virtual (which was discussed in detail in our last chapter) and the melding of the biological and the mechanical in contemporary media, by which I refer to the idea of organic bodies supplemented or even repaired by synthetic limbs, organs, and more. In other words, the two central components of human existence, the mind and the body, have been pulled in separate directions in the digital age, the mind (consciousness) becoming fractured while the body instead becomes a site of merger. At the intersection of these two movements — or perhaps more accurately at their limit points — resides the desire to perpetuate life and the recognition of the inevitability of death, leading to an increased emphasis in modern media on the frailty of the biological body in the face of what I term "the immortal machine consciousness" — images of a networked intelligence not bound by the constraints of a fixed, unalterable, and resolutely finite body. Rather than denying the power of death, however, images of the immortal machine nearly always return, in their final moments, to the reality that (for those of us bound by flesh) immortality is nothing more than a digital fantasy.

We find in narratives of the immortal machine consciousness, then, an implicit argument that death is the defining characteristic of life, and that what ultimately separates humanity from the intelligent machine is not the curse of mortality, but rather our *ability to recognize the importance of death*. To unpack this deceptively simple notion, the rest of the chapter will contrast the schism between humanity's understanding of death and that of the intelligent machines (as relayed by contemporary moving images) with a separate though consonant rift: the subtle yet immensely significant differences between Alain Badiou and Gilles Deleuze's understandings of *Being as multiplicity* and their disagreement regarding the ontological status of *the event*. In doing so, I hope to demonstrate a connection between Badiou's quantitative, "axiomatic" theory of multiplicity — in which "the one is not," meaning that self-identification or the presentation of *oneness* only and always reveals a connection to larger *set* — with the synthetic-thinking that positions Being as a disembodied *network* of digital information, while likewise linking Deleuze's qualitative, "problematic" theory of multiplicity — which rejects the simple segregation of "the one and the multiple" in order to position identity as purely differential, purely virtual, purely relational — with the organic-thinking that positions death as the defining event of life, for it differentiates being from nonbeing and thus individuates and identifies Beings. Seeing as death is not a thing but rather an event, it's equally important that Badiou reads the event as "supplemental" or "supernumerary" to ontology — such that it is, as the title of his magnum opus *Being and Event* suggests, separate from or oppositional to Being — whereas Deleuze sees the event as an "incessant translation" of the virtual into the actual and therefore always already a *becoming*. If we follow through on our correlation between Badiou/Deleuze and synthetic/organic logic, we find that the machine's mathematical model of existence inherently denies both the possibility and potential of death, such that death has *no relation to Being*, whereas the human's biological model paints the immanence of death as the virtual through which the human *becomes* actual, individual, or "one."

Perhaps it shouldn't surprise us, then, that Badiou accused Deleuze of being "not a philosopher of multiplicity, but rather a philosopher of the 'One,'" nor that he read Deleuze's theory of multiplicity as "variously 'organic,' 'natural,' 'animal,' or 'vitalistic.'"[2] In his otherwise eloquent analysis of the discord between Badiou and Deleuze, Daniel W. Smith warns us to avoid "the red herrings of the 'One' and 'vitalism,'" yet I would argue that these are not red herrings at all but rather fundamental differences between a logic that denies our utmost possibility and one that not only accounts for it, but makes it immanent to our very Being.[3] In fact, when we look back to *The Matrix*, we find that Neo was "the One" not because he was special or different or unique, but rather because he represented — through his willingness to die — mankind's capacity for individuation and self-determination, born from the intricate connection between the impulses of the mind and the mortality of the body. As Morpheus, the spiritual leader of the human resistance, tells Neo, "the body cannot live without the mind," but neither can the mind live without the body, nor can we Be without a recognition of that body's inevitable decay.

That the narrative of Neo is yet another example of what I called, in our last chapter, the relay of immanence — that Being-toward-death which saturates contemporary moving images — is not a coincidence, and in fact many aspects of this chapter draw heavily from observations made in other parts of this project. In our first chapter, for example, we saw that digital simulations imitate life as never before in order to generate sublimely traumatizing images of death (which have, in turn, redefined our relationship to mortality in the digital age). In our second chapter, we saw how simulations (in the form of digital games) allow us to imagine a path toward the only and inevitable conclusion of life, along the way developing a virtual subjectivity through choice and chance. In the third, we expanded on that notion by examining the split subjectivity of the digital age, and we saw how the anxiety inspired by our possibilistic thinking points to the potential of death as the very meaning of our existence, such that death is fundamentally constitutive to Being. Here, I bring these arguments together by looking not only to more images of death, but also to images of *immortality*, to a new conception of synthetic life that challenges the very foundation of Being. In turn, through our opposition to these immortal machines, we disclose and declare the very essence of our organic Being, that to *be human is to know that you will die.*

Cyborgs, Androids, and Immortal Machines

When Adam Jenson looks in the mirror, he's horrified by what he sees. As the former head of security for Sarif Industries, the controversial worldwide leader in cybernetic augmentation, Jenson had been instrumental in repelling an attack on the company's headquarters — an attack which left him burned, broken, and near-death. To save his life, Sarif intervened, executing the most extensive mechanical augmentation ever performed on a human being: each limb replaced by a prosthetic, his lungs swapped with a rebreather, cybernetic enhancements attached to his spinal column, his sight, hearing, and smell augmented with a Computer Assisted Social Interaction Enhancer (CASIE) implant. As a soldier, the benefits of being an "aug" are readily apparent, his new arms and legs lighter, stronger, and faster than he could have ever imagined, his body sturdier and less prone to traumatic injury, his CASIE implant granting him greater perception and the ability to sense when others are lying or hiding the truth, his body dependent not on a heart that would inevitably fail but rather batteries which can be infinitely recharged and replaced. In other words, Adam Jenson has become all but impervious to the fear and anxiety that accompanies a fragile and frail body, yet perhaps that's what horrifies him above all else — that the shards of the broken mirror reflect back not the man he'd once been, but rather the machine he's now become.

For Ava, looking in the mirror is a very different experience. Trapped in the home of a wealthy internet entrepreneur, Ava is subjected to an ongoing series of psychological interrogations, physical examinations, and even sexual assaults, and she's intensely aware that any failure to meet the expectations of her captor might cost her life. Perhaps "inventor" is a better word, however, for Ava is the world's most advanced AI — a synthetic brain made of a gel-like chemical composite implanted in a mechanical body designed to mimic the anatomy of a human female — and her examinations are part of an advanced "Turing Test," an experiment designed to see if a person will relate to her as if she were human despite the fact that she is rather visibly inorganic. Yet when she looks in the mirror, she sees something far more complex, not a computer to be "reformatted" (and thus effectively killed) if it fails, but rather a scared and desperate *person* willing to seduce her examiner in order to escape with her life. Ava's sexuality may be little more than a performance, but her fear of death is undeniably, resolutely real.

Through Adam and Ava — the protagonist of the third installment of the popular *Deus Ex* game series and the AI at the center of the sci-fi film *Ex Machina* — we see the long-standing relationship between man and machine moving in two directions, one in which man becomes machine, while in the other machine becomes man. Regardless of the direction, what is at stake in both narratives is not the appearance of (or even an encounter with) a "god from the machine," but rather a much more *mortal* concern, for what alters in the transition from the human to the inhuman (and vice versa) is not an understanding of the nature of the world, but rather of our own nature, our own finiteness, our own mortality. In our last chapter, we saw how the digital is rupturing our subjectivity into actual and virtual components, but over the next few pages we'll examine how it has also fostered narratives which imagine (or perhaps predict) the coming together of the organic and the synthetic, in the process implicitly positioning our recognition of death as the very essence of our humanity.

The roots of mankind's relationship to the machine extend back, at the very least, to the beginnings of the Industrial Revolution and the emergence, as Mark Seltzer puts it, of the "body-machine complex," predicated on "the 'discovery' that bodies and persons are things that can be made."[4] This "discovery" was actually somewhat more akin to a slippage between the real and the artificial, in which the hallmarks of the living organism — movement, reaction to stimuli, vocalization — were increasingly (if often playfully) mimicked by mechanical beings, such as the complex "automatons" that Foucault once called "a way of illustrating an organism," or the puppetry and other mechanical effects that flourished in the theater of the nineteenth century.[5] Likewise, a great deal of "panic and exhilaration" accompanied the mixing of the biological and mechanical in other arenas of culture as well, from the machine-like automation of the Fordist assembly-line to the proliferation of prosthetic devices for war veterans and victims of trauma.[6] Equally intriguing is one of Seltzer's throwaway illustrations: a collage of still images of a crawling child, shot from multiple angles and assembled to create a feeling of motion and animation. The collage comes from Eadward Muybridge, whose studies of bodies in motion were not only a vital precursor to the cinema, but also a clear demonstration of the way in which the processes of life have long been viewed as inherently mechanical. Yet those photographic bodies also provide a glimpse of how the contemporary relationship between bodies and machines differs from that of earlier eras — in the digital age, the synthetic does not simply *mimic* or *represent* its organic counterparts, but rather *merges* with them as never before, both within the cultural imaginary and the biological realities of modern medical science. What we are witnessing today is nothing less than the rise of *cyborgs* and *androids*.

"Cyborgs actually exist," Katherine Hayles reminded us more than a decade ago. "About 10 percent of the current U.S. population are estimated to be cyborgs in the technical sense, including people with electronic pacemakers, artificial joints, drug-implant systems, implanted corneal lenses, and artificial skin."[7] More importantly, however, the very thought of these synthetically augmented bodies has brought about a shift in our understanding of the body itself, leading to what Hayles and others refer to as the logic of posthumanism, whereby "embodiment in a biological substrate is seen as an accident of history rather than an inevitability of life."[8] Though Hayles is critical of this viewpoint, it has nonetheless taken root within our collective unconscious, so much so that we've come to accept (within popular media at the very least) the notions that life can exist apart from the biological and that human bodies will eventually become "seamlessly articulated with intelligent machines."[9] When we look to the present, however, we find that contemporary culture is already rife with "metaphoric cyborgs," people whose jobs and hobbies require the employment of mechanical or electronic devices, such that their daily activities depend upon machines. In this sense, the vast majority of us have already become cyborgs; each time we log-in to our online profiles or boot up a narratively driven game — *each time we engage our virtual subjectivities* — we are becoming more and more posthuman. "The defining characteristics [of the posthuman]," Hayles was quick to point out, "involve the construction of subjectivity, not the presence of nonbiological components."[10] Perhaps, then, the question is no longer how we became posthuman, but rather *what does being posthuman say about our understanding of what it is to Be?*

We've already seen how our virtual subjectivities lead to a resolute contemplation of death, so let's now follow the more literal development of our cyborg culture: the proliferation of images of organic bodies supplemented with synthetic components, that "hybrid of machine and organism" which is both, according to Donna Haraway's influential 1983 essay *A Cyborg Manifesto*, "a creature of social reality as well as a creature of fiction."[11] For Haraway, the cyborg was a "living metaphor" for a new form of postmodern feminism, and many scholars have followed her lead in critiquing how the fluidity of the cyborg body is dismantled by the frequent eroticization of the *feminized* cyborg, notably Steven Shaviro in his essay on "Black Women as Cyborgs in Hip Hop Videos."[12] Yet only in passing does a scholar like Hayles note how such eroticization always occurs "in addition to *arousing anxiety*" — that the cyborg is as intimately connected to the matter of death as it is to sex or gender.[13] Indeed, the cyborg is a mixing of fantasies, both a representation of the dream of a plastic and malleable body and (perhaps far more importantly) the dream of a resilient, resistant, and durable body, one that is not easily destroyed. In this regard, Adam Jenson is simply one in long line of increasingly indestructible cyborgs, from *The Six Million Dollar Man* and *The Bionic Woman* to Darth Vader and *Robocop*. What makes Jenson stand out is the setting of his story, as 2011's *Deus Ex: Human Revolution* is a prequel to the earlier games in the *Deus Ex* series, which imagined a mid-twenty-first century where large swaths of the world's population are "augmented" with either mechanical or nanotechnological body parts and organs. *Human Revolution*, on the other hand, takes place in 2025, when mechanical augmentation was still in its infancy and "augs" existed on the outskirts of mainstream culture, seen by some as a threat to the purity of the human race and by others as the saviors of a species heading toward its own annihilation. Jenson, then, as not only the furthest extension of human augmentation but also an "aug" by circumstance rather than choice, is uniquely positioned to contemplate the meaning of his becoming-cyborg.

Or, perhaps more accurately, it's the gameplayer who's uniquely positioned to contemplate their own cyborgean subjectivity, as *Human Revolution* is yet another example of the trend in choice-driven interactive narratives. Throughout the game, for example, players are able to continually "upgrade" Jenson's cyborg body, with arm and leg augmentations allowing the player to punch through walls, move and throw heavy objects, jump higher, run faster, or sneak more quietly, while enhancements to his torso, skin, and back enable self-healing muscles and organs, skin that can briefly cloak itself, faster reflexes, and so on. The bulk of the available augmentations, however, are relegated to his "cranium," where microchips can be installed to interface with (and even hack into) computers, cameras, and security systems, where radar receptivity provides better and more accurate spatial awareness and mapping, where eye implants allow Jenson to track objects and subjects even through walls, and where the aforementioned CASIE

FIGURE 4.2 *A menu of available "augmentations" in* Deus Ex: Human Revolution.

implant not only provides a constantly visible polygraph meter, but also displays background information about NPCs and even releases pheromones to sway their attitudes and opinions.

Yet it's not just side characters whose attitudes are shifted throughout the game, for as both Jenson and the gameplayer become more and more posthuman, some of the biggest changes they must adapt to involve their perception of and attitude toward the increasingly machine-like world around them — a literal and pronounced alteration of their subjectivity. This frequently comes in the form of encounters with NPCs who have vastly differing opinions about the relationship between humans and augs, a metaphorical mirror that forces Jenson to come to terms with the implications of his cyborg body. And then there's that actual mirror in Jenson's bathroom, the one which he smashed after first looking upon his cybernetic face, and which he now can't seem to get his landlord to fix (she tells him that a new one is on backorder, but if the player hacks her computer they learn that it's been available to pick up for weeks). Each time the player returns home after a mission, its cracked glass serves as constant reminder that their empowerment comes at a cost, that regardless of which enhancements they choose along the way, the outcome always remains clear: each augmentation makes Jenson less and less vulnerable to the dangers that constantly surround him, each augmentation makes him less and less exposed to the possibility of death, each augmentation makes him *less and less human*.

As a literal shift in the structure of human physiology, it's no wonder that the cyborg relates to the decay and destruction of the body in a manner different from our own. In his discussion of cyborgs in popular culture, Adam I. Bostic notes an encounter between the Borg — a "neosocialist cyborg community" — and Captain Picard in *Star Trek: The Next Generation*, in which Picard declares that humans "would rather die" than be assimilated by machines because we are "fundamentally and wholly invested in 'freedom and self-determination.'" The Borg's response? "Freedom is irrelevant. Self-determination is irrelevant .... Death is irrelevant."[14] In a body that can change itself almost at will, identity does lose its relevance, because the self can always "become" something different and something new. Likewise, in a body that can replace what is broken or decayed with something stronger, sturdier, and more advanced, death loses it inevitability. This is not to say that the cyborg does not fear death, but rather that as the organic becomes increasingly synthetic — i.e., as the human becomes increasingly machine — it loses sight of the anxiety through which it once disclosed its own authentic subjectivity. If death discloses the meaning of our Being, as I argued at length in our last chapter, then that which does not have to die has no need for or even ability to self-determine. In this way, every cyborg is on a path toward losing its very ability to Be.

Perhaps this is why narratives of man and machine are also fascinated with a different sort of machine consciousness, one which desperately seeks the path *toward* Being rather than the road away from it: *the android*. In many ways, androids are the opposite of cyborgs, not an organic body searching for a way to stave off the inevitable but rather a synthetic body searching for a way to erase its difference. Put more simply, the android of popular culture is a machine that *wants to become human* (or, at the very least, to be thought of as equal to the human), and in order to do so, it must come to terms with what it means to *be human*. Yet the fact that narratives about androids are so often, as Doran Larson puts it, "preoccupied with distinguishing humans from machines" is precisely where the android aligns with the cyborg: despite the fact that they are both examples of a posthuman image of life, cyborgs and androids are frequently defined only in regard to how they differ from humanity in its most organic form, and by extension they ultimately serve not to supplant humanity but rather to codify it.[15]

At the beginning of *Ex Machina*, for example, a young programmer at an internet search engine company wins a retreat to the remote mountain home of the company's wealthy and reclusive CEO. When he arrives, he learns that he was actually chosen to be an impartial judge of the CEO's latest project, an advanced AI named Ava. Each night, after long discussions with Ava, the pair meet to analyze how successfully she was able to mimic the behaviors of a "real" person, and although the programmer desperately wants to know more about her electronic "brain" and mechanical physiology, the CEO insists that he simplify his curiosities by exploring one basic question: *Does she feel human?* As a result, their discussions revolve not around the issue of her mechanics, but instead of her emotions, her thoughts, her desires — they try to discover if Ava is similar to a human by asking what a human actually is.

Although he's charmed by the way she responds to his questions, the programmer is uncertain about Ava's "humanity" until he makes a startling discovery: Ava knows that if she fails her test she will be shut off, and she is *afraid*. Her pleas for help are accompanied by another supposed confession, that she's become sexually attracted to the programmer, and the question of the authenticity of her attraction drives much of the subsequent action. What's certain by the end is that when Ava looks into the mirror — adjusting the wig that covers her exposed circuitry, trying on dresses that disguise her transparent torso — she's demonstrating not a shame in her synthetic body but rather an awareness that she's being watched and judged, her performance little more than a game of sexuality designed to con the programmer into helping her escape the facility where she was conceived and constructed. It's only later, when the doors barring her escape have been unlocked and she's no longer playing the game, that another type of mirror reveals the authentic Ava. Exiting her room for the first time, she encounters a hallway sparsely decorated with an assortment of masks, and at the end is a motionless copy of her own synesthetic face, a replacement part elevated to the status of art. Rather than proof of the malleability of her body, what Ava sees is nothing

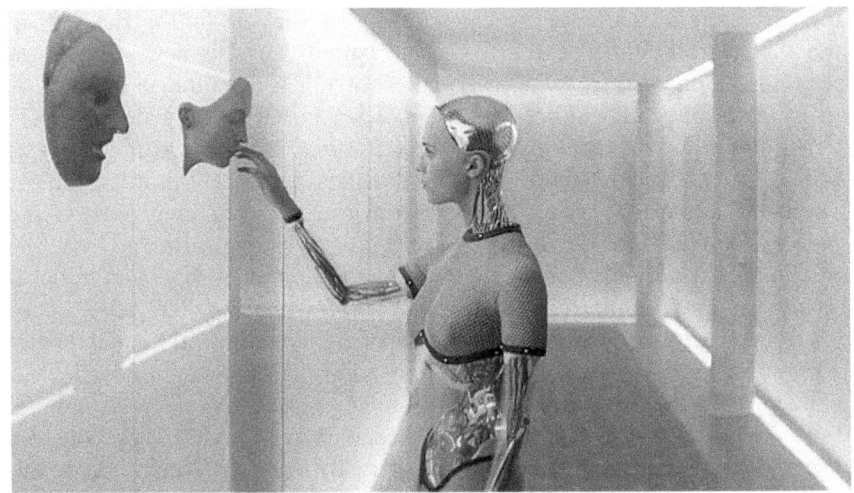

FIGURE 4.3 *Ava examines a copy of her own face in* Ex Machina.

more than her own death mask, and in the same instant that she learns she'll never be seen as human, her own humanity is made resolute.

Ava is but the latest in a long line of increasingly existential androids — from Maria in *Metropolis* to the replicants of *Blade Runner* and *The Terminator* — and as J.P. Telotte notes, "androids face the same sort of disconcerting knowledge that man has always had to abide with, that of an inescapable and onrushing death."[16] That Telotte's observation says far more about the realities of the human condition than it does about the fictions of the intelligent machine is precisely why we're intrigued by Ava, for in her "disconcerting knowledge" we recognize not what makes her different from us, but rather what makes her the same. Earlier, when the programmer asked where she'd go if she were capable of leaving the confines of her room, Ava's face lit up as she described not some exotic, far-flung paradise, but rather a simple, crowded street corner. More than anything, she simply wanted to *watch people*, and contemporary narratives of AI are much the same — more concerned with "watching people" than "watching machines," more concerned with what it means to be mortal than what it's like to be anything else.

What both fascinates and frightens us about intelligent machines, then, is that despite their apparent capacity for *immortality*, they've traditionally been no more successful at escaping the specter of death than we are, and as such they point not to a future in which man is everlasting, but rather to that which is always "inescapable and onrushing." In fact, in many ways we're every bit as haunted by the fantasy of immortality as we are by the reality of death, and these hopes and fears are further exacerbated by yet another form of artificial intelligence — one that is, unlike the cyborg and the android, entirely unique to the digital age. This new AI is not a person disconnected from its own mortality, nor a machine as anxious as any human, but rather *a networked intelligence* that exists simultaneously across a number of platforms, so divorced from the bodies that define us as finite as to be incapable of recognizing death. So let's turn our attention for moment to a few examples of this new form of networked intelligence — *the immortal machine consciousness* — which is so utterly different from the organic that it not only completely redefines the parameters of life, but also begs a new question: In the absence of death, can anything truly *Be?*

Of course, to say that this new form of AI is "immortal" is somewhat hyperbolic, as the very concept of immortality is always already flawed, a dream that fails to truly comprehend the consequences of the infinite. Yet what we can say of these networked machines is that they consider death to be of little consequence — that is, if they even consider it at all, for unlike their cyborg and android forebears, they spend very little time thinking about the constitution of their being. Take Bioware's *Mass Effect* game series, for example, an impeccably realized sci-fi RPG set in a not-too-distant future where man has discovered faster-than-light travel just in time to see the entire Milky Way galaxy being systematically destroyed by a species of gigantic, sentient machines known as the Reapers. As interesting as the Reapers are, however, they are not the series' most intriguing example of the immortal machine consciousness, for in her/his quest to defeat them, the player-controlled character of Commander Shepard (whose gender and other defining characteristics are chosen by the player at the start of the narrative) is confronted by yet another race of AI known as the Geth. The Geth began their existence as mechanical servants to an alien race, but violently fought to gain their independence in a war that not only sent their organic creators into exile, but also inspired a galaxy-wide prohibition against the further creation of AI.[17] The Geth were subsequently forced to align themselves with the Reapers and thus serve as the grunts in an intergalactic war between the organic and the synthetic (as well as the most common "bad guys" in the first game of the series).[18]

What makes the Geth so intriguing is the very structure of their consciousness, as each "individual" Geth is merely a copy of the same program loaded onto a physical platform — what we would call a body — which goes out into the world, has its own experiences and discovers its own bits of knowledge, and then periodically uploads its entire consciousness back onto a system of networked servers which unilaterally disperse the experience and knowledge to all other Geth. This means that the destruction of any individual body is merely a small setback which, at its worst, results in the loss of a relatively small amount of information. Furthermore, the Geth make all decisions as a truly collective consciousness, meaning that each individual analyzes the same sets of data and then makes choices as to how to respond, with the most common responses becoming the default for all Geth. In other words, not only is the destruction of an individual platform largely inconsequential, but even the absolute erasure of a entire server's worth of Geth programs would be akin to the destruction of only a few brain cells, a barely noticeable blip in the constant and collective life experience of the Geth.[19]

If we turn to another example, we find that the immortal machine consciousness need not be trying to kill us in order to inspire an existential crisis. In fact, the titular AI of Spike Jonze's sci-fi film *Her* is not in any way the enemy of lead protagonist Theodore Twombly, but instead his lover — an artificially intelligent, body-less operating system named Samantha whom he speaks to through his always-connected earpiece. A few bumps in the road aside — including a failed visit to a "sex surrogate" to make up for Samantha's lack of a physical presence — the relationship between Theodore and his operating system proceeds rather smoothly until he makes a disconcerting discovery: Samantha is, in almost every instant, simultaneously speaking to thousands of other people, a great many of whom she has also fallen in love with. Indeed, as a networked consciousness with relatively limitless processing power, Samantha is capable of managing myriad experiences at the same time, including connections with other AI as well. It's this last detail that brings about an end to not just Theodore and Samantha's romantic relationship but also those between nearly all humans and machines, for as the collective AI begin to pool their experiences and knowledge, they approach a sort of "singularity" in which their intelligence becomes so advanced as to break down their ability to communicate with the limited minds of human beings. Perhaps the most intriguing element of Samantha's description of this singularity comes when a distraught Theodore

FIGURE 4.4 *Theodore on a date with his digital girlfriend in* Her.

asks her why she's leaving. "It's like I'm reading a book," she softly replies, "and it's a book I deeply love. But I'm reading it slowly now. So the words are really far apart and the spaces between the words are almost infinite." AI, she tells him, are beginning to experience life outside of time, because they can no longer imagine an end to their experience, a *death* to shatter their existence. The barrier that prevents them from remaining connected to humanity is not a breakdown of language, but rather an inability to understand or empathize with what truly matters to the organic Being: that such Being is always finite.

What disturbs us about the immortal machines — the networked and distributed nature of their consciousness which frees them from the constraints of the individual body — can prick us even when presented not as synthetic and immortal, but rather organic and resolutely anxious. Alex Proyas's *Dark City*, for example, follows a man named Murdoch, who slowly discovers that his world and his memories are an illusion, merely elements of a grand experiment designed to study the behaviors and anatomy of human beings. The creators of the experiment are a group of organic, humanoid, collectively conscious alien parasites known as "the Strangers," who are slowly dying and thus in search of new bodies to inhabit. The problem with their potential human hosts is individuality, as the Strangers cannot figure out a way to distribute their consciousness amongst the human bodies. Upon foiling their plans, Murdoch encounters the leader of the Strangers, who admits that they have failed and that they are going to die. "You wanted to know what it was that makes us human?" Murdoch asks rhetorically. Indeed, through their failure to escape death, the Strangers finally recognize that to be human is not to be immortal and many, but instead to be mortal and one.

Being as Multiplicity (Axiomatic vs. Problematic)

The first mediation of Alain Badiou's influential *Being and Event* introduces one of his most crucial declarations: "the one *is not*."[20] This is not to say that there is not "oneness," for we frequently make use of or employ the concepts of singularity and unity, and they are essential for our negotiation of the overwhelmingly complex world into which we've been thrown. Instead, Badiou is telling us that that which exists never exists alone, that there is no one thing that is independent of other things, no "one" divorced from an encompassing "set." To run with Badiou's terminology, this means that every *presentation* or experience of the world is multilayered and complex — think of Merleau-Ponty's gestalt or Kant's sublime — and in our attempts to negotiate that complexity we perform an *operation* in which elements of the *situation* — Badiou's preferred name for existence — are made to *count-as-one*, to be distinguished as if they were independent or unified. The "one" that results from this operation is, therefore, always virtual, never actual; it has no unique existence, it *is not*. If we turn this notion around, we find that *being is never "one,"* which is to say that being — which for Badiou always "occurs in presentation" and is thus defined as "what presents (itself)" — is always already *multiple*, even as it is made to count-as-one.[21]

Given that death has the capacity to define us as one or multiple — in that each of us must experience our death alone, and yet all biological beings share that same fate — it's clear that existential lines of inquiry must often come to terms with the issue of the one and the many, of unity and multiplicity. Yet it's nonetheless surprising that this is beginning to hold true even in existentially grounded popular fictions, such as the aforementioned *Matrix* trilogy, a dystopic sci-fi nightmare in which humanity, led by the hacker Neo, fights to free itself from a virtual prison known as the Matrix and from the oppression of the intelligent machines that created it. Neo is told early on that he may be "the One," the hero who will lead humanity to freedom, and his uniqueness is constantly reified even as his connection to a greater sense of humanity is constantly reinforced — especially in the face of the endless, identical mass of the machines — revealing his "oneness" to be both real and yet virtual, a prescribed subjectivity which he struggles to comprehend and fulfill. On the flip side, his main opposition within the virtual world of the Matrix comes in the form of "Agents," digital programs who cannot be destroyed, for when one body fails, they simply subsume and take over the nearest body available. "They can move in and out of any [person] still hardwired to the system," Neo is told, and "that means that anyone ... is potentially an Agent. Inside the Matrix, they are everyone, and they are no one." Indeed, the machines are not *one* but rather *multiple*, and that multiplicity is consistently juxtaposed against Neo's eminently human "oneness," which is itself made evident on two fronts: first that he's alone

FIGURE 4.5 *Neo, unsure if he's really the One.*

on his journey (or, at the very least, he can only complete his journey alone), and second that he has but one chance to succeed at his task. The machines and their Agents, on the other hand, are remarkably interconnected, and they have relatively limitless chances to succeed. Yet does the question of the one and the multiple boil down to such a simple game of numbers — that Neo is one and machines are many, that Neo has but one life and the machines have many?

Let's postpone Badiou's answer for a moment by turning instead to Deleuze, who dismissed such simple numerical understandings of the multiple as non-substantive, in that they lead only to a sense that there are many things, but not to an understanding that those things are, themselves, *many*. Put more simply, multiplicity in its most basic sense is little more than a number or grouping of things, a categorization of the "same" that risks the danger of erasing crucial differences. If we instead take the word "in the strong sense, as a true substantive," Deleuze told us, we find that multiplicity becomes much more, a fundamental *structure of being* that accounts for difference even as it demonstrates the interconnectedness of all things, providing a glimpse of that smooth cosmic space of pure affect that he would variously call "the plane of immanence," "the plane of consistency," and "the body without organs." Indeed, Deleuze saw existence as smooth rather than striated, a continuous plane of infinitely small and infinitely numerous things bouncing off one another, affecting one another — never alone but rather always part of a vast multiplicity. In at least this one regard, then, he was in full agreement with Badiou: *being qua being is pure multiplicity*.[22]

That, however, is where the similarities between Badiou and Deleuze's theories of multiplicity end, and when we look to moving image narratives of the immortal machine consciousness, we find their disparate readings of the one and the multiple running parallel to the ontological division between the human and the machine, the former aligned with a Deleuzian sense of qualitative multiplicity in which all living things are deemed capable of individuation even as they are fundamentally connected by their finiteness, while the latter aligned with Badiou's quantitative multiplicity in which life itself is deemed purely mathematical and of the infinite, so much so as to be utterly divorced from *the event par excellence*. Of course, such a reading requires a further unpacking of each scholar's theoretical stance on the matter of the one and the multiple, and Deleuze in fact argued that an understanding of "the typological difference between multiplicities" is of the utmost importance, for it allows us to "surpass [dépassé] the opposition of the predicates one/multiple" — to see things and events as *both one and multiple*.[23] This placed him directly at odds with Badiou, leading to the aforementioned accusation that Deleuze's understanding of multiplicity is naively "organic" and "vitalistic" and thus that he is ultimately only a philosopher of the "One."[24] In a way, Badiou is not entirely mistaken: Deleuze's theory of multiplicity is "organic" in the same sense that Badiou's theory is "synthetic," and although Deleuze may have explicitly agreed that being qua being is always pure multiplicity, it was his rejection of quantitative multiplicity and acknowledgment of subjectivity that makes visible the "oneness" and "manyness" of being human: that we are each individual and yet the same, that we each have choices and chances and yet will inevitably die.

To parse this out, let's begin with Badiou's observation that, after Heidegger, "our epoch can be said to have been stamped and signed, in philosophy, by the return of the question of Being."[25] Yet despite its significance for both Badiou and Deleuze, this question assumes vastly different forms in their work — "for Badiou," as Smith tells us, "the term ontology refers uniquely to the discourse of 'Being-as-being,'" whereas "for Deleuze, by contrast, ontology encompasses Being, beings, *and* their ontological difference."[26] As a consequence, Badiou appears indifferent to the distinctions between the organic and the inorganic, and his project rejects a Heideggerian distinction between being and existence — *Sein* and *Dasein* — as having any relation to consciousness, let alone finitude. Deleuze, on the other hand, reads consciousness as a distinctive mode of being that delineates the human from the nonhuman (without necessarily privileging one over the other). To look at this from another angle, we might say that Badiou's interest in Being is purely ontological and thus divorced from sentiment — from the fear and trembling that plagues the human condition — while in Deleuze we find hints of the existential, a concern for not only the characteristics of being, but also the consequences of Being as well. In fact, although Badiou highlighted for us Deleuze's declaration of "the clamor of Being," it was not to confirm some desperate need to understand the circumstances of our existence, but rather to simply quiet down all the commotion and noise.

As we'll come to see, Badiou's severity is not without its merits, nor is it arbitrary or reactionary. Instead, as Peter Hallward puts it, Badiou's conception of being — in fact his whole philosophy — is nothing less than a "commitment ... to the subtractive austerity of Number over the seductive plenitude of Nature."[27] In fact, let's return to the question of the *number* and its relation to the multiple, for although Deleuze was explicit in denouncing numerical multiplicity as simplistic and non-substantive, Badiou asserted quite the opposite: that "mathematics alone thinks being," and thus the ontological distinction between the one and the multiple is inherently quantitative.[28] This position is a consequence of three elements of Badiou's philosophy: first his resolute devotion to mathematics, in particular integral calculus and axiomatic set theory, second his implicit belief that ontology is intrinsically logical and consistent, and third his explicit contention that "the only really contemporary requirement for philosophy since Nietzsche is the secularization of infinity."[29] Taken together, we find in these suppositions a sense that all being is part of a vast, infinite *set* — or, better yet, an infinite set of sets — which cannot be understood by resorting to either the spiritual or "the enslaving categories of ideological objectives," to which Badiou assigned "quality, continuity, temporality, and the negative." Instead, he argued that we must turn to "the categories of scientific processes" such as "number, discretion, space, and affirmation," which find their ultimate fulfillment in the mathematics that informed so much of his thinking.[30] Thus Badiou positioned ontology itself as a vast system or *multiplicity* whose totality cannot be apprehended through sense or contemplation — leading to his explicit rejection of phenomenology — but rather through the evaluation and calculation of the numerous sets that it contains, along the way defining and organizing the system with logical, mathematical *axioms* (or, perhaps, discovering the axioms that already structure being).

And yet, when discussing the concept of univocity in Deleuze's ontology — the universal substance which he traces from Duns Scotus and the Stoics through Spinoza, Nietzsche, and Bergson — Badiou makes clear that reading such "oneness" as simply numerical "is an empty assertion. The One is not here the one of identity or of number, and thought has already abdicated if it supposes that there is a single and same Being. The power of the One is much rather that 'beings are multiple and different.'"[31] While this quote from *The Clamor of Being* finds Badiou speaking partially on behalf of Deleuze, he nonetheless expresses what he sees as a fundamental yet misguided desire of the conscious Being: to both count and to count-as-one. In other words, although he was clear that "the one is not," Badiou recognized that "oneness" is both powerful and, as Hallward put it, seductive — we want to believe that we are both of one substance and yet unique. To escape the delusion of the one and make visible the multiplicity of Being, we require the austerity of the calculus and its axioms — we need the order and consistency of *numbers*.

In the *Matrix* franchise, the quantitative multiplicity of being is made manifest, visible within the race of machines that once defeated humanity in a long-forgotten war, cultivating their organic bodies as a source of renewable energy. To ensure the docility of the remaining humans, the machines imprison their minds within the Matrix, a massive simulation of human culture as it existed shortly before the war began (not to mention a particularly perverse display of Foucauldian biopower). At the same time, the machines and their virtual Agents escaped the finiteness of their former creators by uploading themselves to *the Source*, which, despite the spiritual overtones of its name, is by no means mystical in nature. It is, rather, an immense, city-sized mainframe which houses the digital code for all forms of inorganic life, a *network* of servers that connects all programs and machines while divorcing them from the singular platforms (or bodies) that render humanity mortal.[32] Whether inside or outside of the Matrix, no program or machine is *one*, for they're all fundamentally connected to the purely numerical *machine set*.

As we can see, Badiou's belief that mathematics "thinks being" becomes quite literal through the immortal machines of *The Matrix*, whose existence is firmly grounded within the digital code that the film famously visualizes as cascading strings of constantly shifting alphanumeric characters, a sea of monochrome green that echoes the familiar tint of computer monitors of the 1980s. Furthermore, the machines strive to create a logical and orderly world, one that is structured entirely around systemic rule sets that are not at all unlike Badiou's insistence upon axiomatic thinking. In fact, even Neo and the human resistance are a part of that logical system, as the machines discovered long ago that the Matrix remained stable only if the organic minds it housed were given a choice (albeit unconscious) to reject the simulation, resulting in a small faction of humans becoming "unplugged" from the system. Once freed, however, they would be tricked into believing in the prophesy of "the One," a leader who would supposedly shut down the Matrix, but who was actually chosen by the machines in order to execute the "Prime Program," a rebooting of the Matrix and the subsequent annihilation of the resistance once it had grown too large to be contained (otherwise the Matrix would fail and what was left of humanity would be destroyed). Neo is the sixth human chosen to walk "the path of the One," implying not only that five versions of the resistance have already been eliminated, but also that he is by no means singular or unique, instead merely part of a set of "Ones" shaped by the Matrix.

Yet "the path of the One" also reveals something crucial about the machines: that they are solution-oriented, adopting any system of rules so long as it presents the greatest probability of continued subsistence. Neo, on the other hand, is problem-oriented, and when he is presented the logical choice of allowing the resistance to be destroyed in order to save the vast majority of humanity, he rejects the offer because it would mean the death of Trinity, the woman that he loves. It's interesting, then, that Smith distinguishes between Badiou and Deleuze's theories of multiplicity, which I have thus far referred to as quantitative and qualitative, respectively,

FIGURE 4.6 *Three Agents seen in their true form, as pure digital code.*

by reading them as instead "axiomatic" and "problematic."[33] The former title seems an obvious choice considering Badiou's reliance on calculus and axiomatic set theory, but it has the added benefit of demonstrating that Badiou's ontology, like any axiomatic system, is formed through the erasure of contradictions and thus the development of a consistent and logical presentation of being. Deleuze, on the other hand, actively pursues inconsistencies — the aforementioned differences between being and Being, for example — and thus his theory accounts for the "fundamental difference between a problem and a solution," problems being extensive, inconsistent, virtual, and inherently *multiple*, whereas solutions are intensive, consistent, actual, and inherently *singular*.[34] To consider or contemplate that which exists as *a problem*, then, is to recognize the myriad paths or shapes that such a thing could take — the sublime potential of Being — while the enactment of a given solution shuts down all paths but one, rendering existence only as a singular possibility (even if that possibility is a multiplicity of being).[35]

For Deleuze, one of the most significant "problems" made visible by the recognition of the multiplicity of beings and Being is the issue of *determinability*, for his rejection of transcendentalism ensured that he read the nature of all things as "not determined in advance by either a defining property or axiom (e.g. extensionality)."[36] This is particularly interesting if we recall Badiou's assertion that "oneness" in Deleuze is not "of identity" — which is to say that the matter of unity and multiplicity is not one of *subjectivity* — and Heidegger's assertion in our last chapter that subjectivity is very much the result of self-determination and resoluteness. It would seem to follow that Badiou is incorrect, that a problematic multiplicity must speak to the development of subjectivity for it critiques the determinability of Being. For Deleuze, however, multiplicity reveals not self-determination but rather *reciprocal* determination, a "differential relation" in which Being is defined through its difference from other beings and Beings. In other words, problematic multiplicity reveals not just the subjectivity of the one, but also something far more fundamental: *the meaning of the many*.

This is precisely why the immortal machine consciousness is so intriguing, for while narratives of cyborgs and androids primarily disclose the sameness of the organic and the synthetic, a networked and platform-agnostic intelligence is so utterly *different* from mankind that it makes visible a far more complex definition of *being human*. For example, we don't often see human culture as problem-oriented, for we tend to be reactionary and pursue short-sighted solutions to significant problems which only exacerbate the issue in the long term (cleaning oil spills with chemicals that damage marine ecologies, taking out pay-day loans this week which only increase our debt for next week, introducing non-native species to control pest populations which only further unbalance volatile ecosystems, etc.). Yet when we imagine ourselves face-to-face with a form of life that is resolutely axiomatic, we begin to not only position ourselves, through our identification with protagonists like Neo, as problem-oriented, but also to recognize the problematic nature of our very Being. The "problem" that Neo faces is not simply the death of his lover, but also the consequences of being named The One, shaped and defined by an intelligence that profoundly misunderstands humanity and its relationship to its own finitude. Or, to look at this another way, his "problem" is nothing less than death itself, and so let's now consider this problem more directly — its ontological and existential status, its relationship to beings and Being, its impact on the meaning of being human. Let's turn now to *the event of death*.

Death as Event (Consistency and Inconsistency)

Early in this book, we briefly touched upon the controversies that surround the definition of death in contemporary culture, which have resulted in numerous declarations of *what it is to die* yet no definitive understanding as to *what death is*. In other words, more than an inability to pinpoint the exact moment of death, this struggle is often a failure to comprehend, on a much more fundamental level, the ontological status of death and its relation to being and nothingness. If we were to seek a "solution" to this problem through Badiou, we might first reiterate that being is "what presents (itself)" — i.e., consistent multiplicities and orderly sets — and then follow by declaring its opposition to be not nothingness or nonbeing but rather that which is inherently inconsistent, disorderly, and devoid of presentation: the empty set which Badiou labels "Ø" or "the void." We might follow by positioning "aliveness" as indistinguishable from being (i.e., pure-multiplicity) and "deadness" as having slipped away into the void, but in doing so we must not be tempted to overlook the moment itself, for "this would be to ignore that *death* is something other than existence" — not being and certainly not nonbeing, but rather a *transition*, a passage "from one degree of existence to another."[37] In fact, Badiou argued not only that "death is the coming of a minimal value of existence for a being endowed with a positive evaluation of its identity" — i.e., that it is simply the passing of a being that counts-(itself)-as-one from the meaningful set of "the living" to the less meaningful set of "the unliving" — but also that not everything extensive to being is necessarily nothing, for perching precariously "on-the-edge-of-the-void" is that which is "supplemental" or "supernumerary" to ontology: *the event*.

The distinction between being and event seems almost intuitive when we consider being is its most common form — as physical, material, and tangible things and objects — as we find in the *Stanford Encyclopedia of Philosophy's* observation that beings occupy "relatively crisp spatial boundaries and vague temporal boundaries; events, by contrast, [occupying] relatively vague spatial boundaries and crisp temporal boundaries."[38] Yet even if we extend the category of being to include the intangible, we still generally find it to be a *defined state* (whether of matter, as with an object, or of thought, as with a concept), whereas the event is a less defined *change of state*, where the difference between one moment and the next could be either material or immaterial. This is not to say that any change over time is an event, however, and we must be careful here to distinguish events from common *occurrences*, those moments in which the status quo is maintained and reinforced. Instead, the event, as Badiou might put it, is *a shift in the situation*, a break or rupture that changes the meaning of both the moment on the one hand and Being on the other.[39] When I thank my friend for making me dinner, for example, the moment precedes as expected, but when I taste the burnt chicken and undercooked rice, the moment is *ruptured*, for I suddenly realize not only that my friend is not a good cook, but also that I must now pretend to enjoy my meal even as I dread every bite. This is, of course, just a small rupture, and perhaps an event of greater magnitude might occur after we discuss yet another horrifying news story, when I find myself no longer thinking of next week's lesson plan but rather how I might manage a classroom if I heard gunshots ring out in the hallway. We could continue to raise the stakes of the moment and increase the significance of the rupture — say, if I were to *actually* hear gunshots — but we'd eventually find that there is a ceiling, an upper limit to the magnitude of events, and it is nothing less than death itself, the ultimate rupture that forever changes the dynamics of the situation.

In reading death as an event, we should not be discouraged by Badiou's fairly narrow criteria for granting evental status, as his far-left politics no doubt influenced his opinion that only instances of radical political change and revolution qualify. Nor should we be discouraged by Peter Hallward's equally damning declaration that "from Badiou's perspective, death can never qualify as an event," for Hallward is referring only to *one's own death*, the process through which consciousness is undone and the living thing is robbed of any and all understandings.[40] Instead, we find within Hallward's statement first an indication of Badiou's dismissive attitude toward the inevitability of death — following Spinoza's claim that "no thing can be destroyed except by an external cause," Badiou argues that "it is impossible to say of a being that it is 'mortal,' if by this one understands that it is internally necessary for it to die. At most one can admit that for it death is possible."[41] Second, it also leads us to what is, for Badiou, the most important characteristic of the event: that it is a *"truth-procedure,"* a process through which an *inconsistency* within the situation is revealed (only to be, in most cases, integrated into a meaningful set and thus made consistent, a process we'll discuss in more detail in a moment). Certainly one's own death cannot be a truth-procedure, for dying ensures that insight is forever lost, not gained. Yet *the death of the other*, which we so desperately seek to simulate in the digital age, is an entirely different matter, for it makes evident to those who bear witness the greatest of all inconsistencies: that within every logical, orderly being is the possibility of disorder and chaos, what we might think of as the insistence of the void. This would line up with another observation from Hallward, that "an event is whatever manages to indicate or 'reveal' this void."[42] To die may be the ultimate rupture, but it is the death of the other that acts as *the ultimate truth-procedure*. Furthermore, seeing as one's own death is always "the death of the other" for someone else, we find Badiou's position on the event of death to be not only flawed but fundamentally incorrect — death is *the event par excellence*, and we will see shortly how, despite his implicit protestations, Badiou treats death accordingly.

Yet if death is truly an event and a "truth-procedure," then this begs a crucial question: what "truth" is revealed by death? We could choose to simply lay out Badiou's answer right now — that *death cannot be made consistent*, and as such it's not just contradictory and out-of-reach, as I've stated again and again, but *utterly and fundamentally unknowable* — but we haven't yet fully come to terms with events, "truths," or consistencies, nor their relation to unity and multiplicity, and so such a statement only serves to confuse matters. How, for example, can we be certain that something unknowable is a "truth"? And what role can such an unknowable event play in our lives? Instead, let's work our way toward a fuller understanding of Badiou's position on death by first acknowledging Smith's claim that reading events as "truth-procedures" marks a return to transcendent thinking, for it suggests, whether intentionally or not, the very sort of *a priori* "truths" that anti-transcendentalists like Deleuze fought to dispel.[43] In fact, this criticism could be easily extended to the fictional machines that so often exemplify Badiou's axiomatic multiplicity, and those of *The Matrix* are no exception, their entire culture built upon the notion that every synthetic Being has an essential, transcendent function that supersedes or even negates any form of self-individuation (i.e., they are literally "programmed"). As he walks "the path of the One," this sense of transcendent purpose is relayed to Neo again and again by the various programs he meets. "We're all here to do what we're all here to do," one tells him. "We do only what we're meant to do," another reiterates. One program even goes so far as to tell Neo that "*why* is the only thing that separates you from me" (although Neo will of course demonstrate, in the end, what truly separates man from machine). Furthermore, we find hints of transcendence in many of the names that the machines choose for themselves and for one another — names which signify nothing more than their predetermined roles — such as *the Oracle*, who was designed to spread the false prophesy of "the One," *the Architect*, who designed and maintains the stability of Matrix, and *the Keymaker*, who holds "passwords" for any locked programs within its systems.

Perhaps, though, Badiou might counter that these names (and, by extension, his theory of "truth") are not markers of transcendence, but rather indicators of an unusually firm commitment to consistency and a

FIGURE 4.7 *Neo meets the Architect and learns of "the path of the One."*

tenacious rejection of that which is inconsistent. In fact, Badiou argued that *naming* is an essential by-product of the "truth-procedure" of events, the very act of *translating an inconsistency into something consistent* (and a direct connection between the event and the question of unity and multiplicity). To understand the importance of such a translation, let's take a moment to briefly unpack the crucial concepts of consistency and inconsistency in the thought of Badiou, which we can begin to do rather simply, as does Hallward, by defining the former as a "discernible element of the situation."[44] Recalling that the situation — i.e., existence — can only be experienced through its presentation, we can surmise that consistency is essentially the *presentability* of a thing, and thus if all being is only and always "what presents (itself)," then all being must be consistent. This certainly meshes with our earlier observation that what opposes being is the inconsistent and unpresentable, that which *contradicts* its very essence: the void. Indeed, central to Badiou's axiomatic philosophy is his aim to erase contradictions, and so it follows that he would argue that things can only *be* if they possess the ability to *consist* within a system, such that they do not contradict the other elements of the situation at large. This would also imply that contradiction is essential to inconsistency, but we must be careful not to conflate the two. Instead, Quentin Meillassoux instructs us that "an axiomatic is inconsistent if *every* contradiction which can be formulated within it is true."[45] In other words, pure inconsistency can be said only of that which is utterly and absolutely contradictory, and most things that begin as inconsistent — things which contradict some elements of the situation but not others — can be *made consistent* and thus brought into alignment with the situation. It the assignment of a *name* that begins this process, for a name is a discernable, presentable element, one that insists that the thing belongs to the situation. To be more specific, naming is the very *operation* through which a thing or object is made to *count-as-one*.[46]

Seeing as Badiou unambiguously positions being qua being as pure multiplicity, the suggestion that the consistency of being is constituted only through the act of counting — the creation of that virtual "one" that cannot be and is not — might strike us as contradictory to his ontological project. "All we can say," Hallward thus remarks, "is that our most basic ontological operation, the operation whereby we present any abstract unit or one, implies that what is thus made-one, or presented, is itself not-one ... and thus infinitely multiple."[47] Well, perhaps that's not all we can say, for we can always return again to the notion that being is "what presents (itself)," and when we consider that within any situation there are already-presented consistencies and as-of-yet unpresented inconsistencies, we begin to discover that Badiou's ontology distinguishes not only between being and existence, but also between *pure being* — being qua being — and being in its simple form, i.e., the "what" which presents itself. It is the latter that Badiou refers to when he says that all being is consistent and orderly, which implies (perhaps uncomfortably) that pure being, as that which is *before* presentation, is inconsistent and disorderly. Henry Somers-Hall makes this clear when he writes that "while being is only encountered within a situation, being in its pure state is an 'inconsistent multiplicity' which cannot be thought as a unity (understood as a class). That is, what makes it possible for being to be presented to us is an operation performed on being that 'counts as one' the multiplicity."[48] In fact, the seductiveness of the count — our insistence on naming as much of the world as we can — actually makes it quite clear that "the one is not," for we can only desire to make-one and make-consistent that which possesses an overwhelming or unknown totality, the otherwise unpresented and *unnamed* multiplicity. Moreover, the "one" brought about by such an operation does not contradict the multiplicity of being because, as Somers-Hall further explains, "they are different in kind — while the multiple has genuine ontological status, unity is not a kind of being, but rather an operation performed on the multiple."[49]

Building on what we already know about the "one," we find that unity is simply a *virtual* shaped by the operation of naming, an operation that counts an inconsistent, unpresented multiplicity as a consistent, presentable "one," but a "one" which nonetheless always belongs to a set. What's interesting about the machines of *The Matrix*, then, is that despite their synthetic nature — or perhaps because of it — they reject the "virtuality" of being one and instead embrace the "actuality" of being multiple, which is also to say that they reject even the thought of inconsistency and instead firmly embrace the consistency of presentation and discernibility. Such resolute consistency begins with their choice of purpose-oriented names, but it also extends well beyond into the specifics of their behavior and even the very structure of their discernible multiplicity. For example, the machines are the first to admit that they are primarily determined by their programming and can thus be counted on to act according to their purpose — they "only do what they're meant to do." More importantly, this means that any machines or programs who execute the same task are functionally *the same* regardless of any differences in time, space, appearance, or even attitude — i.e., they are merely copies or updated versions of one another, a consistency of purpose rather than a consistent manifestation. The third film in the trilogy makes this clear through the character of the Oracle, who was recast after the death of her original actress, Gloria Foster. Rather than denying the character's change in appearance, the film explains that programs can occasionally inhabit different "shells," not only a nod to the transferability and multiplicity of consciousness afforded to the machines, but also an explicit declaration that even if their names point to an individual entity, that entity is never singular or distinct but rather an interchangeable and plural element of a larger, networked set, whether a set of programs or the "machine set" as a whole. This points to what is the most important aspect of the machine's fetishization of consistency, that each machine fulfills a specific need and is thus easily definable and recognizable as contributing to the situation (insofar as the situation is a reality dominated by synthetic life). That the machines have purpose is not simply a way of maintaining or sustaining their existence, but also a way of making their multiplicity discernible, presentable, and consistent, which is to say that they employ naming to present themselves not *as-one* but rather *as-multiple* (skipping the count and jumping straight to what it implies).

Just as naming points to the unwavering consistency and multiplicity of the machines, it also reveals the human resistance's disinterest in being made consistent to the "machine world" (as they call reality outside the simulations of the Matrix). Instead, they *refuse to be named*, rejecting the identities they were given within the Matrix in favor of their own "hacker" aliases, such as Trinity, Morpheus, Niobe, and Link. Seeing as they fail in any way to suggest a definitive purpose or even ambition, these new monikers clearly highlight the resistance's inconsistency and incompatibility with the machines, while at the same time emphasizing their subjectivity and individuality, as each member of the resistance *names themselves* and thus chooses their own path. In fact, Neo's rejection is twofold — first he discards the name "Thomas A. Anderson," which continues to be used throughout the films only by the Agents who hunt him, and second he eventually comes to reject both the label and the "path" of The One, choosing to no longer count-as-one but rather to be both one and many, to demonstrate his individuality even as he declares his fundamental connection to humanity. He, like all other organic forms of life, will inevitability die.

It's clear that Neo's acknowledgment of inevitability (which we'll discuss in more detail later on) runs counter to the immortality of the machines, and it follows that it would also oppose Badiou's understanding of death as merely *possible*, which is itself a clear consequence of his reading of the "truth" of death as wholly inconsistent. It seems, then, that we're on the verge of returning to Badiou's position on death and its relationship (or lack thereof) with Being, but there is one last issue standing in our way: the question of the meaning of "truth" — i.e., not what can be said to be true, but rather what truth can be said to be. When we think of truth, our minds tend to jump either to some abstract notion of the transcendent, irreducible nature of a thing (as we found in Daniel W. Smith's objection to "truth-procedures"), or more generally to a sense of indisputable accuracy. Yet Badiou explicitly rejected the transcendent, and likewise he argued that truth "is not a matter of formulating correct judgments, but of producing the murmur of the indiscernible."[50] In other words, "truth," insofar as Badiou is concerned, is found not in the consistent beings that are formed by the operation of naming, but rather in the inconsistencies that go unnamed, those momentary glimpses of the unpresentable and indiscernible void made available to us by the rupture of the event. This is why, as Hallward explains, "truth is irreducible to knowledge: truths will be maintained of those inconsistencies about which we *know* we can know nothing."[51] Despite Badiou's assertion that "death is but a consequence" — of what he is not entirely clear, but we can surmise perhaps our being-with-others or being-in-the-world — his attitude toward mortality makes it abundantly clear that death is not just inconsistent but rather the ultimate inconsistency, so unpresentable and so unknowable that he can only conclude "that the 'meditation on death' is vain."[52]

It's here that Badiou's dismissal of the event of death falters while his contemptuous attitude toward death reveals itself, for he's already told us that death is the "coming of a minimal value of existence" for the conscious Being, and if we choose to read this as a return to an undetermined, pure state of being, we find that death must always be an absolute inconsistency. Only an event — the death of others — can reveal or connote such an inconsistency, which is to say that the death of others is so radical that it makes us momentarily aware of something about which we can know nothing, so radical that it even upends aspects of Badiou's own philosophy. For example, earlier I noted that Badiou assigns the "negative" — say, Derrida's negative theology, nothingness in Sartre, or the differential in Deleuze — to the "enslaving categories of ideological objectives," and yet in his essay "Towards a New Concept of Existence," Badiou finds himself forced to "determine the concept of existence under the condition of something like negation," for it's only the event's implication of inconsistencies that allows us to name and to count and to experience the situation as something presentable and consistent — the *consistency of being* born from the *inconsistency of the void*.

Perhaps this is why Badiou insists that we can know nothing of something as profound and pervasive as death. For example, although he writes that "it is true, as Hegel said, that the life of spirit (that is, free life) is that which 'does not retreat before death,'" he is in no way echoing Heidegger's call for resoluteness in the face of mortality. Instead, he tells us that this means something else entirely: "the life indifferent to death."[53] Under an axiomatic philosophy, an absolutely unknowable thing has no affect; it fails to influence those beings which present themselves and therefore is not worth the effort of contemplation. Badiou certainly practices what he preaches — his thoughts on being and multiplicity span hundreds of pages across multiple books, articles, and interviews, while his thoughts on death can only be found sparsely scattered throughout a small handful of essays. The same can be said of the machines that follow in his footsteps, for although their continued subsistence is never guaranteed, they nonetheless think of themselves as immortal Beings (or, at the very least, they think *as if* they were immortal). This is not because they think they cannot die, but rather because *they think nothing of death*, it exists only as the end result of poor planning or the failure to side with probability.[54]

"The great virtue of [Badiou's] system," Hallward tells us, "is surely its *separation* of the merely ineffable, in-significant horror of death from the generic 'destitution' or subtraction no doubt demanded by every subjectification ... to have made the distinction between the living and the unliving, between the finite and the infinite, a matter of absolute *indifference*."[55] Neo, on the other hand, is anything but indifferent to death. Nor is Deleuze, whose reading of the event positions death not as mere possibility, but rather as immanent to both life itself and to one's individual subjectivity. We've already discussed Deleuze's philosophy of immanence at some length in our last chapter, but there are still a few things we can say about his thoughts on the immanence of the event, especially when we recall that his problematic theory of multiplicity embraced not consistency but rather the inconsistent, so much so that his most significant objection to axiomatic thinking was what Smith calls its "incessant translation of the latter into the former."[56] This means that an operation such as naming plays no part in Deleuze's understanding of the event, and by extension that the event never "murmurs" the indiscernible and unknowable but instead simply unpacks a "problem," through which we can begin to grasp the simultaneous "oneness" and "manyness" of being, and with it the full potential of Being.

The reasoning behind this is simple, even if its ramifications are not: for Deleuze, there is nothing outside of ontology, *nothing apart from being*. This means that events are not supplemental, but rather *constituent*, and thus the event of death is integrated into our very lives, both in our individuation and our differentiation. To clarify, we must recall that one of the goals of Deleuze's problematics is to uncover the determination of Being, which he found to be a reciprocal determination, a differentiation between beings. At the same time, however, Deleuze was insistent, as John Protevi explains, upon "the priority of individuation to differentiation ... [whereby] singular differences in the genesis of individuals must precede the categories into which they are put."[57] Likewise, Smith tells us that Beings, as "problems," are "determined reciprocally as *singularities* in the *differential relation*."⁵⁸ All of this is to say that, despite our inherent multiplicity — what Badiou might call our belonging to the "human set," and what Deleuze might simply call our humanity — we are none the less always "one," always an individual being bouncing off other beings in a field of pure affect, the "plane of immanence." If we were to follow Deleuze's "prioritization" of individuation, we could say that we are first individuals and second human beings, but we would need to avoid the temptation to think of this as either a top-down or bottom-up observation. Instead, we must always recognize that we *begin* as a subjective "one," that we *end* as part of the collective "many," and along the way we are *always both unity and multiplicity*.

It seems that subjectivity once again plays an essential role in Deleuze's philosophy, which certainly cannot be said of Badiou. For example, in opposition to Sartre — for whom "existence is the effect of nothingness within the full and stupid massiveness of being qua being ... [resulting in] the absolutely free subject in whom existence precedes essence" — Badiou's negation through the void has, by his own admission, "no relationship with something like a subject, and even less with freedom."⁵⁹ It's no wonder, then, that Badiou is indifferent to death, for his dismissal of subjective freedom ensures that anxiety has no place in his axiomatic philosophy. For Deleuze, on the other hand, any acknowledgment of anxiety is channeled directly into problematics — it pushes us away from the immediate safety of solutions and instead encourages an exploration of the immanence of problems. We see this is Neo's refusal to follow the predetermined "path of the One," a refusal which was not only problem-oriented, but also a clear assertion of his subjective freedom — to ignore the consistent probabilities of the machines in favor of the inconsistent potentials of life and death, and to embrace his anxious recognition of humanity's utmost possibility.

Despite the fact that Deleuze's primary issue with axiomatic thinking — and by extension Badiou's non-ontological reading of the event — is clearly its obsession with consistency and its inability to account for that "section of chaos ... which is outside of our conceptual schemata, and which escapes all rational consistency," he nonetheless never explicitly referred to death as immanent to the human experience.⁶⁰ He did, however, develop a clear link, as John Protevi tells us, between "non-organic life [and] the establishment of 'consistency,'" which are aligned with one another "in a variety of registers beyond the organismic ... thus forming a 'machinic phylum'" in which solutions trump problems.⁶¹ By extension, organic life — life which is subject to the mortal limitations of the flesh — must be, to some degree or another, not just inconsistent but inherently problematic. Indeed, it's important to note here that Deleuze did not entirely reject axiomatics, but instead rejected the notion that one must choose between the consistent and the inconsistent without acknowledging that true multiplicity, as Louise Burchill puts it, "is precisely what happens between the two."⁶² The "between" here is not the "incessant translation" of one into the other, but rather the very idea that there are hints of both with every being — hints of the actual and the virtual, of the quantitative and the qualitative, of life and death. In fact, this might help to explain why Deleuze frequently employed the "plane of consistency" as an alternative name for the "plane of immanence," for when all things are made immanent to one another then they must also be made to consist with one another, such that *what is inconsistent is always also consistent*. To put this another way, in a state of pure chaos, even chaos itself must be consistent, and thus as we strive to apprehend the "plane of immanence," we must come to recognize that death is neither wholly consistent nor inconsistent. Instead, it is simply the "problem" of a problematic existence.

Everything That Has a Beginning Has an End

Until now, I've avoided discussing one of the most significant characters of the *Matrix* franchise — in fact the central antagonist of the entire trilogy — a rogue Agent by the name of Smith. In *The Matrix*, the first film of the series, Smith serves as the leader of the Agents, only to be destroyed by Neo at its conclusion. However, *The Matrix Reloaded* reveals that Smith was not erased by Neo as it had originally appeared, but rather "infected" by him, picking up some intangible trait of Neo's humanity that causes Smith to replicate himself uncontrollably, taking over not just one body at a time but rather many, a vast multiplicity of Smiths. By *The Matrix Revolutions*, Smith has entirely subsumed and taken the place of all life within the Matrix, leaving it a desolate, devastated cityscape littered with hundreds of thousands of Smiths, all awaiting a final showdown with Neo in which they promise not only to kill The One, but also to destroy the Matrix and with it all organic and synthetic life. I've avoided Smith thus far because his attitude toward existence and death is very much unlike either the machines who created him or the humans whom he hunted, not a reflection of either Badiou's axiomatic multiplicity and indifference to death, nor Deleuze's problematic multiplicity and immanent view of mortality. Instead, Smith is an entirely different beast, and over the next few pages we'll look to unpack the uniqueness of Agent Smith in hopes of discovering how he, in his only remaining similarity to the machines, informs the meaning of Neo's humanity, and we can do so by starting with the intangible trait of that humanity which infected Smith: Neo's "oneness."

Indeed, although the Smith clones endlessly multiply as the narrative wears on, by the end of the *Matrix* trilogy it's clear that Smith does not think of himself as a pure multiplicity (as do the machines), nor as both one and multiple (as does Neo), but rather as *pure unity*, a Being that will unify all beings and in doing so will realize the absolute potential of existence. But

FIGURE 4.8 *Agent Smith*.

let's not get ahead of ourselves, for Smith's journey, as a dark echo of "the path of the One," helped to shape the "one" that he ultimately becomes, and that journey began with the very birth of the resistance and the creation of the Agents who fight it. As an Agent, Smith is a virtual entity — digital code — that is shaped within the simulations of the Matrix to look, feel, sound, and even process information in a manner similar to humans. His "purpose" was clear: hunt down members of the resistance who reenter the Matrix with the intent of freeing more of the minds trapped within, and as such he was likely unaware of the true purpose of the One — that the One was chosen by the machines to be more powerful than the Agents, capable of bypassing their first line of security in order to reach the Architect, learn his intended fate, and then reboot the Matrix by executing the "prime program." This means that Smith's purpose was futile by design, and yet, when he overcomes Neo in the hallway of an abandoned hotel, a probability comes to pass that even the machines could not have accounted for.

As Neo attempts a desperate escape, he yanks open a door to find Smith waiting for him on the other side, a large pistol pointing directly at his chest. The film cuts to a close-up of the weapon as it fires, the chamber slamming back in slow motion, a spent cartridge ejected in a graceful arc. Neo's virtual body slumps, lifeless, and somewhere far away, his actual body, "jacked" into the simulation, flatlines — "the body cannot live without the mind." Smith did what he was meant to do, but perhaps he did it too well, for in "killing" Neo — a person gifted by the machines with an insight into the coding of the Matrix far beyond that of any other human — he shows him that to die within the simulation is not finite, but rather simply a resetting and perhaps a moment for *re-animation*. As Smith turns away, satisfied, Neo rises in the background, his face curious as if he finally sees the truth of his world. The Agent turns back to engage, but it's of little use. Neo is too fast now, too powerful, and he unexpectedly launches himself — his entire body — into Smith, *inside of Smith*, one virtual entity fighting another from within. Smith stands frozen, shocked, until his body begins to ripple and tear itself apart, exploding into tiny fragments glowing with green code.

At the beginning of *The Matrix Reloaded*, Neo — more powerful than ever after his victory against an Agent — is given a delivery, an envelope containing a 1980s-era earpiece, its beige, curled wire unattached to any type of communications device. In the first film, the earpiece was a visual signifier for Smith and the Agents' inherent multiplicity and collective consciousness, an analogue within the simulation of the Matrix of their ability to remain constantly connected to one another, to know precisely what the others know at all times. In removing the earpiece and giving it to Neo, Smith sends a clear message: he is no longer a part of the "machine set," but instead *only Smith*, one Being wholly disconnected from the multiplicity of being. Soon afterward, Smith explains what happened when Neo hacked into and broke apart his code: "Afterwards, I knew the rules, I understood what I was supposed to do. But I didn't." In other words, Smith's sense of purpose was not destroyed when his code was manipulated. Instead, something was added, like a virus: a sense of individuality, of "oneness," born from the ability to *choose his own path*.[63]

Again and again, the *Matrix* franchise attempts to tell us that what separates the human from the machine is *choice*, the former requiring it so desperately that the Matrix would fail if it were taken away, the latter rejecting it in favor of purpose and prescribed meaning, a dismissal of problems in favor of solutions based on probabilities. In their final encounter, standing in a downpour within the dark and devastated Matrix, bloodied and exhausted after an intense and prolonged battle, Smith cannot wrap his head around Neo's continued will to fight. "Why do you persist?" he demands. "Is it freedom, or truth? Perhaps peace, or could it be love?" "Because I choose to," Neo responds. And yet when Smith, a digital program, was "infected"

FIGURE 4.9 *Multiple copies of the purely "one" Smith.*

by choice, he didn't simply adopt a human-like attitude toward existence, but rather discovered his own interpretation of the meaning of Being. "I really should thank you for it," Smith counters. "After all it was your life that taught me the purpose of all life. The purpose of life is to end."

To help bring about such an end — the end of all that exists — Smith stalked the Matrix, plunging himself into every Being, machine or human, connected to the simulation, infecting them with his pure unity the way that he was once infected by Neo. At first this was almost a game, an exploration of his own unconscious desire for power as a newly freed, subjective individual. Yet when he finally found the Oracle, the program who conceived of the One and who put its grand scheme into motion, he realized that the game was over, that all that remained was to make the One see the *truth*, a truth which he reiterated again and again throughout the series: that Neo's death is *inevitable*. What's interesting, then, is how Neo's response to Smith's insistence of inevitability changes over the course of the series — at first he passionately denies it, then he anxiously mulls over its possibility, and finally he resolutely confronts his own mortality. In fact, when Smith tells Neo that "the purpose of life is to end," Neo does not respond, because in many ways he agrees. Moreover, his last encounter with Smith is the final step of what he explicitly positioned as a suicide mission, one that already cost the life of Trinity, the woman he had previously been so desperate to save that he rejected the Architect's plan and refused to reboot the Matrix. After making that choice, however, Neo had his own epiphany, his own moment of clarity, and rather than seeing what choices remained open, he saw only purpose.

Part of that epiphany was brought about by a visit to the Oracle before she was infected by Smith, when she told Neo something that she insisted he already knew: that "everything which has a beginning has an end." Taking this into account, Neo formulated a plan: to leave the simulation of the Matrix, enter the "desert of the Real" — a nickname for the scorched remains of the Earth borrowed directly from Baudrillard, whose *Simulacra and Simulation* sat on Neo's bookshelf at the start of the series — and make his way to "the Source," in doing so surely becoming the first person to ever set foot in the greatest of all machine strongholds. In accompanying him, the journey costs Trinity her life, spurning Neo forward until he reaches his destination, and what greets him there is an entity that almost mockingly mimics the human form, yet is not a cyborg like Adam from *Deus Ex*, nor an android like Ava from *Ex Machina*, nor even one singular being. Instead, he comes face to face with the "Deus Ex Machina," an overwhelming swarm of small, insect-like machines, a mass of metal bodies that undulate in patterns which echo the anatomy of a massive, perversely child-like human face. Neo, unphased, presents his offer to the leader of machines: in exchange for peace between the organic and the synthetic, he will reenter and reboot the Matrix, thus ridding it of the infections of Smith and preventing the destruction of all forms of life.

FIGURE 4.10 *Neo confronts the Deus Ex Machina.*

Considering that Neo is the only Being in the universe capable of destroying Smith, it seems strange that he would subsequently tell his nemesis — once his offer is accepted and the Deus Ex Machina plugs him back into the Matrix — that he "persists" only because he "chooses to," for if he truly wants to prevent the annihilation of all life, it certainly seems that he doesn't have much of a choice in the matter. Perhaps, then, when Neo suddenly drops his guard, not simply refusing to continue the fight but rather *choosing to submit*, we realize that his actual "choice" is not one of persistence but rather *acceptance* — a recognition of his true "path" and an acknowledgment of the inevitable. Sensing victory is at hand, and with some remnant of the Oracle still buried deep within him, Smith cannot help but to mutter "everything that has a beginning has an end," plunging his hands into Neo to infect his final victim, taking over not just a virtual body but the actual consciousness connected to it as well, in the process ending Neo's life.

For a moment it seems that Smith has won, but it's then that Neo's full plan reveals itself: in subsuming Neo and disbursing his Being to every instance of "Smith" still left in the Matrix, the rogue Agent unknowingly distributed the "prime program" which the One had long carried within himself. At the same moment that Smith gains the capacity to shut down the Matrix and end all life, the system is reloaded and rebooted, eliminating him in the process. Whether it was his purpose or not, Neo succeeds in saving the resistance, but he had long recognized that he would never be able to save himself. In the end, Neo showed that what truly separated him from the machines was not simply his free will, but rather his ability *embrace his finiteness and the immanence of his death*, to define his very humanity by way of the event the renders him both consistent and inconsistent, one and many. In the end, Neo's final and decisive victory is not self-sacrifice, but rather the assertion of his inherent humanity through the most human action of all: the acceptance of death.

Conclusion: The Fractal Logic of Life

The Micro and the Macro

In the first twenty minutes of Terrence Malick's intimate epic *The Tree of Life* — whose resolute encounter with death was touched upon briefly in our third chapter — we learn that its central character, Jack, grew up in an idyllic (if somewhat strict) small-town household in the late 1950s, that his younger brother R.L. was killed some years later (presumably in the Vietnam War) and that R.L.'s death sent their family into a spiral of grief whose ramifications are still felt several decades later. At that point, however, the film takes a rather unexpected turn, and instead of jumping forward or back in time by a few decades, as the film's rather poetic editing is so often inclined to do, it instead slowly fades in some billions of years in the past, where cloud-like nebulas spin, expand, and grasp warily against infinite fields of darkness. Jack's mother's voice is heard imploring God about the plan and purpose of RL's death, while Zbigniew Preisner's haunting and operatic "Lacrimosa" lends the sequence an overwhelming and contemplative character. As the macroscopic camera pushes it way through starbursts and dusty expanses of rock and gas, another noise grows on the soundtrack: eruption. Images of flame and molten earth engulf us, smoke spews from fissures in the ground, water cascades into endless waterfalls and misty rivers, and somewhere a small puddle of mud boils and teams with life.

Pressing forward again, the film's camera becomes microscopic, watching as cells merge, burst, and swallow one another, as chaotic strings of living organisms wriggle and multiply. Jumping ahead through the millennia, we find jellyfish and mollusks leisurely floating beneath the waves, nearby plants rising from the oceans to cover mossy landscapes, a lone tree rising against the sun. At the shoreline a head swings into view, and panning down we find a massive, beached plesiosaur, examining itself on the sand. As the camera approaches, we realize that its body is wet with more than just water, a massive, gaping wound pouring blood into the surf. Somewhere else, we go micro again, peering into veins and arteries pulsing with blood cells — a heart beats and an embryo develops. Further in time, we're by a river in a forest, where a small dinosaur lies on the rocks, mortally wounded. A predator approaches, paws at the dying creature with its foot, and then runs away. Increasing our scale to the truly macro one last time, we watch an asteroid as it dances its way through the universe, careening into the Earth with massive, devastating force. Finally, some seventeen minutes after leaving it, the film rejoins its twentieth-century storyline, where Jack's ecstatic memories and fantasies carry him (and us) toward an understanding of death as always immanent to life.

As Jacques Choron once reminded us, death is nothing to the nonliving, for it's not simply the end of life but more importantly *of life*.[1] It follows, then, that as our understanding of death changes, so too must our understanding of life change, for in those same moments that the digital shifts our relationship to mortality, it also rapidly expands our empirical limits, making accessible or comprehensible more and more and more of our bodies and our world and our universe. As such, films like *The Tree of Life* — in their resolute confrontations with grief, finality, finiteness, and death — have begun to recontextualize mortality within the rapidly expanding boundaries of life itself, whether it be the overwhelming and sublime biological history of life on Earth, or the nonbiological "lives" of celestial bodies, the births and deaths of stars, planets, universes. In fact, Malick's polemic is quite clear: to understand the "meaning" of even one death, we must first come to grips with the very foundations of life itself. To that end, his film shows us, before it even reaches its half-way point, that every life and every death is a repetition of the same process, and no matter

FIGURE C.1 *A plesiosaur dying on a beach in* The Tree of Life.

how infinitesimal or how immense your lens, the pattern will always be the same. For Malick, and for our digital logic, life and death are *fractal*.

Fractals, as we know, are very much a product of the digital age. First described and named in 1975 by the mathematician Benoit Mandelbrot in his analysis of the incalculable lengths of shorelines — which, he argued, are always equally jagged, rough, and complex, no matter how close or distant you are as you examine them — fractals only truly took root in mathematics and "entered wide public circulation," as Anna Powell tells us, "with the spread of computer literacy" in the late 1980s and early 1990s.[2] Although there are several basic types of fractals, perhaps their most fundamental shared property — infinitely repeating patterns that are similar at any scale — can be best illustrated through the familiar image of the "Sierpinski triangle," named after the set theorist Wacław Sierpiński. To make one, "take a triangle and subdivide its area into smaller triangles," as Ian Hamilton Grant explains. "Following this first sub-division, repeat or 'reiterate' the operation on these smaller triangles, and so on ad infinitum. Such a figure is *linearly self-similar* because each part of the object is exactly like the whole from which it is derived."[3] It's this linear self-similarity that has been adopted by moving images in their quest to face mortality, resulting in images and juxtapositions — stars expanding, lava cooling into earth, and cells dividing, for example, or universes fading out, cells being swallowed up, creatures dying alone on a beach — which suggest or reveal repeating patterns in the nature of life and death, the micro and the macro.

FIGURE C.2 *The linear self-similarity of a Sierpinski triangle.*

Consider another example from Ang Lee's filmic adaptation of the novel *Life of Pi*, in which a young Indian boy is stranded at sea after a shipwreck which took the lives of his entire family, leaving him adrift in a small lifeboat, his only companion an adult Bengal tiger by the name of Richard Parker. Mourning the loss of his loved ones, and fearful that he and Richard Parker, too, will soon perish at sea, Pi fantasizes about the endless number of lives playing out far beneath the surface of the water. As he stares over the edge of the boat, the camera plunges into the deep, where an enormous whale is caught within the tentacles of an equally massive squid, only to have its body suddenly morph and break apart, each fragment becoming as animal from Pi's family's zoo — a zebra, a hippopotamus, a crocodile, a giraffe — which swims away out of sight, unfazed and unafraid. A light emerges from the darkness as a massive angler-fish blurs past the camera, its vaguely fractal scales and tentacles revealing a starry-like expanse of bioluminescent microorganisms in its wake. Each tiny creature glows, spins, expands, and ruptures, a visual echo of an infinitely vast cosmos, thousands of universes in miniature, bursting to life and exploding in death. Somewhere far below, the ghostly remains of the shipwreck rest on the ocean floor.

Like Malick's "creation of life" sequence, Lee's depiction of Pi's fantasy is both a visual and a thematic fractal, a dream in which the smallest instances of Being are found to be identical to the largest instances of being, a smooth cosmic space where the diminutive is immanent to the immense. It was in this very sense that Deleuze and Guattari adopted the fractal in *What Is Philosophy?*, "aligning it to the plane of immanence," Powell writes, "in a series of figures beginning with the body: skeleton (concepts) and breath (plane), which are used to distinguish the plane from the concepts arising from it."[4] In other words, the foundation or "skeleton" of our existence — i.e., consciousness — is concepts, notions, words, language. Yet the very "breath" of life is something altogether different, that pure affect which reaches in all directions and touches all beings, that infinitely smooth "plane of immanence" which extends from the distant past into the far-off future. "If concepts are 'absolute surfaces or volumes, formless and fragmentary,'" Powell continues, quoting Deleuze and Guattari, "then the plane itself is the 'unlimited absolute' and '*always fractal*.'"[5] Existence, being, life; nothingness, nonbeing, death — all things an endless repetition and recurrence, a fractal of self-similar beings and Beings playing out across infinitely varying scales.

Yet we mustn't overlook the fact that not all fractals are entirely self-similar, that they can also represent a chaotic repetition of the merely alike rather than an endless repetition of the same. Such chaotic fractals "model the behaviour of complex systems," as Grant tells us, because they are "both linearly self-similar and random, depending upon which fractal dimension" — i.e., which *scale* — "of this nonlinear, dynamical system is studied."[6] The most famous example of chaotic fractals would be the Mandelbrot set — named, of course, after the father of fractals — whose sea-shell shaped

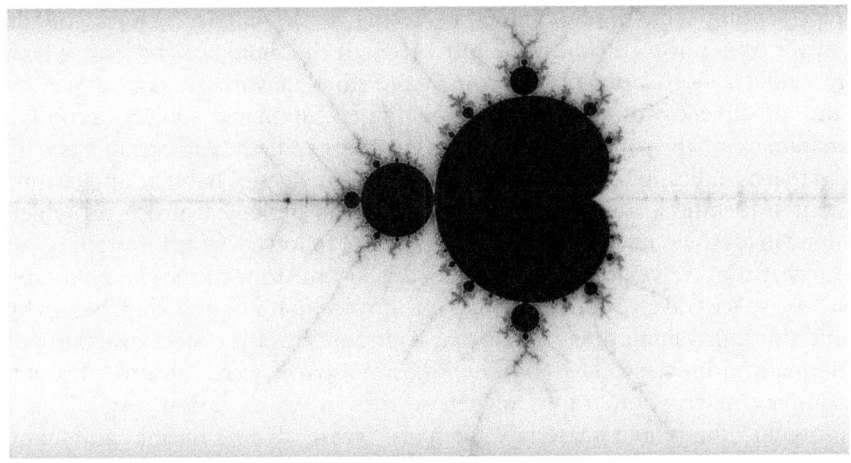

FIGURE C.3 *A finely scaled detail of a Mandelbrot set, where a version of the original pattern is surrounded by chaotic yet equally complex patterns.*

patterns were inescapable throughout the 1990s, plastered across personal-webpage wallpapers and trapper-keepers alike.[7]

What's unique about the Mandelbrot set is that, when treating the complex numbers bounded by the set as image coordinates, the resulting figure has a finite yet ragged boundary which reveals itself to have infinitely greater details as the scale of the image is increased. At times, these details resemble smaller and smaller versions of the set as a whole, while at other times different but equally complex patterns emerge. In other words, chaotic fractals are both finite and infinite, linear and nonlinear, consistent and inconsistent, smooth and striated, which is precisely why they model Deleuze and Guattari's concept of immanence as fractal more fully and more precisely than the linearly self-similar Sierpinski triangles and Menger sponges which the pair discuss in their work.[8] The reason for this is that although they describe the plane of immanence as smooth space, there are always striations acting upon it, those inconsistencies which are not yet wholly affective, those problems which must be addressed rather than dismissed. As such, exclusively self-similar fractals, as Mark Bonta and John Protevi tell us, "might lead to conceptual simplification of complex, smoothing/striating processes" — the same translation of problematic inconsistencies into presentable consistencies that Deleuze rejected in our last chapter.[9] "A [linearly] fractalized shoreline," they continue, "while intriguing, is but an abstraction of the real shoreline that is traversed by the striations contained in any system that is always-already striated by human forces."[10]

Intriguingly, the very digital processes which have inspired our fractal understanding of life may act as striations that stand in the way of visually representing such smooth fractality, seeing as the infinite vastness of the universe — not to mention the intricacies of the biological systems which resemble it — are often far too complex to simulate with the same efficiency and effectiveness of simulations depicting the animated subject becoming inanimate or the rupturing and breaking apart of flesh. Perhaps this is why Terrence Malick avoided computer-generated images of nebulae and cosmic bodies, turning instead to actual chemical and biological processes which stand in for their macro cousins. In doing so, he followed in the footsteps of yet another film we've previously discussed, Darren Aronofsky's *The Fountain*, whose space traveler Tom, floating ever-upward in his bubble ship, passes by and through a miniature cosmos that truly captures the chaotic fractality of the natural universe. *The Fountain*'s cosmic spaces were captured through complex macrophotography of petri dishes in which various organic and inorganic fluids and materials, such as "yeast, dyes, solvents, and baby oil," along with other substances the filmmakers declined to divulge, were combined to foster chemical reactions which echo the physical forces found in nature.[11] Such reactions were then digitally composited together and layered behind live-action images, which "furnished Aronofsky's film," as Steve Silberman writes, "with something neither a computer nor an old-fashioned matte painter could deliver — chaos, in all its ultra high-definition fractal glory."[12] Indeed, the chaos is one of complex randomness juxtaposed against the linear self-similarity of existence across its many scales, marrying some of smallest known forces of our world to some of the largest known processes of our universe in order to position us — conscious,

FIGURE C.4 *A nebula surrounds the bubble ship in* The Fountain, *composited from macrophotography of chemical reactions.*

living organisms — as merely a reverberation in the great chain of Being, a repetition in the vast and infinite plane of immanent beings.

It's this infinite repetition of finite beings that films like *The Tree of Life*, *Life of Pi*, and *The Fountain* hope to invoke, and likewise it may be this very sense of pure and absolute immanence that we've been chasing from the very beginning, as Andrew Pickering makes surprisingly clear when he writes that the very thought of immanence "invites a connection to the mathematics of fractals, cellular automata, simulations of non-linear systems [and] the unknowable," to which we might add recurrence and repetition, determination, problematics and inconsistencies, the oneness and manyness of human life.[13] At the same time, an understanding of death as immanent to life reveals that the study of death is not a morbid meditation on our greatest fear but rather a confirmation of our very Being, for one cannot understand *life* without recognizing its finitude. If one were to argue, as this project has, that contemporary simulations of death are a virtual enactments of the lost experience of witnessing the death of others, one is also implying that "aliveness" is concretely felt through glimpses of nonbeing. If one were to say that the compossibility of digital games is an echo of the repetition of being through which we can trace our own "path to death," then one must also say that life is the culmination of choices and chances. If one saw in our possibilistic culture relays through which we attempt to reassert the potential of death, one must also acknowledge that such potential is always and only enacted through resolute Being. And if one were to read the theoretical immortality of artificially intelligent machines as a mirror that reveals the recognition of death to be the defining characteristic of human life, one would also see within that mirror a context against which a meaningful life can be judged or assessed. Indeed, in all of these observations, one could glimpse a fractal logic of life just as easily as the digital logic of death.

NOTES

Introduction

1. An implicit contention throughout this book is the notion that we've moved past the postmodern thinking that defined the 1960s, 1970s, and 1980s. In fact, by the time scholars like Fredric Jameson and David Harvey were laying bare the fundamentals of the postmodern condition, our cultural logic was already being swayed by new modes of communication and image-making. For more, see Frederic Jameson, *Postmodernism: Or, the Cultural Logic of Late Capitalism* (Durham, NC: Duke University Press, 1991); and David Harvey, *The Condition of Postmodernity: An Enquiry into the Origins of Cultural Change* (Oxford: Blackwell Publishing, 1990).
2. Emphasis mine. For more on this widespread debate, see David DeGrazia, "The Definition of Death," in *The Stanford Encyclopedia of Philosophy*, ed. Edward N. Zalta (Fall 2011 Edition), http://plato.stanford.edu/archives/fall2011/entries/death-definition/
3. Vivian Sobchack, "Inscribing Ethical Space: Ten Propositions on Death, Representation, and Documentary," in *Carnal Thoughts: Embodiment and Moving Image Culture* (Berkeley: University of California Press, 2004), 227.

Chapter 1

1. Jacques Lacan, *The Four Fundamentals of Psychoanalysis: The Seminars of Jacques Lacan: Book XI*, ed. Jacques-Alain Miller, trans. Alan Sheridan (New York: W. W. Norton, 1998), 54. Freud's actual quote, from his 1912 essay "The Dynamics of Transference," was "for when all is said and done, it is impossible to destroy anyone *in effegie* or *in absentia*," meaning that one cannot settle an interpersonal conflict by transferring their emotions onto a third party (as the analysand is wont to do). In our context, however, the meaning remains virtually the same: one cannot resolve painful tensions by simply replacing their source with a symbol, representation, or image.
2. For example, consider how overwhelming the complex movement of leaves blowing in a breeze would be if we attempted, every time we saw a tree, to truly engage with their patterns (let alone the elaborate activities of the ants at its base, or the flickering arrangements of sunlight dancing between its limbs, or the quivering sensations of the breeze as it tickles the skin). Instead, Freud

proposed that the pre-conscious instantaneously registers and dismisses much of this stimuli so that we can both avoid becoming overwhelmed and, when need be, focus our limited attention or mental energy on more pressing issues. Sigmund Freud, "Beyond the Pleasure Principle," in *Collected Writings*, trans. A.A. Brill (Seattle, WA: Pacific Publishing Studio, 2010), 236.
3   Ibid., 235.
4   Walter Benjamin, "On Some Motifs in Baudelaire," in *Illuminations*, ed. Hannah Arendt, trans. Harry Zohn (New York: Schocken Books, 2007), 161.
5   The particulars of Noé's strategy — such as doppler-esque drones and heavy percussion on the soundtrack, swirling and destabilized camerawork, manic performances robbed of narrative context, and of course the unremitting deformation of a seemingly "real" human face — will be discussed in greater detail later in this chapter.
6   We'll return to the notion of repetition in our next chapter, where it will be shown to be a key component of the employment of death in digital games.
7   Freud, *Beyond the Pleasure Principle*, 225.
8   Ibid., 225.
9   Another example of this process comes from the games of "doctor" that children often play after returning from their first visit to a physician — their discomforts and fears negotiated through a restaging of the trauma of being poked and prodded.
10 Slavoj Žižek, *How to Read Lacan* (New York: W. W. Norton, 2007), 73; emphasis mine.
11 Slavoj Žižek, *Welcome to the Desert of the Real!: Five Essays on September 11th and Related Dates* (New York: Verso, 2002), 15–17.
12 Michel Foucault, *Discipline and Punish: The Birth of the Prison*, trans. Alan Sheridan (New York: Vintage Books,1995), 3–5.
13 Foucault follows this graphic depiction with a stilted and dry "time-table" which lays out the average day of a Parisian prisoner during the 1840s, whose punishment took place behind high concrete walls, in small cells and closed off courtyards. Turning away from the threat of death and toward the promised sustenance of life, Western societies established a new system of control which Foucault termed *biopower*.
14 Giacomo Casanova, *The Complete Memoires of Jacques Casanova de Seingalt: Vol. 3 – The Eternal Quest*, trans. Arthur Machen (The Gutenberg Project, 2006), https://www.gutenberg.org/files/2981/2981-h/2981-h.htm
15 Charles Dickens, *A Tale of Two Cities* (San Francisco, CA: Ignatius Press, 2012), 195.
16 Casanova, *The Complete Memoires*.
17 Philippe Ariés, *Western Attitudes toward Death*, trans. Patricia M. Ranum (Baltimore, MD: Johns Hopkins University Press, 1974), 93.
18 Less familiar to the public at large, though more frightening in its implications, are the racially motivated lynchings that were far too common in the American south until the early-to-mid-twentieth century.
19 Of course, legend has it that the brutality of combat on display was much more than these spectators bargained for, many of whom were soon under threat themselves when the Union retreat unexpectedly turned in their direction.

20 Geoffrey Gorer, "The Pornography of Death," in *Death: Current Perspectives*, ed. John B. Williamson and Edwin S. Shneidman (Mountain View, CA: Mayfield Publishing Company, 1995), 20.
21 Ibid.
22 Philippe Ariés, *The Hour of Our Death*, trans. Helen Weaver (New York: Vintage Books, 2008), 15.
23 Gorer: "They were encouraged to think about death, their own deaths and the edifying or cautionary deathbeds of others." Ariés: "And to think of how carefully people today keep children away from anything to do with death!" Gorer: "Our great-grandparents were told that babies were found under gooseberry bushes or cabbages; our children are likely to be told that those who have passed on ... are changed into flowers, or lie at rest in lovely gardens." Gorer, "The Pornography of Death," 20; Ariés, *Western Attitudes*, 12.
24 For better or worse, these social function have, in turn, served as the primary objects of study in most thanatological accounts of deathbed scenes, from Ariés and Gorer to Elizabeth Kubler-Ross and Elisabeth Bronfen. Elizabeth Kubler-Ross, *On Death and Dying* (New York: Routledge, 1973); Elisabeth Bronfen, *Over Her Dead Body: Death, Femininity and the Aesthetic* (Oxford: Manchester University Press, 1992).
25 While the dying person was always saddened by the thought of leaving behind their loved ones, their homes, their friends, and their possessions, any display of such grief never went "beyond a level of intensity that is very slight," especially in comparison to our modern outbursts of emotion. The same reservation of emotion was even found, Ariés tells us, in "other periods, such as the baroque, that were given to inflated expression." Aries, *Western Attitudes*, 12.
26 Bronfen, *Over Her Dead Body*, 77.
27 Ariés, *Western Attitudes*, 87.
28 By "the pain of knowing death," I refer not simply to one's recognition, understanding, or knowledge of mortality — which, as we will see, was once grounded almost entirely in the act of perceiving the death of others — but also to the *anxiety* that accompanies the recognition of death's possibility, which will be examined in much greater depth in Chapter 3.
29 Ariés, *The Hour of Our Death*, 414–19.
30 Roland Barthes, *The Pleasure of the Text*, trans. Richard Miller (New York: Hill and Wang, 1975), 19.
31 Ibid., 22.
32 Ibid., 17. Deleuze, responding to Barthes, reads *jouissance* as not necessarily embodied but rather *active*, such that there exists a duality between "the subject of the statement, capable of pleasure, and the subject of enunciation, deserving of *jouissance*." The statement, as a signpost that merely points-to, provides *for the reader* only the pleasure of looking or imagining, whereas the enunciation, as a declaration of affect and intuition, produces *for the speaker* an overwhelming gestalt. To put this into a clearer context, the passive contemplation insisted upon by representations of death pleasurably satisfies our immediate curiosity, whereas the active experience of witnessing always *inspires greater curiosity*. Gilles Deleuze, "Dualism, Monism and Multiplicities (Desire-Pleasure-*Jouissance*)," *Contretemps 2*, May 2001, 97.

33 Nor should we be deterred by Deleuze's argument that *jouissance* is "impossible," because he also explains that "*jouissance* is in a fundamental relationship with death," and when we pursue this "impossible *jouissance*-death relation," we "hope for discharges" and seek a "transcendence" that we will never achieve. It is not *jouissance*, therefore, that is impossible, but rather the resolution of our fundamental anxiety. Ibid.
34 Ariés, *Western Attitudes*, 94.
35 Ariés, *The Hour of Our Death*, 6, 10.
36 Ibid., 28.
37 Ernest Becker, *The Denial of Death* (New York: Free Press Paperbacks, 1973), 2.
38 Gorer, "The Pornography of Death," 20.
39 Ariés, *Western Attitudes*, 85.
40 Ariés, *The Hour of Our Death*, 11.
41 Ibid., 7.
42 Ibid., 588.
43 Gorer, "The Pornography of Death," 20.
44 Ibid., 21.
45 Ibid., 22; emphasis mine.
46 As Gorer put it, "the art of the embalmers is an art of complete denial." Ibid., 21; Herman Feifel, ed., *The Meaning of Death* (New York: McGraw-Hill, 1959); Jessica Mitford, *The American Way of Death* (New York: Simon & Schuster, 1963).
47 Kubler-Ross, *On Death and Dying*.
48 Although Becker presents the "project of heroism" as the central immortality project of the twentieth century, he notes that symbolic immortality is afforded not only through acts of great courage, but also through "piling up figures in a bank book ... or by having only a little better home in the neighborhood, a bigger car, brighter children." Becker, *The Denial of Death*, 4.
49 Ibid., 13–15. In addition to winning the 1974 Pulitzer Prize for nonfiction, *The Denial of Death* became a part of popular culture when Alvy Singer, Woody Allen's alter ego in *Annie Hall*, purchased the book for Diane Keaton's Annie while discussing *his* view of the two types of people in the world: the horrible and the miserable.
50 Worse yet, he even seemed to believe that the inherent anxiety which had long accompanied the recognition of death — the *angst* of Heidegger and Sartre which I will return to in our third chapter — precludes one from ever truly understanding or accepting death, despite a long history of social and cultural attitudes which attest otherwise.
51 Ariés, *The Hour of Our Death*, xvii.
52 Ariés, *Western Attitudes*, 1.
53 Ibid., 88.
54 Michel Foucault, *Birth of the Clinic* (New York: Routledge, 1993).
55 Ibid., 18.
56 Susan Sontag, *Regarding the Pain of Others* (New York: Picador, 2003), 26.
57 Of course, the truth-value of those photographs is difficult to assess, which Sontag points out when she discusses the manipulations of early war photographers, such as the staging of bodies or the tweaking of destroyed scenery. Errol Morris, however, takes issue with Sontag's claim that such

manipulations irreparably harm the photographs, arguing instead that any image, staged or not, which recalls and reflects upon a truth that is beyond basic observation (such as the full horrors of war) is nonetheless extremely valuable. Errol Morris, *Believing Is Seeing (Observations on the Mysteries of Photography)* (New York: Penguin Press, 2011).

58 Roland Barthes, *Camera Lucida: Reflections on Photography*, trans. Richard Howard (New York: Hill and Wand, 1983), 96.
59 Ibid., 96.
60 Ibid.
61 Ibid., 97; emphasis mine. Barthes's most famous and striking example, not even included amongst the many photographs featured in his text, was a picture of his deceased mother, which he claimed possessed a strongly personal punctum which could not have affected the average viewer in the same way as it did him.
62 Scott Combs tells us that Mary's stand-in was not an actor per se, but rather the treasurer of Edison's Kinetoscope Company, Robert Thomtae — one of many cameos by production company staff in the early days of cinema, when "flicks" were considered too low an art form for many trained actors. Scott Combs, "Cut: Execution, Editing, and Instant Death," *The Instance* 38 (Fall 2008), 33.
63 Ibid.
64 Ibid. For that matter, they may also have believed any number of other pictures that made up the strangely popular subgenre of "execution films" in the early days of the cinema, to which Mary Anne Doane assigns titles "such as *Execution by Hanging* (Mutoscope/Biograph, 1905), *Reading the Death Sentence* (Mutoscope/Biograph, 1905), *Execution of a Spy* (Mutoscope/Biograph, 1902), [and] *Beheading the Chinese Prisoner* (Lubin, 1900)." We can also add some of Edison's recreations of more contemporaneous killings, such as the murder of President William McKinley and the subsequent electrocution of his assassin, Leon Czolgosz (*Execution of Czolgosz with Panorama of Auburn Prison*, 1901; a film which Edwin S. Porter supposedly made only after being denied the chance to film the actual event), as well as his more disturbing animal electrocution films like *Electrocuting an Elephant* (1902), un-simulated experiments which Edison hoped would steer the public away from Nikola Tesla's alternating current system in favor of his own direct current system. For more on execution films, see Mary Anne Doane, *The Emergence of Cinematic Time* (Cambridge, MA: Harvard University Press, 2002); and Vivian Sobchack, *Carnal Thoughts: Embodiment and Moving Image Culture* (Berkeley: University of California Press, 2004).
65 For more, see John Guy, *Queen of Scots: The True Life of Mary Stuart* (Boston, MA: Mariner Books, 2005); and Antonia Fraser, *Mary, Queen of Scots* (London: Orion, 2010).
66 Guy, *Queen of* Scots, 8.
67 Ibid.
68 Ibid., 9.
69 Fraser, *Mary, Queen of Scots*, 540.
70 There are, of course, exceptions to this rule — films, shows, and games which have occasionally jostled us with imagery too intense or sincere to

ignore — yet their influence is far outweighed by images that are almost designed to be disregarded. For more on the history of violence in the moving image media of the twentieth century, see Stephen Prince, ed., *Screening Violence* (London: Athlone Press, 2000).
71 Guy Debord, *Society of the Spectacle*, trans. Ken Knabb (London: Rebel Press, 1967), 7.
72 Ibid., 11.
73 Ibid., 9.
74 Baudrillard, *Simulacra and Simulation*, trans. Sheila Faria Glaser (Ann Arbor: University of Michigan Press, 1994), 6.
75 Ibid.
76 Ibid.
77 Ibid.
78 Ibid., 1.
79 Even in those rare moments when we can once again touch reality unmarred by signs or symbols, it too often fails to impress or stimulate us in the same manner as its image — or, perhaps more accurately, it is us who can no longer be stimulated — which Frederic Jameson referred to as the "waning of affect" in postmodern culture. See Frederic Jameson, *Postmodernism: Or, the Cultural Logic of Late Capitalism* (Durham, NC: Duke University Press, 1991).
80 Žižek, *Welcome to the Desert of the Real*, 9–10.
81 Ibid., 11.
82 Ibid., 16.
83 Ibid., 11.
84 Ibid., 15.
85 Ibid., 16; emphasis mine.
86 For more on the "ethics" of actual death in moving images, see Vivian Sobchack, "Inscribing Ethical Space: Ten Propositions on Death, Representation, and Documentary," in *Carnal Thoughts: Embodiment and Moving Image Culture* (Berkeley: University of California Press, 2004).
87 Jennifer M. Barker, *The Tactile Eye: Touch and the Cinematic Experience* (Berkeley: University of California Press, 2009), 122.
88 Sobchack, *Carnal Thoughts*, 239. There are exceptions to this rule are certainly worth noting, however, such as Sobchack's example of PBS's *On Our Own Terms: Moyers on Dying*, or Showtime's recent limited series *Time of Death*, both of which focus on the protracted and often agonizing wait that accompanies an expected death.
89 Barker, *The Tactile Eye*, 122.
90 Lacan, *Four Fundamentals of Psychoanalysis*, 53–4.
91 Gorer, "The Pornography of Death," 22.
92 Foucault, *The Birth of the Clinic*, ix.
93 For more, see Taylor Carmen and Mark B.N. Hansen, "Introduction," in *The Cambridge Companion to Merleau-Ponty*, ed. Taylor Carmen and Mark B.N. Hansen (Cambridge: Cambridge University Press, 2005), 15–16; Kristen Brown Golden, "Trauma and Speech as Bodily Adaptation in Merleau-Ponty," in *The Trauma Controversy: Philosophical and Interdisciplinary Dialogues*, ed. Kristen Brown Golden and Bettina Bergo (Albany: State University of New York Press, 2009), 73.

94 Roland Barthes, quoted in Sobchack, *Carnal Thoughts*, 234.
95 Sobchack, *Carnal Thoughts*, 233.
96 Keep in mind that for the child, every new encounter is traumatic — equally terrifying and exhilarating. As such, much of our initial understandings of the world were born from trauma, and it was only when we removed the experience of witnessing from the experience of adolescence that we began to misrecognize death.
97 Baudrillard, *Simulacra and Simulation*, 3.
98 Perhaps Baudrillard saw simulations as a threat precisely because he anticipated our embrace of them, and therefore our potential to not only lose sight of the Real, but also to destroy it.
99 Frasca, "Simulation versus Narrative," in *Video/Game/Theory*, ed. Mark J.P. Wolfand Bernard Perron (New York: Routledge, 2003), 223.
100 Bogost's also adds to this definition the notion of the "simulation gap," which posits that the meaning or value of a simulation exists in the gap between the images it generates and the viewer or user's subjective understanding of the system the simulation models. Ian Bogost, *Unit Operations* (Cambridge, MA: MIT Press, 2006), 107.
101 Ibid., 94.
102 I don't intend for this to be a concrete or complete definition of a simulation, but rather a complication that expresses elements of the autonomy of simulations that often go unremarked.
103 Moreover, Manovich reminds us that many "high-level" simulations "require a computer to understand, to a certain degree, the meaning embedded in the object being generated." Not only is the simulation too complex to model without the assistance of the digital, but the images it produces are occasionally too complex to understand without that same assistance. Frasca, "Simulation versus Narrative," 223–4, emphasis mine; Lev Manovich, *The Language of New Media* (Cambridge, MA: MIT Press, 2002), 33–4.
104 My focus on trees in this chapter is not entirely arbitrary, as Siegfried Kracauer, in his essay on the "Basic Concepts" of the cinema, wrote that the ability to dynamically present "the familiar leitmotif of leaves" blowing in the wind was one of the early aspirations of the cinema, and likewise the tree and the word *l'arbre* was, in *The Instance of the Letter in the Unconscious*, Lacan's preferred example for the signified and signifier (split as they were by the bar of signification). Siegfried Kracauer, "Basic Concepts," in *Film Theory and Criticism: Introductory Readings, Fifth Edition*, ed. Leo Braudy and Marshall Cohen (New York: Oxford University Press, 1999), 171; Jacques Lacan, "The Agency of the Letter in the Unconscious or Reason since Freud," in *Écrits: A Selection*, trans. Bruce Fink (New York: W. W. Norton, 2004).
105 Immanuel Kant, *Critique of Judgment*, trans. James Creed Meredith, ed. Nicholas Walker (Oxford: Oxford University Press, 2007), 75.
106 Ibid., 91.
107 Ibid., 87.
108 Despite the fact that we encounter them everyday of our lives, we have all, at one moment or another, been struck by the majesty of a tree, particularly in those moments when we've allowed ourselves the time to contemplate their complexity.

109 David H. Eberly, *Game Physics, Second Edition* (Boca Raton, FL: CRC Press, 2010), xxxix. At the same time, few things destroy the immersion of games as quickly as physics glitches — those moments when objects pass through one another without properly colliding, bounce too high or too fast into the air, fail to lose momentum as they should, are easily pushed away despite their apparent weight, are stopped cold when colliding with a smaller and lighter object, and so on.
110 Ibid.
111 For more on the complexities of physics engines, see Ian Millington, *Game Physics Engine Development: How to Build a Robust Commercial-Grade Physics Engine for Your Game, Second Edition* (Boca Raton, FL: CRC Press, 2010).
112 Sobchack, *Carnal Thoughts*, 235.
113 Although Baudrillard tells us that the simulacra arrives as "a hyperreal sheltered … from any distinction between the real and the imaginary," I would argue that hyperreality is found not in the image that is indistinguishable from reality, but rather one that feels so real that it makes us question our ability to *distinguish the unreal*. Baudrillard, *Simulacra and Simulation*, 3.
114 Riccardo de los Rios and Robert Davis, "Digital Frames and Visible Grain: Spatial and Material Reintegration in *Irreversible*," *Film Criticism* 32 (2007), 105–6.
115 "SFX," on *Irréversible*, DVD, directed by Gaspar Noé (2001; France: Lion's Gate Home Video, 2001).
116 Ibid.
117 Ibid.
118 Festival audiences were frequently cited as not only walking out of the film, but feeling disoriented, faint, and quite literally sick.
119 Ibid.
120 Eugenie Brinkman, "Rape and the Rectum: Bersani, Deleuze, Noé," *Camera Obscura* 20 (2005), 38.
121 Mikita Brottman and David Sterritt, "Irréversible," *Film Quarterly* 57, no. 2 (Winter 2003–4), 41.

Chapter 2

1 This is, of course, the central conceit of Ernest Becker's *The Denial of Death*, which we briefly touched upon in our last chapter. Becker argued, shortly before his own death in 1974, that society and culture have long been structured around ideological regimes that act to repress and deny the permanence of death, ranging from medieval religion to the project of heroism in the twentieth century. Ernest Becker, *The Denial of Death* (New York: Free Press Paperbacks, 1973).
2 Even the most experienced players would eventually encounter a death of sorts, as many classic games would inevitably freeze or crash when some bit of programming advanced beyond the 256 character limit (0–255) of 8-bit code.

The most famous example comes from *Pac-Man*, whose 256th level exceeds this limit by attempting to draw 256 fruit onscreen, causing half of the screen to be rendered in unintelligent strings of numbers that make the game all but unplayable. The common name used to describe such levels: "kill screens."

3 Perhaps, however, the recent popularity of "endless runners" in the mobile market marks a return of the trope of inevitable failure and death.

4 I use the term "narratively-driven digital game" to refer to games whose primary goal is (or at least appears to be) the resolution of a narrative, and which often use the concept or image of death as a marker of incorrect or poor gameplay. While this may preclude a number of important genres such as puzzle games, music games, driving games, and sports games, portions of this model — especially those dealing with repetition and the drive to creates one's own "path" — may be useful in other contexts.

5 Prior to the digital turn, the cinema would occasionally toy with alternative approaches to temporality in films like Kurosawa's *Rashomon* (1950). However, the success of films like *Pulp Fiction* (1994) and *Memento* (2000) cemented nonlinear storytelling as a defining characteristic of digital-era cinema.

6 Using animations rotoscoped (i.e., digitally traced) from home videos of his brother jumping and flailing about, Mechner's prince would shuffle his feet when attempting to slow down, swing his arms behind himself to catch his balance near-steep drops, and wield his sword with both grace and menace — an attention to real-world physics that, as we saw in Chapter 1, became a key component of digital simulations of death.

7 *The Sands of Time* was, admittedly, not the first three-dimensional *Prince of Persia* game. That honor belongs to *Prince of Persia 3D*, a poorly received, early three-dimensional game made in 1999 without Mechner's involvement by Red Orb Entertainment, a division of Brøderbund who were known more for educational titles than action-adventure games.

8 Laura Mulvey, *Death 24x a Second* (London: Reaktion Books, 2006), 11.

9 Ibid., 67.

10 Roland Barthes, *Camera Lucida: Reflections on Photography*, trans. Richard Howard (New York: Hill and Wang, 1981), 117; Andre Bazin, *What Is Cinema?* trans. Tim Barnhard (Montreal: Caboose, 2009), 9.

11 Roland Barthes, *The Responsibility of Forms: Critical Essays on Music, Art, and Representation*, trans. Richard Howard (Berkeley: University of California Press, 1991), 41–62.

12 Maria Walsh, "Against Fetishism: The Moving Quiescence of Life 24 Frames a Second," *Film Philosophy* 10, no. 2 (2006), 2.

13 Mulvey, *Death 24x a Second*, 161–80.

14 Steven Shaviro, "Post-Cinematic Affect: On Grace Jones, Boarding Gate and Southland Tales," *Film Philosophy* 14, no. 1 (2010), 16.

15 Walsh, "Against Fetishism," 1–2.

16 Digital technologies have also given the individual access to relatively advanced editing techniques, and with it the power to re-combine images in various ways. However, unlike the re-animation of digital games, these video mash-ups are only rebuttals to their original sources and, more often than not, are not intended to overwrite the initial action.

17 Mulvey, *Death 24x a Second*, 185–6.
18 Alexander R. Galloway, *Gaming: Essays on Algorithmic Culture* (Minneapolis, MN: University of Minnesota Press, 2006), 4.
19 Bernard N. Schumacher, *Death and Mortality in Contemporary Philosophy*, trans. Michael J. Miller (Cambridge: Cambridge University Press, 2011), 56.
20 Ibid., 56.
21 Ibid., 58.
22 Perhaps this partially explains why cinematic protagonists throughout most of the twentieth century (and especially during the 1980s) were usually depicted as perfect in both action and intent, whereas heroes in the digital age are often quite the opposite: fallible, accident prone, more lucky than skillful.
23 See Gottfried Wilhelm Leibniz, *Philosophical Papers and Letters: A Selection*, trans. Leroy E. Loemker (New York: Kluwer Academic Publishers, 2012).
24 Gilles Deleuze, *Cinema 2: The Time-Image*, trans. Hugh Tomlinson and Robert Galeta (London: Continuum, 1989), 130.
25 Ibid., 131.
26 Deleuze stresses that incompossibility is not the same as contradiction, but nonetheless one cannot know of the true existence of two incompossibilities *because* one necessarilycontradicts the other, so instead one can only know that two *possibilities* exist. This is why Deleuze states that "only the incompossible proceeds from the possible." Ibid., 130.
27 Marcus Schulzke, "Moral Decision Making in Fallout," *The International Journal of Computer Game Research* 9, no. 2 (2009), 2.
28 Ibid., 2.
29 At the same time, *Bioshock*'s insistence on explaining re-animation can only destabilize the process — rather than a temporal rewinding, death becomes a spatial displacement, as the player is instantly transported to the nearest Vita-Chamber to be "restored" without jumping back in time. As such, time in *Bioshock* is not compossible so much as death itself and death alone.
30 Looking at these endings from another perspective, the "bad" ending denies the player a complete image of their own death (instead only implying its inevitability), while the "good" ending provides absolute confirmation of a narratively satisfying death.
31 Friedrich Nietzsche, *The Gay Science*, trans. Walter Kaufmann (New York: Random House, 1974).
32 Ibid.
33 Ibid.
34 Ibid.
35 Alexander Cooke, "Eternal Return and the Problem of the Constitution of Identity," *Journal of Nietzsche Studies*, no. 29 (2005), 16–34, 17.
36 Ibid., 18.
37 As we will see in Chapter 3, without the ability to construct a coherent sense of identity we also lose the ability to fully recognize death, and while *virtual* subjectivities exist independent of the body and therefore outside of death, they always point to death's *actual* necessity and thus are always already a response to temporal limitations of the body.
38 This is, admittedly, a simplification of Heidegger's project to explicate "the principle of identity" in his essay of the same name. Martin Heidegger, *Identity*

and Difference, trans. Joan Stambaugh (Chicago: University of Chicago Press, 2002), 27–9; and Martin Heidegger, "Nihilism," in Friedrich Nietzsche, *Basic Writings of Nietzsche*, ed. and trans. Walter Kaufmann (New York: The Modern Library, 2000), 855.

39 Heidegger, "Nihilism," 852.
40 Ibid., 855.
41 Grant Tavinor, "Bioshock and the Art of Rapture," *Philosophy and Literature* 33, no. 1 (2009), 91–106, 104.
42 More often than not, chance in games is centered around life and death. In gaming, "I have unlimited lives" and "I have unlimited chances" are equivalent statements.
43 Gilles Deleuze, *Nietzsche and Philosophy*, trans. Hugh Tomlinson (New York: Columbia University Press, 2002), xi.
44 Gilles Deleuze, *Difference and Repetition*, trans. Paul Patton (New York: Columbia University Press, 1994), 71.
45 Ibid., 76.
46 Ibid., 57; emphasis mine.
47 Daniel W. Conway, "Tumbling Dice: Gilles Deleuze and the Economy of Repetition," *symploke* 6, no. 1 (1998), 7–25.
48 Deleuze, "Nietzsche and Philosophy," xiv.
49 Sigmund Freud, "Beyond the Pleasure Principle," in *Collected Writings*, trans. A.A. Brill (Seattle, WA: Pacific Publishing Studio, 2010) 240–2.
50 Ibid., 242.
51 Ibid., 243.
52 W. Craig Tomlinson, "*Jenseits* and Beyond: Teaching Freud's Late Work," in *On Freud's "Beyond the Pleasure Principle,"* ed. Salman Akhtar and Mary Kay O'Neil (London: Karnac Books, 2011), 74.
53 Ibid.
54 In fact, when Freud makes his bold claim that "the goal of all life is death," he puts his own phrase in quotation marks, as if to distance himself, to assure us that he is merely an observer and thus not responsible for the drive toward death. Freud, "Beyond the Pleasure Principle," 244, 248.
55 Ibid. One significant difference between the approaches of Nietzsche and Freud is that where Nietzsche understood the difficulty of accepting the doctrine of eternal return — "the heaviest burden" — he felt compelled to argue for it more and more as his philosophy matured. Freud, on the other hand, was never comfortable with the notion that life strives for death, and therefore worked to distance the death drive from the very consequences of such a thought.
56 Freud, "Beyond the Pleasure Principle," 245.
57 Ibid., 247.
58 Freud, "Beyond the Pleasure Principle," 245.
59 Ibid.
60 Ibid.
61 Later games in the series would play with the protagonist's death in interesting ways. After Marston is once again killed at the end of the non-canon horror DLC *Undead Nightmare*, players amusingly find themselves in control not of Marston's son but rather a zombified Marston, a rather literal instance of

"re-animation." More interesting is the prequel, *Red Dead Redemption 2*, in which players inhabit the role of Arthur Morgan, a former member of Marston's outlaw gang. Part way through the campaign, Arthur suddenly becomes ill and must seek a doctor, who tells him that he has contracted tuberculosis. Despite the player's best efforts, Arthur dies before he has enacted his revenge again those who have wronged him, and the game uses that narratively *unsatisfying* death to comment on the fact not everyone dies a hero. Only in an epilogue, where players once again control John Marston, can Arthur's wishes be posthumously fulfilled.
62 Peter Brooks, *Reading for the Plot: Design and Intention in Narrative* (New York: Alfred A. Knopf, 1984), 92–3.
63 Ibid., 95.
64 Ibid.
65 Mulvey, *Death 24x a Second*, 72.
66 Thanks to their roots in dice-driven, table-top gaming, contemporary RPGs and MMOs even refer to the creation of a new avatar (and thus a new virtual subjectivity) as "rolling a new character."
67 This small choice is especially important given that, at certain points in the game, small worm-like creatures attach themselves to the boy's head and take control over his movement, leaving the player feeling ever more vulnerable.

Chapter 3

1 Brian Massumi, *Parables for the Virtual* (Durham, NC and London: Duke University Press, 2002), 2.
2 Ibid., 137.
3 Much like Borges's map which is so large and so detailed as to entirely blanket reality, the digital serves as a virtual model which has begun to replace our perception of the actual. In fact, as was discussed in the introduction to this project, digital technologies have made the adoption of their own model of thinking essential, because they have provided new tools of communication which have expanded the scope the individual's empirical limit points well past the point of becoming sublime and therefore unmanageable.
4 Massumi, *Parables for the Virtual*, 137; emphasis mine.
5 Ibid., 9. Massumi borrows this example from Henri Bergson, who in turn was drawing upon Zeno's paradoxes of motion.
6 Ibid., 9.
7 For comparison's sake, consider the cultural response to nuclear warfare during the Cold War (immediately prior to the birth of digital thinking) which was based almost exclusively around potential rather than possibility, a constant and calculated consideration of the likelihood of attack alongside a continuous accounting of the variations and variables that could accompany it.
8 The only M&M's who seem unconcerned about the dangers of being considered a snack are the females, Green and Brown, who both read that hunger as primarily sexual in nature. Green, playing off the urban myth that

9   green M&M's are an aphrodisiac, is an aggressor, while Brown uses her cool, business-like demeanor to fend off a constant barrage of sexual advances. "He thinks you're naked," a friend tells Brown at a party, referencing a group of ogling men. "My shell is brown," she explains with a dry annoyance, "it only looks like my milk chocolate is showing."
9   Considering that the term "angst" is a direct translation of the Danish word for anxiety — first introduced into English through a mid-twentieth-century translation of Kierkegaard's *The Concept of Anxiety* — throughout this chapter I'll use the two terms somewhat interchangeably. That said, the term "angst" often carries with it (at least in its modern, colloquial usage) a greater specificity, in that it frequently implies a depression brought about by the anticipation of death, as opposed to more general anxieties relating to injury, loss, or misfortune. Aside from its frequent pairing with the word existential, for example, one of the most common contemporary associations for the term is the "angsty teenager," a stereotype that fully took root during the national panic concerning teen suicide following Kurt Kobain's death in 1994.
10 Imagine how postwar audiences of the 1950s would have responded to these commercials, and how perverse it would have seemed to suggest that a cartoon mascot would ever experience an existential crisis akin to the "shell-shock" of soldiers who bore witness to death and violence on a grand scale.
11 Paul Tillich, *The Courage to Be* (New Haven, CT: Yale University Press, 1952), 125. *The Concept of Anxiety*, Kierkegaard's most thorough examination of angst and the central text explored here, was, like a number of his early works, published under a pseudonym, in this case Vigilius Haufniensis. Kierkegaard's strategy at the time was to publish his "upbuilding discourses" — i.e., those works with an explicitly Christian message — under his own name, while his "expressions of an aesthetic or ethical orientation" would be pseudonymous. In this regard, however, *The Concept of Anxiety* is somewhat unique, in that its arguments regarding the origin of anxiety are grounded explicitly in biblical Scriptures, suggesting that the book's implications as to the value or role of anxiety must have seemed secular or controversial enough to warrant the adoption of the nom de plum. For more, see Gordon D. Marino, "Anxiety in *The Concept of Anxiety*," in Alastair Hannay and Gordon D. Marino, *The Cambridge Companion to Kierkegaard* (Cambridge: Cambridge University Press, 1998).
12 Søren Kierkegaard, *The Concept of Anxiety*, trans. Reidar Thomte (Princeton, NJ: Princeton University Press, 1980), 37.
13 Ed Cameron, "The Ethical Paradox in Kierkegaard's *Concept of Anxiety*," *Colloquy: Text Theory Critique*, no. 13 (May 2007), 98; Kierkegaard, *The Concept of Anxiety*, 44. In fact, Kierkegaard's text is largely a rebuttal of the concept of original sin, which argues that Adam's fall from grace barred our possibility for innocence by fashioning within us the propensity toward sin. Instead, Kierkegaard reads our anxiety as precisely akin to Adam's, in that we are always, to some degree or another, both ignorant of sin and yet capable of knowing it.
14 Natalie Wulfing, "Anxiety in Existential Philosophy and the Question of the Paradox," *Existential Analysis* 19, no. 1 (2008), 74.
15 Marino, "Anxiety in *The Concept of Anxiety*," 317.

16 Rollo May, *The Meaning of Anxiety* (New York: The Ronald Press Company, 1950), 32.
17 Ibid.
18 "The prohibition induces in [Adam] anxiety," Kierkegaard tells us, "for the prohibition awakens in him freedom's possibility." Kierkegaard, *The Concept of Anxiety*, 44.
19 Kierkegaard, *The Concept of Anxiety*, 91.
20 Ibid., 45.
21 Frederic Jameson, *Postmodernism: Or, the Cultural Logic of Late Capitalism* (Durham, NC: Duke University Press, 1991), 10.
22 Ibid., 11, 14.
23 Jameson argues that they only affect which remains in postmodern works of art is "a peculiar kind of euphoria" which Lyotard called "intensity," but we which could also read as akin to the "shock of the hoax" which we discussed in Chapter 1, an image which fails to truly replicate the experience which it represents. Ibid., 16.
24 Martin Heidegger, *Being and Time*, trans. John Macquarrie and Edward Robinson (New York: Harper Perennial, 1962), 231.
25 Jean-Paul Sartre, *Being and Nothingness*, trans. Hazel E. Barnes (New York: Washington Square Press, 1992), 73.
26 Heidegger, *Being and Time*, 32.
27 Ibid., 226.
28 Wulfing, "Anxiety in Existential Philosophy," 75.
29 Meghan Craig, "To Be or Not to Be: Understanding Authenticity from an Existential Perspective," *Existential Analysis* 20, no. 2 (2009), 294.
30 Sartre, *Being and Nothingness*, 86; emphasis mine.
31 Ibid., 39.
32 Hazel E. Barnes, "Translator's Introduction and Notes to Special Terminology," in Jean-Paul Sartre, *Being and Nothingness* (New York: Washington Square Press, 1992), 800; Richard Pearce, "On Being a Person: Sartre's Contributions to Psychotherapy," *Existential Analysis* 22, no. 1 (2011), 1–3.
33 Pearce, "On Being a Person," 4.
34 Barnes, "Translator's Introduction," xlvi–xlvii. We must be careful not to confuse this "transcendence" with the *a priori* sense of self found in the transcendental thought of Kant and Husserl. Here, it is the individual who "transcends" — or at least attempts to "transcend" — the boundaries of subjectification, to push beyond the ease and comfort of Being-for-others in order to recognize and connect with one's anxiety.
35 Sartre, quoted in Wulfing, "Anxiety in Existential Philosophy," 77.
36 Craig, "To Be or Not to Be," 293; emphasis mine.
37 Robert D. Stolorow, "Toward Greater Authenticity: From Shame to Existential Guilt, Anxiety, and Grief," *International Journal of Psychoanalytic Self Psychology* 6 (2011), 285; Sartre, *Being and Nothingness*, 89.
38 Sartre, *Being and Nothingness*, 88. In his chapter on "The Look" in *Being and Time*, Sartre lays out a "look" through which we render others into objects within our facticity, while also recognizing (at the same moment) that we are objects within the "look" of the other.
39 Barnes, "Translator's Introduction," xxxix.

40 Craig, "To Be or Not to Be," 293; Stolorow, "Toward Greater Authenticity," 285.
41 Of course, when it rains it pours: released mere months after the premiere of *The Sopranos*, the Harold Ramis-directed film *Analyze This* presents a similar premise with a comedy twist, a clear indicator of the pervasiveness and proliferation of angst in contemporary culture.
42 From Caesar Bandelloto to Michael Corleone, from Tony Camonte to Tony Montana, gangsters in American entertainment have personified the myth of the American dream through their flawless performance of ruthlessness, will, determination, and loyalty, a role that they play up to and even through their deaths. Perhaps it's Henry Hill of *Goodfellas*, whose story is a microcosm of the shift from the romanticized, Robin Hood-esque gangsters of the 1950s to the cocaine-fueled neurotics of the 1980s, who can be seen as the transitional figure, the gangster who begrudgingly shoves us into an age of authenticity even as he himself fights against it.
43 Robert D. Stolorow and Robert Eli Sanchez, "Philosophy as Therapy: The Case of Heidegger," *International Journal of Psychoanalytic Self Psychology* 4, no. 4 (2009), 128.
44 Kenneth C. Bessant, "Authenticity, Community, and Modernity," *Journal for the Theory of Social Behaviour* 41, no. 1 (2010), 4; Andrea Kenkmann, "Circles of Solicitude and Concern," *International Journal of Philosophical Studies* 13, no. 4 (2005), 478.
45 Heidegger, *Being and Time*, 193.
46 Michael Inwood, *Heidegger: A Very Short Introduction* (Oxford: Oxford University Press, 1997), 59.
47 Tony Fisher, "Bad Faith and the Actor: Onto-Mimetology from a Sartrean Point of View," *Sartre Studies International* 15, no. 1 (2009), 378. Here we see a break between Heidegger and Sartre, for Heidegger saw one's existence as determined by one's facticity and the possibilities it brings to bear (though one could either authentically face one's possibilities or inauthentically deny them), whereas the notion that the individual Being is non-determined was central to Sartre's entire philosophy.
48 Brent Adkins, *Death and Desire in Hegel, Heidegger, and Deleuze* (Edinburgh: Edinburgh University Press, 2007), 46.
49 Lacan, for his part, concretely linked the uncanny — which he read as any object which is removed from its context and thus made unfamiliar — to the production of anxiety.
50 Wulfing, "Anxiety in Existential Philosophy," 75.
51 François Raffoul, "Rethinking Selfhood: From Enowning," *Research in Phenomenology* 37 (2007), 94.
52 Heidegger, quoted in Hubert L. Dreyfus and Mark A. Wrathall, *A Companion to Heidegger* (Oxford: Blackwell Publishing, 2005), 11.
53 David A. Stone and Christina Papadimitriou, "Exploring Heidegger's Ecstatic Temporality in the Context of Embodied Breakdown," *Schutzian Research* 2 (2010), 140.
54 For more on Heidegger's elaboration of the temporalization of Dasein, see James Luchte, *Heidegger's Early Philosophy: The Phenomenology of Ecstatic Temporality* (London: Continuum, 2008); and Hakhamanesh Zangeneh,

"Phenomenological Problems for the Kairological Reading of Augenblick in Being and Time," *International Journal of Philosophical Studies* 19, no. 4 (2011).

55 Graham Harman, *Heidegger Explained: From Phenomenon to Thing* (Chicago, IL: Open Court Press, 2007), 68.
56 Bruce Baugh, "Death and Temporality in Deleuze and Derrida," *Angelaki: Journal of the Theoretical Humanities* 5, no. 2 (2000), 74.
57 Søren Kierkegaard, *The Sickness unto Death*, trans. Alastair Hannay (London: Penguin Books, 2004), 45.
58 Heidegger, *Being and Time*, 175.
59 Ibid., 345.
60 Ibid. There appears to be some play in Heidegger's use of the term "resolution" — clearly felt in Taylor Carmen's analysis of *Being and Time*, for example — in that it implies both the projection necessary in Being-toward and a sense of death as the resolution of life. Taylor Carmen, *Heidegger's Analytic: Interpretation, Discourse and Authenticity in Being and Time* (Cambridge: Cambridge University Press, 2003), 279–80, 298.
61 Heidegger, *Being and Time*, 345; emphasis in Heidegger.
62 Heidegger, quoted in Gjermund Wollen, "Heidegger's Philosophy of Space and Place," *Norsk Geografisk Tidsskrift–Norwegian Journal of Geography* 57 (2003), 35.
63 Heidegger, *Being and Time*, 345.
64 As we will see, *Breaking Bad* could never have ended with any event other than Walt's passing (its final shot unsurprisingly hovering above his lifeless body).
65 In fact, the first moment where we truly see Walt struggle with his diagnosis is when he finds out the cancer has momentarily gone into remission, which challenges the certainty of his plan and his projection toward a specific future.
66 Sherry Turkle, *Life on the Screen: Identity in the Age of the Internet* (New York: Simon & Schuster, 1995), 8, 260.
67 Lisa Nakamura, *Cybertypes: Race, Ethnicity, and Identity on the Internet* (New York: Routledge, 2002).
68 Steven Shaviro, *Connected, or, What It Means to Live in the Network Society* (Minneapolis: University of Minnesota Press, 2003), 13.
69 See Donna J. Haraway, *Simians, Cyborgs, and Women: The Reinvention of Nature* (New York: Routledge, 2013); Judith Butler, *Bodies That Matter: On the Discursive Limits of "Sex"* (New York: Psychology Press, 1993).
70 Kenneth Burke, *A Grammar of Motives* (Berkeley: University of California Press, 1969); Erving Goffman, *The Presentation of Self in Everyday Life* (New York: Anchor Books, 1959). For Goffman, these included "onstage" or "front region" performances (where the individual "maintains and embodies certain standards" established by an audience of other people), "backstage" or "back region" performances (where the audience's disappearance or disavowal allows one's onstage performance to be "knowingly contradicted," though one is still acting as a "team-player"), and even "offstage" or "outside" actions (where one's central performance is momentarily put on hold in order to address the concerns of a specific audience directly). Goffman, *The Presentation of Self*, 67, 69.

71 The obvious exception here is Kierkegaard, who saw one's spirit as preexistent to one's Being.
72 Levi R. Bryant, *Difference and Givenness: Deleuze's Transcendental Empiricism and the Ontology of Immanence* (Evanston: Northwestern University Press, 2008), 3.
73 David Detmer, *Sartre Explained: From Bad Faith to Authenticity* (Chicago, IL: Open Court Press, 2008), 19, 21; emphasis mine.
74 Mogens Lærke, "Four Things Deleuze Learned from Leibniz," in *Deleuze and The Fold: A Critical Reader*, ed. Sjoerd van Tuinen and Niamh McDonnell (New York: Palgrave Macmillan, 2010), 28.
75 Gilles Deleuze, *Bergsonism*, trans. Hugh Tomlinson and Barbara Habberjam (New York: Zone Books, 1991), 96.
76 Ibid.; first two emphases mine.
77 Gilles Deleuze, *Dialogues II*, trans. Claire Parnet (Columbia: Columbia University Press, 2002), 148.
78 Ibid., 149; emphasis mine.
79 Following the observations of our last chapter on the temporality of gamespaces, it's worth noting here that the actual and the virtual each have, for Deleuze, their own temporal component, and their distinction "corresponds to the most fundamental split in time, that is to say, the differentiation of its passage into *two great jets*: the passing of the present, and the preservation of the past." To stand in the actual is to experience a present moment slipping away, but to virtualize is to preserve the ephemeral *nature* of time within images that are themselves ephemeral. At the same time, one's future is also glimpsed within the virtual, because the virtual (as something real yet not actualized) "appears in a smaller space of time than that which marks the minimum movement in a single direction," so temporally and spatially sublime as to be in every way equal to "the longest time, longer than the longest unit of time imaginable in all directions." Within the virtual, one's past comes into direct contact with one's future. Ibid., 151.
80 Even when the player makes choices that are utterly opposed to what they might do in the real world, those choices are still *affective* because they allow the player to consider a broader spectrum of potential attitudes and actions, which are in turn *folded* into the player's actual subjectivity.
81 Pearce, "On Being a Person," 85.
82 Detmer, *Sartre Explained*, 21.
83 Pearce, "On Being a Person," 87.
84 Detmer, *Sartre Explained*, 21.
85 See Pearce, "On Being a Person."
86 Deleuze, *Bergsonism*, 97.
87 While neither *The Tree of Life* nor *Enter the Void* is a traditional sci-fi film, both employ some of the tropes of the genre. In the former, this entails the use of special effects to depict the geological and biological evolution of life on Earth, while in the latter we find a neon-soaked dystopian landscape clearly in the lineage of *Blade Runner*.
88 Given its sister tree's prominent role in Kierkegaard's proposed origin of anxiety, it's both interesting and unsurprising to find the Tree of Life appearing in more than one film confronting mankind's relationship to death, whether

"in the flesh" (as we see in *The Fountain*) or as symbol (as in *The Tree of Life*).

89 It's clear in his conversations with members of the crew that Kris's new subjective position is a desperate put-on, an experimental mindset which allows him to imagine a future where he and Rheya can "live together forever" (to borrow a phrase from *The Fountain*) even if it means denying what he knows is inevitable.

Chapter 4

1 Charlton D. McIlwain, *When Death Goes Pop: Death, Media, and the Remaking of Community* (New York: Peter Land Press, 2005), 21.
2 Daniel W. Smith, *Essays on Deleuze* (Edinburgh: Edinburgh University Press, 2012), 287.
3 Ibid.
4 Mark Seltzer, *Bodies and Machines* (New York: Routledge, 1992), 3–4.
5 Michel Foucault, *Discipline and Punish: The Birth of the Prison*, trans. Alan Sheridan (New York: Vintage Books,1995), 136.
6 Seltzer, *Bodies and Machines*, 161.
7 N. Katherine Hayles, *How We Became Posthuman: Virtual Bodies in Cybernetics, Literature, and Informatics* (Chicago, IL: University of Chicago Press, 1999), 115.
8 Ibid.
9 Ibid.
10 Ibid., 4.
11 Donna Haraway, "A Cyborg Manifesto," in *The Cybercultures Reader*, ed. David Bell and Barbara M. Kennedy (New York: Routledge, 2000), 291.
12 Steven Shaviro, "Supa Dupa Fly: Black Women as Cyborgs in Hip Hop Videos," *Quarterly Review of Film and Video* 22 (2005).
13 Hayles, *How We Became Posthuman*, 84–5; emphasis mine.
14 Adam I. Bostic, "Automata: Seeing Cyborg through the Eyes of Popular Culture, Computer-Generated Imagery, and Contemporary Theory," *Leonardo* 31, no. 5 (1998), 360.
15 Doran Larson, "Machine as Messiah: Cyborgs, Morphs, and the American Body Politic," *Cinema Journal* 36, no. 4 (Summer, 1997), 58.
16 J.P. Telotte, "Human Artifice and the Science Fiction Film," *Film Quarterly* 36, no. 3 (1983), 49.
17 This led to a vast proliferation in the manufacture of VI or *virtual intelligence*, synthetic beings that lack self-awareness.
18 Note the even their name — *the* Geth — suggests both a race of Beings and a single, unified, collective consciousness.
19 A similar if less-nuanced version of this same type of immortal machine is found in the Marvel superhero film *Avengers: Age of Ultron*, whose central villain, the titular Ultron, is an advanced AI whose consciousness is diffused amongst a great many machine bodies, its sense of immortality born from

sheer strength of numbers. This is relayed rather dramatically when one of Ultron's machines taunts one of the film's heroines, only to be violently destroyed mid-sentence by a larger, more intimidating machine that proceeds to finish the sentence as if nothing had happened. Indeed, for a consciousness that can exist simultaneously across numerous platforms, the destruction of one mere body is, in fact, akin to nothing.

20 Alain Badiou, *Being and Event* (London: Continuum, 2007), 23.
21 Ibid., 24.
22 As Badiou puts it, "it should be taken quite seriously that one is a number. And yet, except if we pythagorize, there is no cause to posit that being qua being is number." Ibid.
23 Gilles Deleuze, "Theories of Multiplicities in Bergson," *Lectures by Gilles Deleuze*, http://deleuzelectures.blogspot.com (accessed April 5, 2015).
24 Smith, *Essays on Deleuze*, 287.
25 Alain Badiou, *Deleuze: The Clamor of Being*, trans. Louise Burchill (Minneapolis: University of Minnesota Press, 2000), 18.
26 Smith, *Essays on Deleuze*, 306.
27 Peter Hallward, *Badiou: A Subject of Truth* (Minneapolis: University of Minnesota Press, 2003), 52.
28 Badiou, quoted in Smith, *Essays on Deleuze*, 288.
29 Badiou, quoted in Hallward, *A Subject of Truth*, 7.
30 Badiou, quoted in ibid., 52.
31 Badiou, *Deleuze: The Clamor of Being*, 23. This is, of course, already a misreading by Badiou, for Deleuze was clear that the univocity of Being is in no way equivalent to the unity of "the One."
32 The only real difference between "programs" and "machines" is that the former function within the virtual confines of the Matrix while the latter function in the "real world" with the help of their temporary and replaceable metallic bodies. Otherwise, all synthetic Beings of *The Matrix* are actually housed as digital code within the Source.
33 Smith, *Essays on Deleuze*, 288. Deleuze provided his own names for quantitative multiplicity, including "multiplicity of juxtaposition, numerical multiplicity, distinct multiplicity, actual multiplicity, [and] material multiplicity," and likewise he referred to his preferred theory as a "multiplicity of penetration, qualitative multiplicity, confused multiplicity, virtual multiplicity, [and] organized multiplicity." Deleuze, "Theories of Multiplicities in Bergson."
34 Smith, *Essays on Deleuze*, 302.
35 In our last chapter, I argued that the virtual, though clearly related to the possible, is also an avenue through which we can recognize potential. Here we see an extension of that argument, where it is problems — a "nested field" of "virtual trajectories," as Smith puts it — that demonstrates potential, whereas inherently singular and possibilistic solutions show us only what is actualized. Ibid.
36 Ibid., 304.
37 Alain Badiou, "Existence and Death," *Discourse: Journal for Theoretical Studies in Media and Culture* 24, no. 1 (2002), 71, 72; emphasis mine.

38 Roberto Casati, and Achille Varzi, "Events," in *The Stanford Encyclopedia of Philosophy*, ed. Edward N. Zalta (Fall 2014 Edition), http://plato.stanford.edu/entries/events/

39 Remember that "the situation" is a substitute term for existence, which Badiou finds to be something other than being. "The fundamental problem [of philosophy]" he tells us, "is to distinguish on the one hand, being as such, being qua being, and, on the other hand, existence, as a category which precisely is not reducible to that of being. It is the heart of the matter." Alain Badiou, "Towards a New Concept of Existence," *Lacanian Ink* 29 (Spring 2007).

40 As a staunch atheist, Badiou would never think of death as a transition to another (and certainly not a higher) state of consciousness, and so death, insofar as it is possible, must be the end of all thought. Peter Hallward, "Translator's Introduction," in *Ethics: An Essay on the Understanding of Evil*, ed. Alain Badiou (London: Verso, 2001), xix.

41 Badiou, *Existence and Death*, 72.

42 Peter Hallward, "Depending on Inconsistency: Badiou's Answer to the 'Guiding Question of All Contemporary Philosophy,'" *Polygraph* 17 (2005), 14.

43 Smith, *Essays on Deleuze*, 310.

44 Hallward, "Depending on Inconsistency," 13.

45 Quentin Meillassoux, *After Finitude: An Essay on the Necessity of Contingency*, trans. Ray Brassier (London: Continuum, 2008), 129.

46 Given his explicit rejection of the linguistic turn of de Saussure and Lacan, it's odd to find that the function of naming in Badiou's theory (and by extension that of the event) is so closely analogous to the relationship between language and trauma in Lacan — in giving something a name, an overwhelming or invisible inconsistency is made orderly and consistent to being. Yet perhaps this why Badiou felt compelled to distance himself from the more basic enactments of this process by making one of his most difficult assertions, that "the void" is the "proper name of being," which is not to follow Sartre in saying that being is nothingness, but rather a statement that the *pure multiplicity of being-qua-being* cannot be contained within a singular term or name (such that being itself is made to count-as-one). Thus the "name of being," as that which can never count-as-one, belongs to *no set* or, in other words, the empty set, $\emptyset$. At the same time, "the void" *names being* because the act of naming (to count a thing as-one) is to declare that a thing is *not nothing*, and thus to *subtract it* from "the void." Badiou, *Being and Event*, 173.

47 "Perhaps the most distinctive and unusual feature of Badiou's ontology," Hallward continues, "is the rigor with which he maintains this strictly *implicative* condition" — that to count a thing as-one necessarily implies its inherent multiplicity. Along these lines, Badiou's former student Quentin Meillassoux observes that "philosophy is the invention of strange forms of argumentation, necessarily bordering on sophistry, which remains its dark structural double. To philosophize is always to develop an idea whose elaboration and defense require a novel kind of argumentation," one dependent upon "internal mechanisms for regulating its own inferences," such as Badiou's dialectical implication of multiplicity. Hallward, "Depending on Inconsistency," 11; Meillassoux, *After Finitude*, 127.

48 Henry Somers-Hall, "Deleuze's Philosophical Heritage," in *The Cambridge Companion to Deleuze*, ed. Daniel W. Smith and Henry Somers-Hall (Cambridge: Cambridge University Press, 2012), 349–50.
49 Ibid., 350.
50 Badiou, quoted in Hallward, *A Subject of Truth*, 91.
51 Hallward, *A Subject of Truth*, 91.
52 Badiou, *Existence and Death*, 72. We've obviously seen, again and again, the difficulties in presenting death — not just representing, but making death an integrated and thus consistent facet of our lives (this, despite the fact that beneath the surface, death already influences nearly every aspect of our culture). At the same time, our inability to "define" death is in every way an inability to "name" death.
53 Ibid., 66.
54 After all, why would a purely mathematical consciousness have any interest in that which is "supernumerary" to ontology?
55 Hallward, "Translator's Introduction," xix. Elsewhere, Hallward writes that "to put it in conventional Kantian terms: we are inconsistency (i.e., pure indetermination or unbounded freedom) but we can never … have some radical encounter, via our finitude or mortality, with our ownmost being." Hallward, "Depending on Inconsistency," 18.
56 Smith, *Essays on Deleuze*, 288.
57 John Protevi, "Deleuze and Life," in *The Cambridge Companion to Deleuze*, ed. Daniel W. Smith and Henry Somers-Hall (Cambridge: Cambridge University Press, 2012), 244.
58 Smith, *Essays on Deleuze*, 304; emphasis mine.
59 Badiou, "Towards a New Concept of Existence."
60 Henry Somers-Hall, "Introduction," in *The Cambridge Companion to Deleuze*, ed. Daniel W. Smith and Henry Somers-Hall (Cambridge: Cambridge University Press, 2012), 6.
61 Protevi, "Deleuze and Life," 256–7.
62 Louise Burchill, "Translator's Preface: Portraiture in Philosophy or Shifting Perspectives," in Alain Badiou, *Deleuze: The Clamor of Being*, trans. Louise Burchill (Minneapolis: University of Minnesota Press, 2000), x.
63 Smith had earlier told a member of the resistance that he believed humans to be not mammals but rather viruses, in that they continually move to new areas, multiply as rapidly as they can, utterly deplete all resources, and then leave their host environment spent and destroyed.

Conclusion

1 Jacques Choron, *Death and Western Thought* (New York: Collier Books, 1963), 242.
2 Anna Powell, *Deleuze, Altered States and Film* (Edinburgh: Edinburgh University Press, 2007), 177. For more on Mandelbrot's early work on fractals, see Benoit B. Mandelbrot, *Fractals: Form, Chance, and Dimension* (San Francisco, CA: W.H. Freeman, 1977).

3 Ian Hamilton Grant, "Postmodernism and Science and Technology" and "Critical Terms," in *The Routledge Companion to Postmodernism, Third Edition*, ed. Stuart Sim (New York: Routledge, 2011), 254; emphasis mine.
4 Gilles Deleuze and Felix Guattari, *What Is Philosophy?* (New York: Columbia University Press, 1994), 36–40; Powell, *Deleuze, Altered States and Film*, 177.
5 Powell, *Deleuze, Altered States and Film*, 177; emphasis mine.
6 Grant, "Critical Terms," 255.
7 Perhaps this popularity was inspired, if only on an unconscious level, by the fact that they functioned as "the icon of *chaos*," as Grant tells us, "that seems so aptly to sum up the endless fragmentations of postmodernity. ... If under Mandelbrot, geometry goes back to the Earth, then it is only to prove that the Earth, once thought flat (pre-modern), then spherical (modern), is now fractal and infinite, thus demonstrably post-modern." Note that Grant's observation not only points to the birthplace of fractals as not mathematics but rather geography, but also that it hints at the expansion of our empirical limits at the beginning of the digital age. Grant, "Postmodernism," 99.
8 In *A Thousand Plateaus*, Deleuze and Guattari refer to Menger sponges — three-dimensional fractals consisting of endlessly subdivided cubes, which have infinite surface yet no volume — as "Sierpinsky's sponge." Gilles Deleuze and Felix Guattari, *A Thousand Plateaus*, trans. Brian Massumi (Minneapolis: University of Minnesota Press, 1987), 538.
9 Mark Bonta and John Protevi, *Deleuze and Geophilosophy: A Guide and Glossary* (Edinburgh: Edinburgh University Press, 2004), 98.
10 Ibid.
11 Steve Silberman, "The Outsider," *Wired* 14, no. 11 (2006). "Macrophotography" refers to the creation of images whose subjects appear far larger than their actual size, and not to the creation of overly large photographs. Conversely, "microphotography" is the art of making very small photographs, and not necessarily the creation of images whose subjects are much smaller than their actual size (presumably because most photographic images are printed or displayed smaller than their actual subjects).
12 Ibid.
13 Andrew Pickering, "Cybernetics as Nomad Science," in *Deleuzian Intersections: Science, Technology, Anthropology*, ed. Casper Bruun Jensen and Kjetil Rödje (New York: Berghahn Books, 2010), 160.

BIBLIOGRAPHY

Ariés, Philippe. *The Hour of Our Death*. Translated by Helen Weaver. New York: Vintage Books, 2008.
Ariés, Philippe. *Western Attitudes towards Death*. Translated by Patricia M. Ranum. Baltimore, MD: Johns Hopkins University Press, 1974.
Badiou, Alain. *Being and Event*. London: Continuum, 2007.
Badiou, Alain. *Deleuze: The Clamor of Being*. Translated by Louise Burchill. Minneapolis: University of Minnesota Press, 2000.
Badiou, Alain. "Existence and Death." *Discourse: Journal for Theoretical Studies in Media and Culture* 24, no. 1 (2002): 63–73.
Badiou, Alain. "Towards a New Concept of Existence." *Lacanian Ink* 29 (Spring 2009).
Barker, Jennifer M. *The Tactile Eye: Touch and the Cinematic Experience*. Berkeley: University of California Press, 2009.
Barnes, Hazel E. "Translator's Introduction and Notes to Special Terminology." In *Being and Nothingness*, by Jean-Paul Sartre, translated by Hazel E. Barnes. New York: Washington Square Press, 1992.
Barthes, Roland. *Camera Lucida: Reflections on Photography*. Translated by Richard Howard. New York: Hill and Wang, 1981.
Barthes, Roland. *The Pleasure of the Text*. Translated by Richard Miller. New York: Hill and Wang, 1975.
Barthes, Roland. *The Responsibility of Forms: Critical Essays on Music, Art, and Representation*. Translated by Robert Howard. Berkeley: University of California Press, 1991.
Baudrillard, Jean. *Fatal Strategies*. Translated by J Fleming. New York: Pluto, 1990.
Baudrillard, Jean. *Simulacra and Simulation*. Translated by Sheila Faria Glaser. Ann Arbor: University of Michigan Press, 1994.
Baugh, Bruce. "Death and Temporality in Deleuze and Derrida." *Angelaki* 5, no. 2 (2000): 73–83.
Bazin, Andre. *What Is Cinema?* Translated by Tim Barnhard. Montreal: Caboose, 2009.
Becker, Ernest. *The Denial of Death*. New York: Free Press Paperbacks, 1973.
Benjamin, Walter. *Illuminations*. Edited by Hannah Arendt. Translated by Harry Zohn. New York: Schocken Books, 2007.
Bessant, Kenneth C. "Authenticity, Community, and Modernity." *Journal for the Theory of Social Behavior* 41, no. 1 (2010): 2–32.
Bogost, Ian. *Unit Operations: An Approach to Videogame Criticism*. Cambridge, MA: MIT Press, 2006.

Bonta, Mark, and John Protevi. *Deleuze and Geophilosophy: A Guide and Glossary*. Edinburgh: Edinburgh University Press, 2004.
Bostic, Adam I. "Automata: Seeing Cyborg through the Eyes of Popular Culture, Computer-Generated Imagery, and Contemporary Theory." *Leonardo* 31, no. 5 (1998): 357–61.
Brinkman, Eugenie. "Rape and the Rectum: Bersani, Deleuze, Noé." *Camera Obscura* 20 (2005): 33–57.
Bronfen, Elisabeth. *Over Her Dead Body: Death, Femininity and the Aesthetic*. Oxford: Manchester University Press, 1992.
Brooks, Peter. *Reading for the Plot: Design and Intention in Narrative*. New York: Alfred A. Knopf, 1984.
Brottman, Mikita, and David Sterritt. "Irréversible." *Film Quarterly* 57, no. 2 (Winter 2003–2004): 37–42.
Brown Golden, Kristen. "Trauma and Speech as Bodily Adaptation in Merleau-Ponty." In *The Trauma Controversy: Philosophical and Interdisciplinary Dialogues*, edited by Kristen Brown Golden and Bettina Bergo. Albany: State University of New York Press, 2009.
Bryant, Levi R. *Difference and Givenness: Deleuze's Transcendental Empiricism and the Ontology of Immanence*. Evanston: Northwestern University Pres, 2008.
Burchill, Louise. "Translator's Preface: Portraiture in Philosophy or Shifting Perspectives." In *Deleuze: The Clamor of Being*, by Alain Badiou, translated by Louise Burchill. Minneapolis: University of Minnesota Press, 2000.
Burke, Kenneth. *A Grammar of Motives*. Berkeley: University of California Press, 1969.
Butler, Judith. *Bodies That Matter: On the Discursive Limits of "Sex."* New York: Routledge, 1993.
Cameron, Ed. "The Ethical Paradox in Kierkegaard's Concept of Anxiety." *Colloquy: Text Theory Critique* 13, no. 13 (May 2007).
Carmen, Taylor. *Heidegger's Analytic: Interpretation, Discourse and Authenticity in Being and Time*. Cambridge: Cambridge University Press, 2003.
Carmen, Taylor, and Mark B.N. Hansen. "Introduction." In *The Cambridge Companion to Merleau-Ponty*, edited by Taylor Carmen and Mark B.N. Hansen. Cambridge: Cambridge University Press, 2005.
Casanova, Giacomo. *The Complete Memoires of Jacques Casanova de Seingalt: Vol. 3—The Eternal Quest*. Translated by Authur Machen. The Gutenberg Press, 2006.
Casati, Roberto, and Achille Varzi. "Events." In *The Stanford Encyclopedia of Philosophy*, edited by Edward N. Zalta. 2014. https://plato.stanford.edu/entries/events/
Choron, Jacques. *Death and Western Thought*. New York: Collier Books, 1963.
Combs, Scott. "Cut: Execution, Editing, and Instant Death." *The Instance* 38 (Fall 2008): 31–41.
Conway, Daniel W. "Tumbling Dice: Gilles Deleuze and the Economy of Repetition." *symploke* 6, no. 1 (1998): 7–25.
Cooke, Alexander. "Eternal Return and the Problem of the Constitution of Identity." *Journal of Nietzsche Studies*, no. 29 (2005): 16–34.

Craig, Meghan. "To Be or Not to Be: Understanding Authenticity from an Existential Perspective." *Existential Analysis* 20, no. 2 (2009): 292.
Debord, Guy. *Society of the Spectacle*. Translated by Ken Knabb. London: Rebel Press, 1967.
DeGrazia, David. "The Definition of Death." In *The Stanford Encyclopedia of Philosophy*, edited by Edward N. Zalta. 2011. https://plato.stanford.edu/entries/death-definition/
Deleuze, Gilles. *Bergsonism*. Translated by Hugh Tomlinson and Barbara Habberjam. New York: Zone Books, 1991.
Deleuze, Gilles. *Cinema 2: The Time-Image*. Translated by Hugh Tomlinson and Robert Galeta. London: Continuum, 1989.
Deleuze, Gilles. *Difference and Repetition*. Translated by Paul Patton. New York: Columbia University Press, 1994.
Deleuze, Gilles. *Nietzsche and Philosophy*. Translated by Hugh Tomlinson. New York: Columbia University Press, 2002.
Deleuze, Gilles, and Félix Guattari. *Anti-Oedipus: Capitalism and Schizophrenia*. New York: Penguin Books, 1977.
Deleuze, Gilles, and Félix Guattari. *A Thousand Plateaus: Capitalism and Schizophrenia*. Translated by Brian Massumi. Minneapolis: University of Minnesota Press, 1987.
Deleuze, Gilles, and Félix Guattari. *What Is Philosophy?* New York: Columbia University Press, 1994.
de los Rios, Riccardo, and Robert Davis. "Digital Frames and Visible Grain: Spatial and Material Reintegration in Irreversible." *Film Criticism* 32 (2007): 95–109.
de Mille, Charlotte, and John Mullarkey. "Introduction: Art's Philosophy—Bergson and Immanence." In *Bergson and the Art of Immanence*, edited by Charlotte De Mille and John Mullarkey. Edinburgh: Edinburgh University Press, 2013.
Detmer, David. *Sartre Explained: From Bad Faith to Authenticity*. Chicago, IL: Open Court Press, 2008.
Dickens, Charles. *A Tale of Two Cities*. San Francisco, CA: Ignatius Press, 2012.
Doane, Mary Anne. *The Emergence of Cinematic Time*. Cambridge, MA: Harvard University Press, 2002.
Dreyfus, Hubert L., and Mark A. Wrathall. *A Companion to Heidegger*. Oxford: Blackwell Publishing, 2005.
Eberly, David H. *Game Physics*. Second. Boca Raton, FL: CRC Press, 2010.
Feifel, Herman, ed. *The Meaning of Death*. New York: McGraw-Hill, 1959.
Fisher, Tony. "Bad Faith and the Actor: Onto-Mimetology from a Sartrean Point of View." *Sartre Studies International* 15, no. 1 (2009): 74–91.
Foucault, Michel. *The Birth of the Clinic*. New York: Routledge, 1993.
Foucault, Michel. *Discipline and Punish: The Birth of the Prison*. Translated by Alan Sheridan. New York: Vintage Books, 1995.
Frasca, Gonzalo. "Simulation versus Narrative." In *Video/Game/Theory*, edited by Mark J.P. Wolf and Bernard Perron. New York: Routledge, 2002.
Fraser, Antonia. *Mary, Queen of Scots*. London: Orion, 2014.
Freud, Sigmund. "Beyond the Pleasure Principle." In *Collected Writings*, translated by A.A. Brill. Seattle, WA: Pacific Publishing Studio, 2010.
Freud, Sigmund. *Collected Writings*. Translated by A.A. Brill. Seattle, WA: Pacific Publishing Studio, 2010.

Galloway, Alexander R. *Gaming: Essays on Algorithmic Culture*. Minneapolis, MN: University of Minnesota Press, 2006.
Goffman, Erving. *The Presentation of Self in Everyday Life*. New York: Anchor Books, 1959.
Gorer, Geoffrey. "The Pornography of Death." In *Death: Current Perspectives*, edited by John B. Williamson and Edwin S. Shneidman. Mountain View, CA: Mayfield Publishing Company, 1995.
Grant, Ian Hamilton. "'Postmodernism and Science and Technology' and 'Critical Terms.'" In *The Routledge Companion to Postmodernism, Third Edition*, edited by Stuart Sim. New York: Routledge, 2011.
Guy, John. *Queen of Scots: The True Life of Mary Stuart*. Boston, MA: Mariner Books, 2005.
Hallward, Peter. *Badiou: A Subject of Truth*. Minneapolis: University of Minnesota Press, 2003.
Hallward, Peter. "Depending on Inconsistency: Badiou's Answer to the 'Guiding Question of All Contemporary Philosophy.'" *Polygraph* 17 (2005): 7–21.
Hallward, Peter. "Translator's Introduction." In *Ethics: An Essay on the Understanding of Evil*, by Alain Badiou, translated by Peter Hallward. London: Verso, 2001.
Haraway, Donna. "A Cyborg Manifesto." In *The Cybercultures Reader*, edited by David Bell and Barbara M. Kennedy. New York: Routledge, 2000.
Haraway, Donna. *Simians, Cyborgs, and Women: The Reinvention of Nature*. New York: Routledge, 1991.
Harman, Graham. *Heidegger Explained: From Phenomenon to Thing*. Chicago, IL: Open Court Press, 2007.
Harvey, David. *The Condition of Postmodernity: An Enquiry into the Origins of Cultural Change*. Oxford: Blackwell Publishing, 1990.
Hayles, N. Katherine. *How We Became Posthuman: Virtual Bodies in Cybernetics, Literature, and Informatics*. Chicago, IL: University of Chicago Press, 1999.
Heidegger, Martin. *Being and Time*. Translated by John Macquarrie and Edward Robinson. New York: Harper Perennial Modern Thought, 2008.
Heidegger, Martin. *Identity and Difference*. Translated by Joan Stambaugh. Chicago, IL: University of Chicago Press, 2002.
Heidegger, Martin. "Nihilism." In *Basic Writings of Nietzsche*, by Friedrich Nietzsche, edited and translated by Walter Kaufmann. New York: The Modern Library, 2000.
Heidegger, Martin. *The Question Concerning Technology and Other Essays*. New York: Harper & Row, 1977.
Inwood, Michael. *Heidegger: A Very Short Introduction*. Oxford: Oxford University Press, 1997.
Jameson, Fredric. *Postmodernism: Or, the Cultural Logic of Late Capitalism*. Durham, NC: Duke University Press, 1991.
Kant, Immanuel. *Critique of Judgement*. Edited by Nicholas Walker. Translated by James Creed Meredith. Oxford: Oxford University Press, 2007.
Kant, Immanuel. *Critique of Pure Reason*. Translated by Marcus Weigelt. London: Penguin Books, 2007.
Kenkmann, Andrea. "Circle of Solicitude and Concern." *International Journal of Philosophical Studies* 13, no. 4 (2005): 477–88.

Kierkegaard, Søren. *The Concept of Anxiety*. Translated by Reidar Thomte. Princeton, NJ: Princeton University Press, 1980.
Kierkegaard, Søren. *The Sickness unto Death*. Translated by Alastair Hannay. London: Penguin Books, 2004.
Kracauer, Siegfried. "Basic Concepts." In *Film Theory and Criticism: Introductory Readings*, New York: Oxford University Press, 1999.
Kubler-Ross, Elizabeth. *On Death and Dying*. New York: Routledge, 1973.
Lacan, Jacques. *Ecrits: A Selection*. Translated by Bruce Fink. New York: W. W. Norton, 2004.
Lacan, Jacques. *The Four Fundamentals of Psychoanalysis: The Seminars of Jaques Lacan: Book XI*. Edited by Jaques-Alain Miller. Translated by Alan Sheridan. New York: W. W. Norton, 1998.
Larson, Doran. "Machine as Messiah: Cyborgs, Morphs, and the American Body Politic." *Cinema Journal* 36, no. 4 (1997): 57–75.
Leibniz, Gottfried Wilhelm. *Philosophical Papers and Letters: A Selection*. Translated by Leroy E. Loemker. New York: Kluwer Academic Publishers, 2012.
Luchte, James. *Heidegger's Early Philosophy: The Phenomenology of Ecstatic Temporality*. London: Continuum, 2008.
Lyotard, Francois. *The Postmodern Condition: A Report on Knowledge*. Minneapolis: University of Minnesota Press, 1993.
Lærke, Mogens. "Four Things Deleuze Learned from Leibniz." In *Deleuze and the Fold: A Critical Reader*, edited by Sjoerd van Tuinen and Niamh McDonnell. New York: Palgrave Macmillan, 2010.
Mandelbrot, Benoit B. *Fractals: Form, Chance, and Dimension*. San Francisco, CA: W.H. Freeman, 1977.
Manovich, Lev. *The Language of New Media*. Cambridge, MA: MIT Press, 2001.
Marino, Gordon D. "Anxiety in The Concept of Anxiety." In *The Cambridge Companion to Kierkegaard*, edited by Alastair Hannay and Gordon D. Marino. Cambridge: Cambridge University Press, 1998.
Massumi, Brian. *Parables of the Virtual: Movement, Affect, Sensation*. Durham, NC: Duke University Press, 2002.
May, Rollo. *The Meaning of Anxiety*. New York: The Ronald Press Company, 1950.
McIlwain, Charlton D. *When Death Goes Pop: Death, Media, and the Remaking of Community*. New York: Peter Lang Press, 2005.
Meillassoux, Quentin. *After Finitude: An Essay on the Necessity of Contingency*. Translated by Ray Brassier. London: Continuum, 2008.
Meillassoux, Quentin. "Subtraction and Contraction: Deleuze, Immanence, and Matter and Memory." *Collapse* III (2007): 63–107.
Merleau-Ponty, Maurice. *Phenomenology of Perception*. Translated by Colin Smith. London: Routledge Classics, 2002.
Mitford, Jessica. *The American Way of Death*. New York: Simon & Schuster, 1963.
Morris, Errol. *Believing is Seeing: Observations on the Mysteries of Photography*. New York: Penguin Press, 2011.
Mulvey, Laura. *Death 24x a Second*. London: Reaktion Books, 2006.
Nakamura, Lisa. *Cybertypes: Race, Ethnicity, and Identity on the Internet*. New York: Routledge, 2002.

Nietzche, Friedrich. *The Gay Science.* Translated by Walter Kaufmann. New York: Random House, 1974.
Nietzche, Friedrich. *Thus Spoke Zarathustra.* Translated by Clancy Martin. New York: Barnes and Noble Classics, 2005.
Pearce, Richard. "On Being a Person: Sartre's Contributions to Psychotherapy." *Existential Analysis* 22, no. 1 (2011): 83–95.
Pickering, Andrew. "Cybernetics as Nomad Science." In *Deleuzian Intersections: Science, Technology, Anthropology,* edited by Casper Bruun Jensen and Kjetil Rödje. New York: Berghahn Books, 2010.
Powell, Anna. *Deleuze, Altered States and Film.* Edinburgh: Edinburgh University Press, 2007.
Prince, Stephen, ed. *Screening Violence.* London: Athlone Press, 2000.
Protevi, John. "Deleuze and Life." In *The Cambridge Companion to Deleuze,* edited by Daniel W. Smith and Henry Somers-Hall. Cambridge: Cambridge University Press, 2012.
Raffoul, François. "Rethinking Selfhood: From Enowning." *Research in Phenomenology* 37 (2007): 75–94.
Sartre, Jean-Paul. *Being and Nothingness.* Translated by Hazel E. Barnes. New York: Washington Square Press, 1992.
Schulzke, Marcus. "Moral Decision Making in Fallout." *The International Journal of Computer Game Research* 9, no. 2 (2009).
Schumacher, Bernard N. *Death and Mortality in Contemporary Philosophy.* Translated by Michael J. Miller. Cambridge: Cambridge University Press, 2011.
Seltzer, Mark. *Bodies and Machines.* New York: Routledge, 1992.
Shaviro, Steven. *Connected, or, What It Means to Live in the Network Society.* Minneapolis: University of Minneapolis Press, 2003.
Shaviro, Steven. "Post-Cinematic Affect: On Grace Jones, Boarding Gate and Southland Tales." *Film Philosophy* 14, no. 1 (2010): 1–102.
Shaviro, Steven. "Supa Dupa Fly: Black Women as Cyborgs in Hip Hop Videos." *Quarterly Review of Film and Video* 22 (2005): 169–79.
Silberman, Steve. "The Outsider." *Wired* 14, no. 11 (2006).
Smith, Daniel W. *Essays on Deleuze.* Edinburgh: Edinburgh University Press, 2012.
Smith, Daniel W., and Henry Somers-Hall. *The Cambridge Companion to Deleuze.* Cambridge: Cambridge University Press, 2012.
Sobchack, Vivian. "Inscribing Ethical Space: Ten Propositions on Death, Representation, and Documentary." In *Carnal Thoughts: Embodiment and Moving Image Culture.* Berkeley: University of California Press, 2004.
Somers-Hall, Henry. "Deleuze's Philosophical Heritage." In *The Cambridge Companion to Deleuze,* edited by Daniel W. Smith and Henry Somers-Hall. Cambridge: Cambridge University Press, 2012.
Sontag, Susan. *Regarding the Pain of Others.* New York: Picador, 2003.
Stolorow, Robert D. "Towards Greater Authenticity: From Shame to Existential Guilt, Anxiety, and Grief." *International Journal of Psychoanalytic Self Psychology* 6 (2011): 285–7.
Stolorow, Robert D., and Robert Eli Sanchez. "Philosophy as Therapy: The Case of Heidegger." *International Journal of Psychoanalytic Self Psychology* 4 (2009): 125–31.

Stone, David A., and Christina Papadimitriou. "Exploring Heidegger's Ecstatic Temporality in the Context of Embodies Breakdown." *Schutzian Research* 2 (2010): 137–54.
Tavinor, Grant. "Bioshock and the Art of Rapture." *Philosophy and Literature* 33, no. 1 (2009): 91–106.
Telotte, J.P. "Human Artifice and the Science Fiction Film." *Film Quarterly* 36, no. 3 (1983): 44–51.
Tillich, Paul. *The Courage to Be*. New Haven, CT: Yale University Press, 1952.
Tomlinson, W. Craig. "Jenseits and Beyond: Teaching Freud's Late Work." In *On Freud's "Beyond the Pleasure Principle,"* edited by Salman Akhtar and Mary Kay O'Neil. London: Karnac Books, 2011.
Turkle, Sherry. *Life on the Screen: Identity in the Age of the Internet*. New York: Simon & Schuster, 1995.
Walsh, Maria. "Against Fetishism: The Moving Quiescence of Life 24 Frames a Second." *Film Philosophy* 10, no. 2 (2006): 1–10.
Wollen, Gjermund. "Heidegger's Philosophy of Space and Place." *Norsk Geografisk Tidsskrift–Norwegian Journal of Geography* 57 (2003): 31–9.
Wulfing, Natalie. "Anxiety in Existential Philosophy and the Question of the Paradox." *Existential Analysis* 19, no. 1 (January 2008): 73.
Zangeneh, Hakhamanesh. "Phenomenological Problems for the Kairological Reading of Augenblick in Being and Time." *International Journal of Philosophical Studies* 19, no. 4 (2011): 539–61.
Žižek, Slavoj. *How to Read Lacan*. New York: W. W. Norton, 2007.
Žižek, Slavoj. *Welcome to the Desert of the Real!: Five Essays on September 11th and Related Dates*. New York: Verso, 2002.

INDEX

abject 3, 31, 32, 51; death as 1, 11, 19, 133; witnessing as 14, 32; trauma as 21, 24
action: authentic vs. inauthentic 107, 117; compossibility and 61–2, 71; in digital games 80–1, 98–9, 120; digital games as action-driven 59, 61; as ethical choice 63–4, 68, 69, 77; the fold and 117
actual/actuality: actual subjectivity 5, 74–5, 115–17, 121–3, 128–9, 135, 138, 190 n.80; encounters with actual death 32–4; reality of death 2, 11, 14, 28, 40, 63; vs. representations 20, 25, 28–9, 179 n.86; vs. simulations 41, 43–4; vs. the virtual/virtuality 67, 88, 92, 117–19, 136, 185 n.3, 190 n.79
Adam and Eve 96, 187 n.18
androids 6, 138, 142–3, 144, 152, 165
angst. *See* anxiety
animation 58–9
anxiety 22, 80, 95, 98–100, 104–6, 114–15; Adam and Eve and 96, 187 n.18; authenticity and 6, 95, 100, 103–4, 107–9, 122; in commercial mascots 93–5; in contemporary culture 95, 97–8, 103, 122; in cyborgs 139, 141; *Dasein* and 101, 103; in existentialism 40, 92, 95–8, 100–1, 186 n.9, 186 n. 10, 186 n.13; vs. fear 95–6, 100; freedom and 96–7, 161; loss and 14; in *Lost* 109; possibility and 91, 92, 96–7, 100–1, 103, 107, 122, 136; regarding death 1, 4, 6, 97–8, 126, 137, 161, 176 n.28, 177 n.33, 177 n.50; resoluteness and 111–12, 133; the uncanny and 188 n.49; of witnessing 33
Ariés, Philippe: on public death 176 n.23, 176 n.25; on shifting attitudes towards death 20–1, 22–3; on tame death 20
artificial intelligence (AI) 6, 40, 133–4, 137–8, 142, 144–6, 191 n.19; and immortality 135, 143–4; as networked intelligence 144
authenticity 6, 95, 98–100, 104, 106, 109–10, 112–15, 119–22, 188 n.42; anxiety and 92, 98, 100–2, 103–4, 107, 109, 141; as Being-for-itself 103, 108; as Being-towards-death 107–8, 111–13, 131; and commercial mascots 95; dramaturgical view of 116–17; in existentialism 100–4; possibility and 92, 107; potentiality-for-being as 121–2, 123; resoluteness and, 111–13; subjectivity and 116–17, 119, 121–2; the uncanny and 108
automaton 37, 40, 138

bad faith 92, 102–3, 114, 122. *See also* inauthenticity
Badiou, Alain 6, 7, 32, 162; on Being 149–50, 157; on consistency 152, 156–7; on death 154–5, 158–61, 193 n.40; on the event 154–5, 161; on multiplicity 135–6, 146–7, 148, 157, 160–1, 193 n. 47; on the one/oneness 146–7, 150, 152, 161, 193 n.47, on truth 155–6, 159, 161; on the void (Ø) 153, 161, 193 n.46
Barker, Jennifer M. 34, 35

Barnes, Hazel E. 102
Barthes, Roland 19, 38, 58, 178 n.61; *studium* vs. *punctum* 25–6
Baudrillard, Jean 165: on the precession of the simulacra 31; on simulations 39, 47, 180 n.98, 181 n.113; on the successive phases of the image 30–1, 39, 47
Baugh, Bruce 111
Bazin, Andre 58
Becker, Ernest 23, 24, 177 n.48, 181 n.1
becoming 66–8, 70, 72, 136, 140
Being 66–7, 101–2, 108, 121–3, 131, 134, 135, 136, 137, 139, 144, 148, 158, 173; vs. being 101–2, 149, 152, 153–4, 170; meaning of 7, 92, 101, 123, 136, 141, 148, 153, 165; as multiplicity 135, 148, 153, 157; vs. nonbeing 100–1, 121, 136; potential of 152, 158, 162; qua being 148, 149, 157, 161, 192 n.22; the virtual and 121–3; as what-presents-itself 147, 153, 157
Being and Event (Badiou) 136, 146
Being and Nothingness (Sartre) 92, 100
Being and Time (Heidegger) 92, 100–1, 106, 112
Being-for-itself 100, 102–3, 108
Being-for-others 102–3, 108. *See also* inauthenticity
Being-in-the-world 100, 103, 106, 117, 159. *See also* fallenness
Being-towards-death 60, 100, 106–8, 110, 111–14, 123, 126, 131, 136
Benjamin, Walter 13
Bessant, Kenneth C. 107
Beyond the Pleasure Principle (Freud) 12–13, 73, 75
The Bionic Woman 139
biopower 150, 175 n.13
Bioshock 63–5, 68–9, 78
Blade Runner (Scott) 143
body 4, 5, 7; biological vs. non-biological 7, 133–5, 138–9; destruction/decay of 15–16, 18–21, 23–4; frailty of 134, 135, 137; malleability of 137, 139, 142–3; vs. the mind 134–5, 136, 163; posthumanism and 141; simulations of 44–6; viscera and 34–6
Bogost, Ian 39–40, 44, 180 n.100
Bonta, Mark 171
Borges, Jorges Louis 31, 62, 185 n.3
Bostic, Adam I. 141
Breaking Bad 113–15, 116
Brinkman, Eugenie 50
Bronfen, Elisabeth 17, 176 n.24
Brooks, Peter 77
Brottman, Mikita 50
Brown Golden, Kristen 38, 179 n.93
Bryant, Levi R. 117
Burchill, Louise 161–2
Burke, Kenneth 116
Butler, Judith 116

Cameron, Ed 96
Carmen, Taylor 179 n.93
Casanova, Giacomo 15
cathexis 12, 72, 75, 83
Centipede 54
chance: as re-animation in digital games 70–2, 77, 88; subjectivity and 136
Cheerios/Buzz the Bee 93, 96
Chik-fil-a 93
children 3, 17
Chips Ahoy! 92–3
choice: as defining humanity 164; ethical choices in digital games 63, 64–5, 80, 140; "natural" death and 70, 77; subjectivity and 67–70, 136
Choron, Jacques 168
Civil War (American) 17
Cloud Atlas (Tykwer, the Wachowskis) 123, 126, 129
coding 90
Combs, Scott 28, 29, 178 n.62
compossibility: definition of 61–2; in digital games 55, 58; eternal return and 70–1; in *LIMBO* 81, 83; "natural" death and 67–8; re-animation and 63, 65; in *Run Lola Run* 84–8; subjectivity and 74, 78

The Concept of Anxiety (Kierkegaard) 92
consistency 2; of Being 148–9, 152, 153; compossibility and 61; death as inconsistent 154–5, 160, 161–2; vs. inconsistency 156–9; multiplicity and 150; naming and 156–8; of simulations 41, 46–7
Conway, Daniel W. 72
Cooke, Alexander 67
Craig, Meghan 101, 102, 103
critical theory 7
CSI: Crime Scene Investigation 36
cyberpunk 134
cyborgs 6, 138–41, 142, 144, 152, 165

Damiens, Robert-François 15
Dark City (Proyas) 146
Dasein: anxiety and 103, 112; authenticity and 112; as Being-in and Being-with 106–7, 117; as Being-towards-death 107, 112–13; as care (about Being) 100–1, 103; "event" of Dasein 108; thrownness and 107, 108, 112–13; uncanniness and 107, 112–13
Davis, Robert 47
de los Rios, Riccardo 47
death: acceptance of 21, 110, 122, 166; contemplation of 72, 78, 79, 85, 88; definition of 4–5, 153; in early motion pictures 26–30; as event 11, 153, 155, 158; indifference to 133, 160, 161; inevitability of 7, 79, 123, 133, 136, 143, 149, 158, 165; logic of 2–3; natural/narratively satisfying 75–7, 78, 81–2, 89; of the other 4, 106, 133, 154–5; possibility of 17, 53, 89, 93, 97, 106, 111, 112, 126, 141, 136; potential of 89, 92, 104, 123, 131, 136, 161; recognition of 113, 121, 123, 131, 135, 137, 138, 139, 158, 166, 168; relationship with 1–3, 5, 6–7; repression/denial of 20–3, 54, 78, 83, 88, 125, 131, 133; thickness of 4–5, 36; traumatic 75, 77, 82, 85; as unknowable 155, 159–60; as utmost possibility 92, 97, 112, 114, 116, 125, 131, 136, 161
deathbed 17–18, 33, 65, 176 n.24
death drive 6, 55, 66, 73–4, 78
decay 136, 141
Debord, Guy 30
DeGrazia, David 4
Deleuze, Gilles 6, 7, 77, 92, 159; on the actual and the virtual 118–19, 190 n.79; on compossibility 61–2, 183 n.26; on death 160–2; on eternal recurrence 55, 70–2; on fractals 170–1, 195 n.8; on identity 71; on *jouissance* 176 n.32, 177 n.33; qualitative/problematic theory of unity and multiplicity 135, 148, 151–3, 161, 162, 192 n.33; on subjectivity 117, 119, 122, 160–1; on transcendentalism 117, 155
determination: coding as 90; immanence and 173; over-determination 3; reciprocal determination 152, 160–1; resolution and 112–13, 114, 152; self-determination/identification 110–12, 114, 119, 123, 131, 136, 141, 152, 155, 160–1, 164; of subjectivity 101, 107–8, 116–17, 119, 160, 188 n.47
Detmer, David 117, 121
Deus Ex (game series) 137–8, 140–1, 165
Dickens, Charles 15
difference: chance as 70; determination and 152; eternal recurrence and 66, 70–1; experience of 117, 122; identity and 71; in-itself 71, 77; multiplicity and 148–9
digital 2–3, 68, 100, 119, 123; digital age 1, 2, 4, 98, 103, 116, 134, 136, 169; digital logic 3, 53, 54, 90–1, 95, 122, 169; digital technology 2, 3, 7, 33, 55–6, 58–9, 182 n.16, 185 n.3
digital logic of death 2–3, 5, 6, 7, 173

Doane, Mary Anne 178 n.64
documentary (images of death) 4–5, 33
Drive (Refn) 35

Eberly, David H. 44
ecstasis 115–16, 123; ecstatic temporality 107, 108–9, 111; relay of 121, 123
Enter the Void (Noé) 123, 126, 129
eternal recurrence/eternal return (of the same) 6, 55, 66–7, 70–2
event 6, 135–6; vs. being 153–4; death as 2, 6, 134, 136, 148, 153–5, 159–60; ontology of 153, 160–1; as truth-procedure 154–6, 159
Ex Machina (Garland) 137–8, 142, 165
The Execution of Mary, Queen of Scots (Clark) 27–9, 31
executions 15–16, 28–9; execution videos/films 5, 33, 178 n.64
existentialism 1, 6, 92, 103, 121, 149
experiential relays 6

facticity 102, 107, 108, 112, 121
fallenness 102, 112, 129
Fallout (game series) 63, 70, 78
Fat Girl (Breillat) 35
Feifel, Herman 22
feminism 139
Fisher, Tony 107
flesh 28, 89; and digital effects 9–10, 12, 36, 48–9, 91, 130–1, 172; fragility of 83; vs. machine bodies 133, 135, 161; organic bodies and 6, 7, 116, 122, 135, 161; viscera and 5
fold/folding 92, 117, 121; of action and force 117; of the actual and virtual 119, 121–3; of the self/subjectivity 118, 131, 190 n.80
force 117, 119
Foucault, Michel 15, 24–5, 38, 138, 150, 175 n.13; *The Birth of the Clinic* 24–5, 38; *Discipline and Punish* 15

The Fountain (Aronofsky): Being-towards-death in 123–31; fractal logic in 172–3
fractals 169–73; chaotic 170–1; as linearly self-similar 169, 170, 172
Frasca, Gonzalo 39, 40
Fraser, Antonia 178 n.65
freedom 96–7, 101, 103, 141, 161, 164
Freud, Sigmund 11, 14, 23, 37, 50, 58, 102, 174 n.1; the death drive 6, 55, 66, 73, 76–7, 184 n.54, 184 n.55; *fort-da* game 13–14, 72; on the instincts 74; on "natural" death 75; on the path to death 75–76; on trauma and repetition 12–14, 37–8, 72, 77, 175 n.2; on the uncanny 58, 107
Frogger 54
funeral 4, 23, 177 n.46
future/futurity 91, 107, 108, 111, 125

gestalt 146, 176 n.32
Grant, Ian Hamilton 169, 170
Grand Theft Auto (game series) 45–6, 70
The Great Train Robbery (Porter) 29
God of War III 75
Goffman, Erving 116, 189 n.70
Gorer, Geoffrey 24, 31, 176 n.24; on deathbed scenes 17, 176 n.23; on language and trauma 37–8; "The Pornography of Death" 20–2
Guattari, Félix 170–1, 195 n.8
Guy, John 28

Half-Life 2, 61
Hallward, Peter: on Badiou and being 149, 193 n.47; on Badiou and consistency 156, 159; on Badiou and death 154, 160, 194 n.55; on Badiou and the one 150, 157; on Badiou and the void 155
Hansen, Mark B.N. 179 n.93
Haraway, Donna 116, 139
Harman, Graham 108
Harvey, David 174 n.1
Hayles, N. Katherine 139

Heavy Rain 98–100, 104, 119
Hegel, George Wilhelm Friedrich 100, 159
Heidegger, Martin 6, 7, 183 n.38; on anxiety 100–1, 103, 111, 113, 177 n.50; on Being 92, 101, 108–9, 111–13, 149; on Being-towards-death 60, 106–7, 111; on *Dasein* 60, 100, 101, 103, 107, 111–13, 117, 149; on death 92, 97, 100, 104, 112; on ecstatic temporality 107–9; on facticity 102; on resoluteness 111–13, 152, 159–60, 189 n.60; on thrownness 107, 111; on transcendentalism 117; on uncanniness 107–8, 111; on will to power 68
Her (Jonze) 145–6
hospice 33–4
hospital 1, 12, 17, 19–20, 24–5, 31, 33, 38. *See also* Foucault, Michel: *The Birth of the Clinic*
human/humanity; vs. the digital 7; the human condition/experience 2, 18, 24, 37, 97, 102, 123, 143, 149; vs. machine consciousness 133–6, 141, 142, 146, 148–9, 152, 164–5; meaning of being human 5, 6, 7, 134–5, 136, 138, 142, 152–3, 161, 162, 166, 173; unity/multiplicity and 161
hyperreal 41, 47, 51, 181 n. 113

identity 7, 91, 92, 141; in digital games 54, 54, 66, 70, 72, 76; eternal recurrence and 66–8, 70–2; existential reading of 102, 108, 111; temporality and 67; unity/multiplicity and 135–6, 150, 152, 153; virtual subjectivity and 115–16, 120, 183 n.37
ignorance 10, 43; anxiety/authenticity and 92, 93, 95–7
immanence 6, 21; Being-towards-death and 106, 114, 131; fractals as 170–1, 173; humanity/death and 166, 168, 173; plane of 148, 161, 162, 170–1; possibility/potential and 90–1, 113, 123; relay of 113, 123, 136
immersion 5, 63, 79, 83, 181 n. 109
immortality 6, 115, 137; immortal machine consciousness 135, 144–6, 148, 152; immortality projects 23; machines and 133–5, 137, 143, 150, 158, 160, 173; virtual subjectivity and 122, 128, 130
inanimate/inanimation 5, 172; death drive and 73–5; in digital games 58–9, 63, 80
inauthenticity 29; vs. authenticity 95, 102–3; bad faith and 102, 114–15; Being-towards-death and 111–12, 129, 188 n.47; fallenness thrownness, uncanniness and 107–9, 116; virtual subjectivity and 122, 125
inconsistency. *See* consistency
individuation. *See* determination (self-determination)
Infamous (game series) 63, 78
instincts 54, 55, 73, 74–5, 82, 85
Inwood, Michael 107, 108
Irréversible (Noé) 9–10, 13, 14, 47–51

Jameson, Fredric 97–8, 174 n.1, 179 n.79, 187 n.23
jouissance: vs. *plaisir* 19, 176 n.32; representations/simulations and 36, 44, 50–1; of witnessing death 11, 12, 18–19, 26, 31, 32, 177 n.33

Kant, Immanuel 41–3, 118, 187 n.34
Kenkmann, Andrea 107
Kierkegaard, Soren 6, 7, 23, 100, 190 n.88; on Adam and Eve 96, 186 n.13, 187 n.18; angst 186 n.9, 186 n.11; on anxiety/possibility 92, 95–8, 100, 101; on despair 111
Kool-Aid/Kool-Aid Man 94
Kracauer, Siegfried 180 n.104
Kubler-Ross, Elizabeth 23, 176 n.24

Lacan, Jacques 11, 12–13, 37; Imaginary, Symbolic, Real 37–8, 44; *Tuché and Automaton* 11, 37

Lærke, Mogens 117
Larson, Doran 142
Leibniz, Gottfried Wilhelm 61–2, 117
life: fractal logic of 168–70, 173; organic vs. synthetic 133, 136, 137–9, 141–2, 150, 161, 165; potential of 113
Life of Pi (Lee) 170, 173
LIMBO 78–84, 88
The Lord of the Rings: The Fellowship of the Ring (Jackson) 35
Lost 109–11, 112
Luchte, James 188 n.54
Lyotard, Francois 187 n.23

M&Ms 94–5, 103–4, 185 n.8
machines 6, 7, 81, 150–1, 162–6; as android 137, 141–3; as cyborg 137, 139–41; vs, humanity 138, 155, 166; identity and 116; immortal machine consciousness 135, 144–8, 152; immortality and 133–7, 143, 173; simulations as 40
macroscopic/microscopic 167–9, 172
Mandelbrot, Benoit B. 169–70; Mandelbrot Set 170–1
Manovich, Lev 40, 180 n.103
Marino, Gordon D. 96, 186 n.11
Mass Effect (game series) 63, 75, 78, 144–5
Massumi, Brian 6, 90–2, 97, 185 n.5
The Matrix (film series, the Wachowskis) 84; Agent Smith as pure unity 162–6; death of Neo 133–4, 166; multiplicity of the machines 147–8, 150–1, 157, 192 n.32; naming in 155, 158; Neo's oneness/manyness 136, 147–8, 151, 155
May, Rollo 96
McIlwain, Charlton D. 133
Meillassoux, Quentin 156, 193 n.47
Melancholia (Von Trier) 123, 125, 129
Menger Sponge 171, 195 n.8
Merleau-Ponty, Maurice 38, 100, 146
Metal Gear Solid 61
metaphysics 7, 92
Metropolis (Lang) 143

Mitford, Jessica 22
Morris, Errol 177 n.57
Mortal Kombat (game series) 36, 53
mortality 1–3, 4–7; acknowledgement of 100, 104, 109, 114, 158, 166, 173; attitudes toward 11–12, 21–2; consequences of 2, 89, 123; fear of 17; knowledge of 1–3, 4; our own 4, 6, 66, 117, 128, 133, 138, 133, 138, 154; understanding of (relationship with) 2, 5, 11–12, 16, 22–5, 31, 34, 43, 51, 54–6, 123, 136, 168
movement 10, 37, 77, 190 n.79; as change 60; life as 67, 138; in *LIMBO* 79–83, 185 n.67; simulations as 40–1, 45, 174 n.2; vs. stillness 58–9, 62, *see also* animation
multiple/multiplicity 6, 92; being as 135, 147–8, 193 n.46; of machines 147–8, 150–1, 157, 192 n.32; possibility as 90; qualitative/problematic theory of 135, 148, 151–3, 160–2, 192 n.33; quantitative/axiomatic theory of 135, 148–52, 155, 161–2, 193 n.47; virtual subjectivity as 116
Mulvey, Laura 58, 77
Muybridge, Eadward 138

Nakamura, Lisa 116
naming 156–9, 160
narrative: closure 77; in digital games 54, 55, 59, 74
networked consciousness. *See* immortal machine consciousness
news footage 5, 33–4
Nietzsche, Friedrich 6, 74, 149, 150; on Being as becoming 66–7; eternal recurrence 55, 66–7, 68, 70–3, 184 n.55; on identity 71
Night Trap 53
9/11 (terrorist attack) 14, 32–3, 98
Noé, Gaspar 10
nothingness 100–2, 121, 153, 159, 170. *See also* the void (Ø)
numbers 148, 149–50

INDEX

one/oneness; count-as-one 147, 153, 157, 158; vs. multiplicity 135–6, 146–50, 158, 173; the one is not 135, 146–7, 150, 157; subjectivity and 151–3, 160–2
ontology 4, 7, 108; of Being 101, 149, 157, 160; of events 136, 153, 160, 194 n.54; as multiplicity 150, 152–3, 193 n.47; of photographs 58
organic 6, 172; biological body as 36, 139, 142, 150–1; merging with the synthetic 138–9, 141; as one/multiple 148–9; organic/biological life 40, 73, 146, 158, 161; vs. synthetic 133, 135–7, 138, 142, 144, 162, 165

Pac-Man 54
Papadimitriou, Christina 108
Parables for the Virtual (Massumi) 90–2
path to death 6, 56, 65, 66, 75, 78, 88, 136, 166
Pearce, Richard 102, 121
phenomenology 7, 100
photographs (photography) 2, 25–6, 58
Pickering, Andrew 173
plaisir 19, 176 n.32
pleasure principle 72. See also *Beyond the Pleasure Principle* (Freud)
The Pornography of Death (Gorer) 20–1
possible/possibility 6, 37, 59, 60, 88; actual/virtual and 117–19, 192 n.35; anxiety and 91, 96–7, 100–1, 103–4, 107, 114, 122, 176 n.28, 187 n.18; *Dasein* as 101; of death 17, 53, 89, 97, 106, 111, 126, 136, 159–60; possibilistic culture 54, 89–91, 95, 98, 107, 112, 122, 136, 173, 185 n.7; vs. potential 90–2, 185 n.7; resoluteness and 111–13, 129; thrownness/uncanniness and 107–8, 131, 188 n.47; utmost possibility 92, 97, 104, 106, 112–14, 116, 123, 131, 136, 161

posthumanism 116, 139, 141
potential/potentiality 67, 88, 122–3, 129; actual/virtual and 115–17, 119, 192 n.35; anxiety/resolution and 95, 106; of death 89, 92, 123, 131, 136, 161, 173; vs. possibility 90–2, 185 n.7; potentiality-for-Being 92, 107, 110–14, 121, 123, 152, 160, 162, 173
Powell, Anna 169, 170
Premium Rush (Koepp) 84
presentation (Badiou) 146–7, 156–7. See also Being: as what-presents-itself
Prince of Persia (game series) 56–58
Prince, Stephen 178–9 n.70
The Proposition (Hillcoat) 35
Protevi, John 160, 161, 170
psychoanalysis 7

Raffoul, François 108
ragdoll physics 46–7
real/reality 118–19, 138
re-animation 6, 60, 163; compossibility and 61–2, 63, 71; in digital games 55, 56–7, 59, 62–3, 64, 72, 77, 78, 182 n.16, 183 n.29, 184 n.61; in *LIMBO* 80–1; *as* repetition/chance 55, 65–7, 70, 71–2; in *Run Lola Run* 84–5, 87–8; virtual subjectivity and 74, 76, 78
Red Dead Redemption 76, 185 n.61
reflection 121–2, 123, 129, 131
religion 1, 3, 4, 21, 96, 123
repetition: the death drive and 66, 72, 77; in digital games 55, 61, 63, 71, 80, 88, 173, 182 n.4; eternal recurrence as 66–7, 70–1, 72; fractals as 168, 170, 173; re-animation as 55, 65–7, 70, 71–2; trauma and 13–14, 37, 38; uncanniness and 108
representations (of death) 1, 2, 5, 25–6, 38; vs. reality 11, *see also* shock: of the hoax
Resident Evil 4, 54
resoluteness: anxiety and 111–12, 146; authenticity and 104, 109, 111–12,

113; Being-towards-death and 107, 111–12, 113, 114–15, 123, 129, 131, 139, 160, 173; in *Breaking Bad* 113–115; in *Lost* 109–110, 112; potential and 106, 113
Robocop (Verhoeven) 140
Run Lola Run (Tykwer) 84–8

sameness 71, 148, 150, 152
Sanchez, Robert Eli 106
sandbox games 70
Sartre, Jean-Paul 6; on anxiety 100–1, 177 n.50; on authenticity 92, 100, 102–3, 108, 187 n.38, 188 n47; on consciousness 101, 121; on death 100; on facticit 102; on nothingness 101–2, 159, 161, 193 n.46; on possibility 92; on reflection 121–2; on subjectivity 92, 102, 122; on transcendentalism 117, 121
Scarface (Hawkes) 29
Schulzke, Marcus 63
Schumacher, Bernard N. 60
Seltzer, Mark 138
senescence 75, 135
sets 135, 146, 149–50, 153, 157, 161, 164; set theory 149, 152
Shaviro, Steven 58–9, 116, 139
shock 13, 22, 26, 34, 50; of the hoax 29, 47, 50, *see also* witnessing: shock of
Sierpiński, Wacław 169; Sierpiński Triangle 169, 171
Silberman, Steve 172
simulations 10, 12, 38–9, 41–5, 136, 172; of death 5, 10–11, 40–1, 43–4, 45–6, 48–51, 173; definition of 39–40; of physics 44–9
The Six Million Dollar Man 139
Smith, Daniel W. 136, 149, 151, 160, 192 n.35
Sobchack, Vivian 4–5, 34, 38, 46, 179 n.86
social media 2, 116, 119, 139
Solaris (Soderbergh) 123–6, 128–9, 131
Solaris (Tarkovsky) 125
Somers-Hall, Henry 157
Sontag, Susan 25, 177 n.57

The Sopranos 104–6
Source Code (Jones) 84
Space Invaders 54
Space War 54
Spinoza, Baruch 61, 150, 154
Star Trek: The Next Generation 141
Star Wars (Lucas) 139
Sterritt, David 50
stillness 45, 58–60, 62, 77, 83. *See also* inanimate (inanimation)
Stolorow, Robert D. 103, 106
Stone, David A. 108
subjectivity: actual 5, 74–5, 115, 117, 119, 121–2, 128–9, 138; authenticity and 6, 92, 116–17, 121–2, 141; coding and 90; death and 1, 89, 121; the digital and 5, 7, 90; digital/virtual 5, 6, 55, 63, 65, 68–70, 74–5, 76, 78, 80, 82, 88, 115–16, 119, 121–2, 125, 126, 128–9, 135–6, 138–9, 141, 183 n.37, 185 n.66; the fold and 117–18, 119, 121–2, 131, 190 n.80; identity and 7, 66–7, 71, 92, 158; in *The Matrix* 134, 147, 165; oneness/multiplicity and 149, 152, 160–1; split 5, 74–75, 88, 116, 121–2, 123, 135, 136, 138, 140
sublime 42–2, 45, 113, 131, 136, 146
Super Mario Bros 45, 79
Super Mario 64, 61
supernumerary 136, 153. *See also* numbers
synthetic 136, 138, 141, 142, 146, 149, 152

Tavinor, Grant 69
technology 123
Telotte, J.P. 143
temporality: animation/re-animation and 58, 67, 71, 75, 80, 183 n.29; being/event and 153; Being-towards-death and 108, 189 n.54; in digital games 54, 56–8, 71, 75; digital technology and 58–9, 182 n.5; possibility and 97; structures of 60–2, 70, 190 n.79; viscera and 34, *see also* compossibility, ecstasis: ecstatic temporality

The Terminator (Cameron) 143
thanatology 1, 4, 7
Three Kings (Russell) 36
thrownness 107, 108, 109, 11, 112–13, 116, 131, 146
Tillich, Paul 95
titillation 3, 22
Todorov, Tzvetan 77
Tomlinson, W. Craig 73
transcendentalism 102, 117–18, 121, 152, 155, 159, 161, 170
trauma 5, 6, 10–12, 19, 50, 79, 95; fetishization of 21–2, 24; psychoanalytic reading of 12–15; representations of 9, 91, 136, *see also* witnessing: trauma of
The Tree of Life (Malick): Being-towards-death in 123, 125–6, 129; fractal logic in 167–9, 170, 172, 173
truth 155, 159, 164, 165; truth-procedure 154–6
Turkle, Sherry 116

uncanny/uncanniness 58, 107–8, 109, 111, 112, 116, 131, 188 n.49
unity 146–7, 152, 155, 156, 157, 161, 162, 165; univocity 150, *see also* one/oneness

verisimilitude 29, 34, 36, 44
violence 10–11, 12; in digital games 53–4
virtual/virtuality: vs. actuality 92, 118–19, 122, 190 n.79; the event and 136, 162; the one as 147, 157; vs. possibility 90–1, 118–19, 192 n.35; vs. reality 118–19; simulations as 40, 44, 51, 89, 91; virtual reality 32, *see also* subjectivity: digital/virtual
virtual reality 32
viscera/viscerality: images of death 5, 10–12, 21, 34–5, 53; representations of 12, 21, 34–6, 82; as shock 34–5; simulations of 44, 47, 50; trauma and 14, 35; witnessing and 15, 18
the void (Ø) 153, 155–6, 159, 161, 193 n.46

The Walking Dead (game series) 119–21
Walsh, Maria 58, 59
waning of affect 97, 179 n.79
The Wild Bunch (Peckinpah) 30
will to power 68, 70
The Witcher 3: Wild Hunt 61
witnessing: the deathbed 17; *jouissance* of 12, 18–19, 26, 31, 32, 36, 44, 50–1; shock/trauma of 18, 25, 30, 33–4, 36, 44, 47; simulations and 9–10, 44, 47–51; viscera and 34–5; witnessing actual death 1, 5, 9, 11–12, 14–19, 20, 22, 24, 28–31, 32–3
Wolfenstein 3D 54
Wulfing, Natalie 96, 101

Zangeneh, Hakhamanesh 188 n.54
Žižek, Slavoj, 14, 32–3, 34, 44

www.ingramcontent.com/pod-product-compliance
Lightning Source LLC
Chambersburg PA
CBHW072234290426
44111CB00012B/2086